What Others Are Saying

A Father Turns Tragedy into Hope after the 1999 Disappearance of His Son in the Colorado Mountains

I had only been in Congress for a very short time when I received news of a missing child by the name of Jaryd Atadero. All I could think of was the anguish of the family and how frightened the young child could have been. I soon came to know the family, and the depth of their pain was palpable. There are no words to describe the helplessness in this kind of situation. We did what we could do to console the family and to aid Mr. Atadero. Eventually, I was able to pass legislation to dedicate the Big South Trail to Jaryd Atadero and his legacy. I have a picture of Jaryd outside my office, and every time I see it, I am reminded how precious and fragile life is. All I want to do is hug my grandchildren. We take comfort in knowing that he is in Christ's loving embrace.

—Tom Tancredo
Member of Congress

When I first covered the Jaryd Atadero story, I was a reporter in Denver. The story moved me beyond belief, and I became close with Allyn, Jaryd's father. Now a father myself, I have a deeper sense of empathy for the pain Allyn has felt. His story and that of Jaryd's disappearance is a must-read for any parent. Other lives may be saved because he shared his heartbreaking story.

—Chris Schauble
KNBC-TV

As a reporter covering Jaryd's disappearance, I was always haunted by the pain that little boy must have felt. After reading the book, I am haunted by the pain his father and his family will feel for the rest of their lives. The book is eye-opening and heart-wrenching. I believe it will help other parents of missing children understand they are not alone.

—Heide Hemmat
Reporter, FOX TV Denver

A true story of a father's loss and sacrifice and, finally, acceptance. Allyn Atadero's love for his young son and his faith are evident on every page—the story of a real-life nightmare, the loss of a child. How coping with the tragedy helps a father gain strength from his faith. I was there from the day after Jaryd went missing through the end of the search when rescuers finally gave up. As a parent myself, it was so very hard to have to stand apart from Allyn and his family and watch while they went through the many stages of disbelief and grief. But as a reporter on the scene, that was my job. Throughout the years that I've known him, I've been amazed at Allyn's strength. I think many people in his place would have found it extremely difficult, if not impossible to go on after losing a child. I know it was hard for him, but with a young daughter to care for, Allyn simply had to. It would have been easy for him to become a bitter man, but he did not. In this book, you can share his experiences and watch how he turned tragedy into hope.

—Ronda Scholting
Former reporter of KMGH-TV
Denver, Colorado

Allyn Atadero displays the same candor and the same grace in *Missing* as he did during those same achingly sad days on the mountain. The book exudes a raw emotion, illustrating the love between father and son.

—Adam Shrager
9News reporter of KUSA-TV
Denver, Colorado

Allyn, I first must say that writing about Jaryd, obtaining his case from the sheriff, having our team travel to the site four times, and later writing about it was a life-changing event. Each of our investigators are seasoned law enforcement professionals, and we were each bothered by many aspects and facts surrounding the case and loss of Jaryd. We cannot ever understand the pain and suffering you have gone through. Our prayers are forever with you and your family.

—David Paulides
Missing 411

MISSING

When the Son Sets

ALLYN AND ARLYN ATADERO

SECOND EDITION

THE JARYD ATADERO STORY

MISSING

When the Son Sets

TATE PUBLISHING
AND ENTERPRISES, LLC

Published by Tate Publishing & Enterprises, LLC
127 E. Trade Center Terrace | Mustang, Oklahoma 73064 USA
1.888.361.9473 | www.tatepublishing.com

Tate Publishing is committed to excellence in the publishing industry. The company reflects the philosophy established by the founders, based on Psalm 68:11,
"The Lord gave the word and great was the company of those who published it."

Book design copyright © 2015 by Tate Publishing, LLC. All rights reserved.
Cover design by Joana Quilantang
Interior design by Gram Telen

Published in the United States of America

ISBN: 978-1-68097-456-0
True Crime / General
15.09.03

This book is dedicated to my beautiful daughter, Josallyn. I know you didn't understand everything that happened, but you knew every moment I was hurting and exactly what to do to comfort me.

You watched as I cried and called out for Jaryd, and you always knew the right moment to sneak up, put your arms around me, and ask, "Daddy, is Jaryd bothering you right now?"

How did you know your love would have a way of calming my pain? Your presence was like your brother's, and each time I held your hand, it made me realize Jaryd was alive in you.

Our lives were touched by a handsome little boy, and with the blink of an eye, he was gone forever. I'm sorry I wasn't there to protect him. I know that each step we take, our lives will never be the same.

I wrote this book to help you understand my moods and to help you remember the moments we shared with our little man, Jaryd. I'm sorry he won't be there for you anymore.

I love you,
Daddy

P.S. I wrote this dedication to you at least twelve years ago, and now you are twenty-one. I'm very proud of what you've become and how you live your life full of integrity. If Jaryd grew up to be half the person you are, we'd have a great young man!

Remember, no one can take him away from you. He will always be your little brother!

This book was written to tell the story of my life after the disappearance of my son, Jaryd. I've taken the time to document many theories and ideas provided to me by others, but the documentation doesn't translate into any belief, on my behalf, concerning any theory. I present what was given to me, and I leave it up to the reader to draw his or her own conclusions.

Please visit my Facebook page "Missing – When the Son Sets" to post any comments you may have. Please like the page when you are finished!

Acknowledgments

I want to thank Rod "Seaux" Larreau for being a hero to all of us. His insights provided answers to questions that went unanswered for years, and I believe others may be saved because of his skills. Seaux is a Green Beret presently serving in the Tenth Group Special Forces in Iraq. Good luck, my friend, and come home safe.

I appreciate Ernie Hudson for his compassion and understanding. He is a man I wish my son would have had the opportunity to meet. Mr. Hudson is the type of man whose character serves as a model for others to follow, and I am sure Jaryd would have learned a lot from him. Mr. Hudson, you are a gift from God and an inspiration to my family.

Don Bendell will always have a special place in my heart for his dedication and understanding. Don and I met several times during the year that followed Jaryd's disappearance, and we explored options concerning Jaryd's whereabouts. Don is a Vietnam Special Forces veteran who uses his skills to track those who become lost or missing.

I truly appreciate Anthony Bruno for standing by my side and providing inspirational support. His kindness and friendship mean more to me each and every day that passes.

My wife, Debbie, stood by my side as I tried to find the answers to the questions that eluded me. Her support and kindness were always there when I needed it the most. I give her my deepest thanks.

I could not have finished this story without the help of my twin brother Arlyn. I'm truly blessed to have had the opportunity to live my life with him by my side.

I want to thank my friend LES for providing support and meaningful feedback. Thanks for the help and for all the special memories. I know you understand.

I want to thank Joni Aldrich and Chris Jerry from the show Advocacy Heals U. They have both experienced the loss of a loved one, and they understand what it takes to survive in this world. Thank you for your support and understanding.

My heart cries for all who have lost a child. Peace!

Contents

Foreword

This dreadful story is about my brother and his quest to discover the truth in his son's disappearance in October 1999. The story made world news, and through the tragic events, he developed many wonderful relationships that will last throughout his lifetime. For years, it was difficult for any of our family to escape the tragedy of my brother's plight. Like a leaky faucet, questions continuously dripped from a vast well of facts, rumors, insinuations, and clairvoyant attention seekers. Most fragments of information only blurred the truth as his search turned into a true-life mystery.

Although I lived over a thousand miles from where my nephew vanished, I often found myself face-to-face with his innocent, and what seemed to be, bewildered gaze. One afternoon, I decided to visit our local Walmart. I had been there over a hundred times, but this time, I felt compelled to glance to my right as I entered the store. To my amazement, I came face-to-face with a missing person's poster of my nephew. His eyes were so captivating and piercing that I instantly felt as though I were in a freefalling elevator. I often opened magazines to discover those eyes again. The Center for Missing and Exploited Children often included my nephew's picture in national publications. The Internet was definitely a haunting ground that provoked many more questions than answers. New stories and photos constantly materialized, challenging the events and evidence surrounding that October day. My aunt Molly, in the state of Washington, said she had deposited some money in a jar for missing children. As she walked away, she noticed the picture of the little boy on the jar was her nephew. My uncle Adolpho, while visiting Germany, intently listened to the news as he watched the story about a little lost boy. It was his nephew. A Poudre Canyon neighbor, who was a friend of ours, later shared the shock he experienced when he saw the Ataderos on the news while visiting friends in South Korea.

This story, in my brother's words, is a gripping tale of a parent's true nightmare. Many parents have experienced that fleeting moment when they couldn't account for the location of a child. Those few seconds conjure up fears so devastating that the horror of actually living them is unimaginable to our human spirit. Thankfully, most of these experiences are only glimpses of the shock, panic, and terror of the wicked reality commonly referred to as a living hell. The rediscovery of our lost children produces euphoria equally as powerful as what the wrenching pain could have been. We become overjoyed to realize we only flirted with disaster and the taunting reality of a lost child. Like a sucker punch to the stomach, the thought of such an ordeal actually takes our breath away. But when it really happens, a darkness so sinister will overshadow one's will to survive. The only thing that kept Allyn from giving up on life was the fear that he would be abandoning his son, who may have been patiently waiting, and possibly watching, his immanent rescue unfold. Constant doubt eroded the tiny slivers of hope to which he struggled to hold.

This story is sure to challenge your emotions. The day my three-year-old nephew walked off into the mountains was only the beginning of my brother's private, unimaginable ride that would last for several years. As he attempted to find the answers to his many questions, the puzzle seemed to only become more complex. Although each path offered a semblance of resolution, it was the many forks in the road that worked to create a web of confusion in which he found himself more and more entangled.

I stood by and helplessly watched my identical twin produce sounds of grief that I could never duplicate, nor do I ever wish to experience them myself. They were sounds so primal that I was sure they originated somewhere deep from within his soul. Although I grieved, it was obvious through our private moments that he was at a depth that I had never imagined existed.

Our lives have paralleled each other in many respects, but that probably is because we are identical twins. After we both entered the teaching profession, we actually spent five interesting years teaching on the same campus in Calexico, California. While teaching at De Anza Junior High, we decided to go into business together. We purchased some cabins and a store in Colorado's Poudre Canyon. We operated that business for about two years. It was there that my brother and nephew spent their last day together.

As a twin, I was often asked if I could feel my brother's pain, but it usually accompanied an additional comment about when he was hit or had gotten hurt. On the day my brother's life came crashing down, I was in San Diego with my wife. We had just experienced a wonderful day with the company of several teachers from McCabe Elementary School. That night, my wife and I decided to not return to El Centro. We stayed in San Diego and didn't tell anybody where we were. After all, my logic was, *What could possibly go wrong in a day?* In the back of my mind, that thought silently tormented me, and no matter how hard I tried, I couldn't shake the feeling that something wasn't right. Little did I know, Allyn and the rest of my family were desperately attempting to contact me. Maybe, in a peculiar way, I was feeling his pain. This is his story.

—Arlyn Atadero

In the Beginning

In all of our lives, we have those days that are forever etched into our memory. Many of us know exactly what we were doing when Kennedy was shot or when three planes changed the heartbeat of our nation on September 11, 2001. For you, October 2, 1999, may have been just another day. You could have been mowing your lawn, taking your kids to the movies, planning an evening with your spouse. For me, this was the day that began the most painful and unpredicted chapter of my life. In retrospect, I often find that my life is broken into two sections: the days before Jaryd's disappearance and those after. Thankfully, I treasure the memories of him, and the sweetness of his existence will always be with me. He was the light that melted away the darkness from the many challenging days I had to endure. Like precious jewels, each of our days together represents a piece of my life's treasure, and as long as I live, he will live in me. I am the man I am today because of my children, and my only regret is that I was not able to spend more time with one of the two gifts God graciously provided to me. Life is delicate, and each day we spend together is much more significant than what we can imagine. My heart was pierced by this fact, and the remaining wound has become a constant reminder of what once was.

It was eleven thirty on Friday evening, October 1, 1999. Jaryd was still awake because his favorite movie, *Godzilla*, was on. It had been a long day, and I was very tired, but Jaryd wouldn't let me go to sleep. How could I sleep when, according to my son, the greatest movie ever made was playing on our TV? I actually tried to fall to sleep several times, but each time I closed my eyes, he yelled, "Daddy, watch this part!" He was pretty persistent because I ended up watching a movie I'll never forget.

As long as I live, I'll always cherish this simple experience we shared. For a boy who was only three years old, Jaryd had a remarkable sense of humor. In fact, it took Jaryd to make me realize *Godzilla* was actually a comedy. During one part of the movie, Godzilla chased a helicopter while running through the streets of New York. As the monster turned to run down another street, Jaryd yelled, "Daddy, did you see that? Did you see that?"

"Did I see what, Jaryd?" I asked. He was obviously pretty excited about something that must have gone right over my head.

With the thrill only seen in the eyes of a little boy, Jaryd replied, "Daddy, when Godzilla turned, you could see his wee-wee."

I can't remember the last time I laughed so hard. Sadly, it would be awhile before I could laugh like this again. The movie ended about twelve thirty, and our final nine hours together had begun to count down. Even now when I think of this, it makes me nauseated. As I sit here typing, I can't help but notice the tears welling up in my eyes. No one understands how much I miss my son because his disappearance was like a nuclear bomb. The original impact made me want to die, and although the fallout has blown away, the radiation from the bomb entered my system, and I feel as if I'm slowly wasting away.

After the movie, I put Jaryd and his six-year-old sister, Josallyn, to sleep on the floor, next to the couch where I slept. At about 4:00 a.m., I was awakened by a presence I felt above me. When I opened my eyes, Jaryd was standing there, looking at me with his deep, penetrating, brown eyes. I asked him if he was okay, and he told me he had wet the bed. I noticed he was shaking, and his pants and underwear were missing. I cleaned him up and placed him on the couch next to me. We snuggled and drifted back to sleep for another two hours.

It was about six thirty when Jaryd and I woke up. Unbeknownst to me, the final three hours of our being together were inconspicuously drifting by. I dressed him for the day in a pair of blue sweatpants and a hooded gray sweatshirt. I then told him to find his shoes and put them on. Of course, I didn't bother with his socks because Jaryd hated them as if they were some sort of disease.

As soon as Jaryd put his shoes on, we went into the store area of the resort to make some coffee and hot chocolate. That's how Jaryd wished he could start every day—a cup of hot chocolate and a cookie. After he was gone, it was these little details about our mornings that became extremely haunting and hard to live with.

The Day Jaryd Disappeared

Saturday, October 2, 1999

The Poudre River Resort is located about thirty miles up the Poudre Canyon on Highway 14, northwest of Fort Collins, and is nestled between the cool waters of the Poudre River and the majestic peaks of the Colorado Rocky Mountains. We were having a retreat for the Christian Singles Association that doubled as a work weekend because we would be doing some repairs on the resort that my twin brother, Arlyn, and I had purchased about a year and half earlier. When not working, everyone in the group would enjoy the natural beauty of the surroundings and the outdoor activities, especially hiking, offered by the resort. Little did I know, this weekend would be different, and it would change my life forever.

When Josallyn woke up Saturday morning, she and Jaryd went to Janet's cabin to spend some time with her. They both liked Janet because she had a warm heart, and she genuinely enjoyed their company. Like most parents, I only trust certain people with my children, and at that time, Janet was one of them.

It was about 9:00 a.m. when Josallyn ran up to me and asked if she could go on a hike. I wasn't sure who she was going with, because this was supposed to be a work weekend. That was the deal: the weekend was free as long as the members from the Christian Singles Association helped with cleaning the premises.

Before long, a crowd of about fifteen people, including Janet, gathered outside, preparing to go for a hike. Again, I had no idea what was going on, and I was confused because I thought people were up here to work.

Deciding not to cause a ruckus, I asked Josallyn if it was okay with Janet if she tagged along. Josallyn was very animated when she told me yes. Never in my wildest dreams did I think Jaryd would come running up to me with the same request. I thought, *Now what do I do?* To this day, I made it a practice never to let Jaryd out of my sight. Once again, I asked Josallyn and Jaryd if it was okay with Janet. "Yes!" they said and jumped up and down like two dogs knowing the Frisbee competition was about to start.

Jaryd's face glowed with excitement when I gave in and said, "Okay, but be careful."

Both kids ran, like a couple of rabbits, to put their jackets on. They came back down to the gathering area and climbed into a white Chevy Blazer. The vision of Jaryd sitting there, with a smile on his face, is etched into my mind forever. Someone made a comment about going to a trail just up the road about three to five miles from the resort next to the trout fishery. I thought, *The kids should enjoy the area because it's an easy area to hike.* The Blazer drove up to the front of the resort, parked in front of the store, and waited for the rest of the group to arrive.

As they waited, I walked up to the Blazer and looked at my children through the window. "Jaryd, roll the window down! I haven't given you a good-bye kiss yet."

He pushed the button, and the window slowly came down. I stuck my head through the window, kissed Jaryd's face, and said, "I love you. Be careful." I had no clue I was truly kissing my son good-bye for the last time.

Jaryd looked at me with his killer smile and said, "I love you too, Daddy."

I replied, "I love you more."

Josallyn, sitting on the other side of the Blazer, yelled, "Daddy, you haven't kissed me good-bye either." I ran to the other side to kiss my other angel good-bye.

....

The group had originally stopped at Poudre Falls but changed their plans when they realized there were no hiking trails in the immediate area. It was midmorning when the party of eleven adult hikers and two children arrived at the trailhead of the Big South Trail. The group was part of Denver's Christian Singles Association, an organization created to facilitate fellowship between single Christians in the Front Range area of Colorado. The hike would be a pleasant getaway with friends and would surely provide an opportunity to create memories for those in attendance.

The Big South Trailhead sits approximately forty-eight miles up the Poudre Canyon on the south side of the road. It's a beautiful, meandering drive that's worth experiencing anytime of the year, but especially during autumn. Nature has a keen ability to captivate the visual sense of humans with majestic displays of orange, yellow, and bronze, and has drawn many people to the mountains to witness its annual spectacle. October 2, 1999, was no different.

The hikers were relaxed as they eagerly hit the trail. The large gathering slowly divided into two smaller groups, as the lead hikers pressed ahead of the others. With spectacular scenery all around, it was easy to become overwhelmed by the awe of God's creation. There's something about the mountains that appeals to the human soul. Our own existence becomes strangely insignificant as we stand in the shadow of the works of a great creator. The adults were consumed by the glorious abundance of beauty displayed around them. The children were just happy to be there!

The little boy in the slower group was full of energy and ready for the Saturday adventure. He slowly pulled away from his chaperone, but she wasn't alarmed, considering he was headed directly toward the other group; and even though she couldn't see them, she knew they couldn't be too far ahead. He vanished on the trail before her.

The little boy scrambled past the second group of adults. He was in his own world controlled only by the limits of his imagination. He relished the freedom to run and explore in hopes of quenching the energy in his inquisitive spirit, and nobody seemed to care. How much better could it get for a three-year-old?

"Somebody needs to keep a closer eye on that little boy before something happens," noted one of the women in the second group of adults as the little boy charged ahead of her. She told Jaryd not to go too far ahead, and he responded, "Okay."

"The mountains are beautiful during this time of the year. It's no wonder they call this God's country."

"Listen to the river. It's so relaxing here," observed another.

The Big South Trail dipped, twisted, and climbed through the pines and aspens while the river to the west gently splashed over boulders as it made its way to the Poudre. The morning air was cool and extraordinarily refreshing. A mild breeze pressed through the small canyon, tickling the aspens, whose leaves danced and shimmered in the wash of the sun. The little boy ventured farther into the depths of the inviting mountains in total awe of his newly gained freedom. In the back of his mind, he knew his dad would never allow this type of liberty, but Dad was back at the resort. The stories he could later share were being formed at this very moment. And when the time came, his excitement would surely captivate the amazement of his father. Fixed on the challenges immediately before him, the young boy continued on.

The little boy ran up the narrow dirt trail away from the adult voices as a Steller's jay flew overhead and announced its presence. All around him, nature was in motion, beckoning him closer. He reached down with his small hand and picked up a rock. After studying its shape, he flung it toward the river below. The projectile disappeared in the underbrush and cracked against the stone surface of a piece of granite, causing a sharp echo. A second rock was retrieved and, accompanied by a little grunt, was given a similar fate. A smile of satisfaction overwhelmed his face as he brushed his hands together to remove the left-behind grit. He thought, *Time to run again*, so off he went, consuming more of the trail beneath him.

As his feet thumped against the dirt path, leaving the adults farther behind, the little boy came upon a stick. He was always able to entertain himself with the simple things provided by the Rocky Mountain wilderness. He gripped the stick in both hands and inspected it. A quick swing through the air and he was satisfied with his newfound toy. Off he went again, the stick pointed in front of him toward the trees ahead. A three-year-old could only experience the imaginary world that he eagerly rushed into, and as the mountain welcomed his charge, not a single person seemed to notice the enthusiasm he displayed.

The trail and the river's edge finally paralleled each other. The boy walked up to the river's brim and studied its flow. For over a year, the river had been the rear boundary of his backyard. It wasn't moving with the fury it usually had in late spring or during the summer months. Instead, there was a more relaxed gentleness about the way the water passed. He dipped his fingers into its coolness and then yanked them back out, fully expecting to be reprimanded for his actions, but the flow of the water and the breeze wrestling through the trees was all he heard. He quickly glanced over his left shoulder then his right, and when he was sure that trouble had no intention of seeking him, he triumphantly slapped at the current, sending a myriad of independent beads of water through the air before him, each one sparkling as the sun's rays penetrated its mass. Amazingly, he heard not a single adult voice.

The boy stood quickly, causing the bangs of his straight dark hair to bounce. He considered, but only for a fleeting second, whether to continue up the trail or go back toward the grownups. With the stick in his left hand and remnants of the river dripping from his right, he began a more casual pace toward the higher elevations of the Colorado Rocky Mountains. Life had dealt him his first real opportunity to learn and explore at a pace only he controlled. *If my sister could see me now, she would be so jealous.* The thought created a smirky grin of achievement he was sure she would never experience. But throughout his experience of freedom, he found himself missing her. When something is this good, it's always more fun to share it with another person.

....

The pole whipped through the air several times as more and more fishing line was fed through the rod's eyelets. Finally, the tiny artificial fly at the end of the leader sailed over a provocative area of the river before touching down on its surface. Floating, it navigated its way up and over stones in quest of an unsuspecting trout, searching for a meal. The fisherman patiently observed the fly darting over the water toward him as his partner readied his own line for a cast. The two men had located the perfect quiet spot far away from the noise of civilization, and nothing could spoil the adventure they had set out to enjoy. As the two anglers worked the river, a strange cracking noise interrupted the typical sounds of the wilderness. It started from somewhere back down the trail and then stopped. The two men eyed each other as if the other knew the source of the clamor, but after each shrugged his shoulders, their attention returned to the task of fishing.

Crack! Crack! Crack! There it was again, but this time louder. Silence, then cracking, then silence again. Strangely, and seemingly from nowhere, a small boy appeared on the trail. He was extremely intent on beating the huge rocks along the river's edge with what appeared to be a walking stick. He hadn't noticed the fishermen on the trail and was obviously very satisfied with the rhythm he was creating.

Annoyed, the two men looked around to see who was accompanying the distracting child, but no one appeared. There had to be somebody they could communicate their dissatisfaction to, somebody who could put an end to the racket created by this kid, but nobody came. What were they to do now?

"Hey, kid, where are your parents?"

Startled, the young boy looked up to see who had spoken to him. *Ah, big people*, he thought. Being on this trail alone wasn't as great as he thought it would be. After all, this was the wilderness that his dad had warned him about. In his high-pitched, young voice, he asked, "Are there any bears here?" It may have been the first sign of concern he experienced, but surely, these big men would protect him. He asked again, "Are there bears here?"

"Yes, but I've never seen one."

After the quick response, the fishermen worked their way to the river and watched as Jaryd continued up the trail.

....

"I thought you were watching him," said one of the ladies back in the group in an effort to appear as though she hadn't considered watching the children. "After all, I didn't bring him up here."

"Well, he's gotta be 'round here somewhere. I figured you guys would see him and keep an eye on him," said a different female as she placed her hands on her hips in frustration. She couldn't believe what she was hearing. "So *nobody* saw him?"

"Come on, you guys. A little boy doesn't just disappear in the mountains," said one of the men in the group. "He's around here somewhere."

The boy's sister watched the drama unfold around her as the adults questioned each other about her brother's whereabouts. Unaware of the potential magnitude of the situation, all she wanted was to head back home.

"He did go past us," responded another woman, "but I don't remember seeing him come back. What about any of you guys?"

Eleven adults stood in bewildered disbelief as the gripping reality of a nightmare began to play its hideous hand. The manifestation of an event that is usually only read about in the paper or watched on the news had leaped upon them. Regardless of the actual role each had played, one by one the cards were dealt, and it was looking like everybody was about to become an instant loser. It was time to ante up.

"Jaryd!" The search had begun.

....

Back at the resort, it was as routine of a Saturday as one could be. Nothing earthshaking had occurred, and who really anticipates a catastrophic event prior to its arrival? I had just finished cleaning our hot tub; knowing my friends in the singles group, I knew the hot tub had the potential of being a big draw.

I'll never forget that day, October 2, 1999. I completed my cleaning chores around two in the afternoon and retreated to our apartment for some well-earned relaxation. As I collapsed on the couch, it caressed my tired body like never before. I'm a big sports fan, so I checked the results of the day's college football games, but even that couldn't keep me awake. Before long, sleep overcame my tired body. I must have drifted off for about ten minutes or so when a commotion coming from the store jolted me awake. The apartment and the store are connected, so it's not unusual to hear what's going on there. Since I was very tired, it was easy at first to ignore the clamor because I could also hear the voice of Melvin "Butch" Shoning, our resort manager. He's very capable of rendering assistance to those in need of service and neutralizing potential problems, but this time, the disturbance continued.

There are times when an event on the premises demands my attention as co-owner, regardless of how tired I may be. As the disturbance continued, I assumed this was turning into one of those times. Sleep was calling my name, but fate was about to rob me of sleep for many days to come. I had no idea of the collision course with disaster I was on.

One of the ladies who had taken my children on the hike abruptly entered my apartment. There was something very strange about her behavior. In fact, she seemed severely frustrated and panicked beyond anything I had ever witnessed. It was so bad; I felt my own tension mounting in response. She made me nervous, and I wasn't sure why. She fidgeted as her eyes roamed about the room, never actually focusing on anything. Confusion reigned, and the order of the day was about to turn into a game of twenty questions.

Our eyes finally met and locked in a sense of despair that was somewhat hypnotic. She tried to communicate something to me that lacked verbal description, and this caused her breathing to be considerably labored. She had been chosen to be the bearer of news that no one else was willing to give. This grave information was the source of a distinct separation between her thoughts and her reality. This wedge that was lodged between her soul and spirit was about to be hammered into the very essence of mine.

Then she spoke, "Allyn, everything is okay, but Jaryd had a little problem."

What an opening statement to an awkward situation that was! Besides, what's a parent to think when suddenly confronted with words of that nature? From her actions alone, I had a dreadful feeling she was giving me a glance at the tip of an iceberg.

"What do you mean 'Jaryd had a little problem?' Is he okay? What happened?" No answer. The questions streamed from my mouth as if they had a life of their own. My voice wasn't normal either. The uneasy feeling this woman had was spreading to me, and I didn't like it. An uncontrollable shiver swept across the surface of my skin as I kept my eyes fixed on her every move, but she just stood there. As if on autopilot, I continued to probe. "Did he fall and cut himself?" I waited, yet there was no answer. "Did he break his arm?"

"No, no, no, no." Her voice had turned to suffering, which only troubled me more. The craving for sleep, which only minutes ago had been so strong, now totally deserted me. I raised my voice and took a more aggressive approach.

"Then what happened? Where is he?" I demanded. My stare seemed to drill right through her, and the response she gave continues to haunt me to this day. In the private stillness of my nights, it echoes a chilling message that monopolizes my mind. The vision of my son dances before me as her words reverberate. I question life as the echo leaps back and forth through me. What she said has become part of my motivation.

"He's okay. We just can't find him."

The statement immediately brought me to my feet. When I first heard these words, they made no sense at all—and they still make no sense today. How could he possibly be okay if he was lost? I stood there, light-headed and bewildered, sure that this was a dream from which I was about to wake. As blood flowed through my body, it actually became peculiarly audible to me. My senses became so keen they were raw and nearly unbearable. How could my son be alone on that mountain? How could he be okay if they couldn't find him? No parent ever wants to hear what she really should have said, especially in a wilderness environment with an elevation of nine thousand feet. *Allyn, your son is lost!* That's what she really wanted me to know, but those words eluded her.

I can't adequately explain the horror that raged through me. In some ways, it was like a falling sensation I've had in dreams when I couldn't wake up. In other ways, it was as though a beast had been turned loose inside of me, and it was ripping at the fibers of life that make me who I am. I was under a siege of fear, and it ran rampant through me, twisting and kicking as it delivered grief and distress to every cell in my body. It was a parent's worst nightmare, and I was engulfed by the evil reality that it wasn't going away. I had been snared by a cruel event that mocked my emotions. The more I thought I could gain control, the tighter it gripped me, choking off the free flow of air that I had taken for granted every day of my life. If I could only breathe!

I staggered around the room, speaking to Jaryd as if he were there with me. No matter what direction I looked, I could see his concerned eyes calling for help. How could they take my son on a hike and lose him? How could they?

"They may have lost you, but I promised I would always be there for you." The words flowed past my lips with a zealous passion to hold my son even though he wasn't there. Then I yelled with a crackling voice, "Hold on, Jaryd! Daddy's coming to get you!"

I prayed, and I hoped God heard every word gushing from my mouth. "Please, God," I pleaded. "Let him be okay, and let me find him. Let Jaryd know that his dad is on his way and comfort him."

As I gathered my thoughts, I ran into the store. It was obvious from the looks that greeted me that the magnitude of the situation was unbearable to everyone. Although Jaryd is my son, he was the male child of the Poudre River Resort too. My pain was also theirs, and the concern for Jaryd's safety had become the group's burden. Butch was so worried that he wanted to contact search and rescue right then and there, but I was naive. I thought I would be able to go to the area where Jaryd disappeared, and as soon as he heard my voice, he would come charging over to me. In my best hopes, the trial of my life would be short and come to a jubilant conclusion. Then as the day ended, we would all go home and thank God for the joyful reunion.

I grabbed my jacket and sweatpants and impatiently hunted for the keys to my Blazer. While I was behind the store counter, I yelled at Butch to get me one of the resort radios. I planned to be on my way up the trail by the time the rest of the group returned to the trailhead, and I wanted to be able to communicate with Butch from my location. As I located my keys and hurried out of the store's front door, the turmoil of emotions jolting through me settled into a knot of panic in my stomach. It was crazy. I just couldn't believe Jaryd was missing!

I got into my Blazer and waited in the parking lot for the people I needed to follow. Patience was a virtue I lacked as I yelled, "Hurry, hurry, hurry!" Brenda, the leader of the Christian Singles Association, came out to my car and informed me the trail was sixteen miles up the road. That didn't make sense to me. When the group initially departed the resort, I was under the impression they were on their way to a trail four or five miles away. What else could go wrong? Even under the best conditions, the drive could take up to thirty minutes or more, assuming I was going to follow the speed limit—which I didn't. I shook my head in disbelief as I started the long journey to the Big South Trail.

As I drove, my world slowly crumbled. I glanced at the odometer over and over, hoping to discover I was almost there, but each time my eyes focused on the numbers in front of me, only a tenth of a mile had gone by. It was then I realized I was experiencing the longest drive of my life. My body trembled uncontrollably, and I became a person I didn't know. I was possibly going into some sort of shock as I physically and emotionally transformed into survival mode. I yelled, screamed, beat my steering wheel, and pounded my dashboard. Fate had impaled my heart with an imaginary knife, and the pain was excruciating. I beat at my chest in an attempt to lessen its sting, but the pain wouldn't stop.

I remembered how the day before I had dreaded coming up to the resort and making the two-and-a-half-hour arduous drive, fighting the Denver area traffic monster, only to then climb a thirty-three mile winding ribbon of highway called the Poudre Canyon. I remembered how I kept hearing a voice inside of my head, pleading with me, *Don't go!* I thought I had little choice; I had already promised a very good friend of mine, Lynne Snyer, that I would give her a ride, and I didn't want to let her down. Lynne had called to let me know she was running late and was thinking about driving up on her own. Inside, my mind pleaded with my reason telling me, *Let her go, just let her go.* I really did not want to go. I could not stop thinking about the last two trips up the mountain and how they both had caused problems in my life.

The first trip started with a rock hitting my windshield and cracking it. The second trip ended at about eleven thirty on a Sunday night with my kids and me arriving home tired and eager for bed. I couldn't wait to get them inside. Unfortunately, the comfort of our own beds would have to wait. When I approached the front door, I realized I had left my keys at the resort. Having neither the time nor the energy to drive back to the resort and then back home again, I called our apartment hotline and requested someone come and unlock our door for us. That situation cost me a little money and a lot of aggravation. As I thought about those two events now, an odd echo of a line from the *Lord of the Rings* came to haunt my thoughts—*third time takes all.*

A current of tears fell from my eyes and down my cheeks, many of them dripping onto my lap. I wiped at them, but my efforts were in vain as the tide continued its progression down the crevices of my face, making it difficult to see where I was going. "Jaryd, Jaryd, Jaryd!" I wailed as I fought the onslaught of guilt nibbling away at the remaining fragment of control to which I desperately needed to hold on. It was a guilt born of not being there when one of my children needed me. No parent ever wants to let a child down, and it was this notion that was eating away at my remaining sanity.

"Calm down, Allyn, you're going to find him," I said in an attempt to reassure myself that everything was going to be okay, but the more I told myself to calm down, the more I felt myself losing control.

"How could you people lose my son?" My sobbing grew louder as I continued to wipe the tears from my face. "How could you take my son up the mountain to his death? He's a three-year-old who should never have been out of your sight! He's my son, not yours! What have you people done to my son—to me?" My feelings were changing so fast I found myself questioning what was real. The actual world I had perceived became distorted as it mingled with an imagination infused with denial and anger.

Where's my daughter? I asked myself, realizing I had to regain some sort of composure. I'd never been on the Big South Trail, but I knew there were only a few more curves in the road and I would be there.

When I reached the trailhead, I leaped out of the Blazer. I don't remember turning my vehicle off or setting the parking brake. Noticing a few people standing around who had gone on the hike with my kids, I ran up to them. "Where's my daughter?" I demanded.

For a couple of years prior to Jaryd's disappearance, life had confronted me with several significant challenges. Many people face obstacles that appear large enough to destroy their will to live. Tragically, some even succumb to the challenges of living by taking their own lives. In spite of my own difficulties, I knew I had a lot to live for because I believe God works in mysterious ways; thus, I focused my thoughts on my daughter, Josallyn. She must be devastated because her little brother—her best friend—was missing. Even though she was growing so fast, Jaryd was just a little boy to her who loved to play. He was so full of life and always tried to play with her, sometimes much to her chagrin, but I know she loved him without a doubt. I desperately wanted to see her and comfort her as best I could. We were the only two on the mountain who were about to experience the shattering of our family.

One of the hikers said that Josallyn was up on the trail somewhere with Janet. The two of them were still looking for

Jaryd. Both of my kids were crazy about Janet, and she treated them extremely well. My kids had gone on the hike because they wanted to be with her.

With my radio in my pocket, I ran south past the wooden signs at the head of the trail, sure I would at least meet up with Josallyn. At first glance, one would never believe the trail was evil enough to consume my son, but after about a hundred feet, it was obvious the terrain could easily take on the role of predator. It's fascinating how something so attractive can actually lure people into letting their guard down. Then, when it's least expected, the trap is sprung, and the victim can only sit and wonder what caused the complacency. The trail narrowed and huge unforgiving drop-offs silently waited for any hiker's mistake. There were a million things to attract the curiosity of a child, and a million things to extinguish a child awash in that same curiosity. The farther I ran, the more I questioned why my babies were on this trail. I would never have brought them here, and if by chance I did, I would never have let go of their hands even for a second.

"Jaryd!" I screamed. The sound of my voice carried through the canyon. It was an eerie reality to hear my son's name being shouted in the wilderness, but I had no choice but to continue.

"Bro, where are you?" I waited for a response and was only greeted with deafening silence—a silence that squeezed a portion of my life out of me as each second passed unanswered. "Hey, little man, Daddy's here!" As I searched the forest for any sign of him, an excruciating anguish continued to push at the hope that had previously filled my spirit. I was gradually dying from a vanquished heart. *It was just too soon for Jaryd to be a memory!*

I hustled up the path, eager to locate anything or anyone who could aid me in my quest. After several minutes of probing and exploring, I heard voices coming from beyond where I could see. As they came into view, I immediately recognized three faces belonging to members of the hiking party. Although they had been attempting to locate Jaryd, they were now on their way back to the trailhead. They asked if the sheriff's office had been contacted. I told them no, recalling how I had asked Butch to refrain from contacting the authorities. A new wave of frustration washed over me. How could I have ever imagined I would be able to locate Jaryd in this vast forest region that seemed to grow each time I turned my head? I prayed that Butch realized I wasn't being rational, and he contacted the necessary people who would initiate a formal search.

One of the hikers volunteered to accompany me back up the mountain so I could continue searching for Jaryd. I know I was chasing my son's vision as it came to rest at the forefront of all my thoughts. I wondered what he was doing that very moment. *Maybe he can see me, but is he injured and unable to call my name? Have I passed his still and lifeless body resting in the folds of the forest?* It would have been easy for him to vanish over the edge of the trail to the river below or disappear into one of the huge boulder fields that lined many areas of the trail to the east. No matter what, I knew we would find him. There simply was no other option.

While the two of us talked, a broken voice came over the radio. I'm not sure what was said, but it was Butch, and he was trying to contact me. As I removed the radio from my pocket, I could hear him, yelling. "Hey, Allyn, are you there? Allyn, do you copy?"

I keyed the radio and held it to my face. "Yes, Butch, I can hear you. Please go back down the road and call the sheriff." The Trading Post store was a couple of miles away, and they had the nearest phone. I knew Butch realized that was where I was asking him to go.

The news he shared with me made me happy that he was my friend. As soon as I was out of the store, he had sounded the alarm, and help was already on the way. The local deputy in the canyon was a tall, friendly man who oversaw that area with a kind and considerate heart. His name is Jose Romero, and I was overwhelmingly relieved to learn he would soon be on location.

God had looked into the troubled face of a desperate father and provided his first allotment of peace. It may have been small, but I willingly accepted it.

I radioed Butch and asked him if he thought I should continue up the mountain or wait for Jose. Considering the state I was in, his conclusion was I should return to the trailhead and let search and rescue do the job for which they were trained. However, there were other factors tugging at my heart, and they were as real to me as the ground I stood on. I couldn't set aside the fact that the temperature had already peaked and was now beginning to drop. To make things worse, the sun was racing toward the jagged edge of the abutting horizon, and daylight was about to be squeezed from the blueness overhead. The eminent and approaching darkness would surely usher in a night of horrors that I was not prepared to deal with, nor was I sure I could survive the pain waiting to accompany it. As I looked around, I wondered again where my daughter was.

At that moment, I wasn't prepared to abandon my efforts, no matter how feeble they appeared, so up I went. I'm not sure if I thought I was racing against time or if I was running away from the army of demons that seemed to pursue me, but I was determined to locate both of my kids.

When I thought of the darkness and the dropping temperature, time seemed to race by uncontrollably. As I thought of Jaryd in the midst of my search, my mind was flooded with events of our past. I remembered talks we shared and how I used to tell him to always be careful so we could spend another day together. His smile exhibited happiness, and his eyes gleamed in a way that caused tremendous warmth to overwhelm me. The way he held my hand each night as he drifted to sleep was a precious daily event to which I looked forward. I'm not so naive that I believe our days together weren't numbered, but I never realized that yesterday might have been the last. As I reflected on our lives, time stood still.

The radio blurted out some sort of message again and interrupted my private moment of recollection. I knew it was Butch, so I asked him to repeat his last transmission. He said, "Allyn, Jose is here, and he wants somebody to go back to the resort and get some of Jaryd's clothes for the dogs." I called back to Butch and told him to wait for me. I was on my way, and for some reason, I felt I needed to return to the resort with him. The information greeted me with a mixture of excitement and distress. I was thankful the search was about to go to the next level, but it was still my son they were looking for. Dogs were coming to the forest to sniff out my child, and the facts surrounding his disappearance would be known soon. A burst of chills exploded over me as goose bumps crawled down my arms.

With a brisk pace, I headed back toward the trailhead. The trip down gave me the opportunity to rescan the terrain from a different angle, but still no sign of Jaryd. When I emerged into the parking lot, I noticed Jose gathering information for the search, so I went to where he was and asked for Butch. Jose informed me that Butch had already departed for the resort to expedite the return of Jaryd's clothing. We were about to wave my child's clothing under the noses of dogs, and although I knew this was the right thing to do, it made me sick to think about.

Curiously, I looked around and inventoried who was on-site. As different groups came into view, I realized others had also noticed me, and I could feel their stares weighing heavily on me. I wasn't sure what to say or even how to react, but I quickly understood I was the "on-scene" focal point to the others. Things were happening so fast, and the role I had been cast into was beyond anything I had ever imagined.

Then it happened. There she was, standing in front of me. Our eyes met and locked as we became fixated on each other. Janet broke down and wept uncontrollably as she ran toward me. Although I was glad to see her, I could feel waves of torment chewing at my insides.

When she reached me, she threw her arms around my shoulders. I could feel her body convulsing as she mumbled, "Allyn, I'm so sorry. I'm *so* sorry." For some reason, an aura of confidence seemed to engulf me as I held her. I'm not sure what it was, but I actually felt we were standing at the threshold of a marvelous event that only appeared to be sinister. It still amazes me how feelings can be so misleading. The troubling mixture of emotions had returned, and they were swimming through my head again, ready to dig in for the long haul.

In a reassuring voice, I told her, "Don't worry, we're gonna find him." I'm not sure where that came from, but my ability to be a comforter surprised me. "Where's Josallyn?"

Janet told me she had taken her back to the resort, hoping to discover that someone had found Jaryd and taken him home. When Janet realized Jaryd wasn't there, she returned to the trail without Josallyn. It was a detail that would later trouble me as I attempted to put the pieces of Jaryd's disappearance together. The more complex the puzzle became, the more people retreated from it. I had fully expected to see Josallyn, and when I learned she was no longer around, another surge of depression fluttered through me. No matter what I did, I couldn't escape the tribulations that ensnared me. Once again, confusion and pain were on the move as they swirled through my mind.

Jose interviewed Janice in the front seat of his car. She told him the last time she saw Jaryd, he was behind two men and one woman who were part of the singles' group. She also witnessed two fishermen along with four other people from the group. She said she lost sight of the front group and the fisherman after they turned a corner. She never caught up with the front group or saw them again.

A few months after Jaryd's disappearance, Josallyn informed me that Janet was tired while she was on the trail and decided to lie down on a rock to take a small nap. Josallyn lay with her and closed her eyes for a few moments. When they awoke, Jaryd was gone. It pains me to think my daughter now understands this action could be the very reason her brother vanished. *How could someone take their eyes off a three-year-old little boy, regardless of how tired they were?* I find it interesting because Janet never disclosed this in the final sheriff's report.

After I spoke with Janet, Jose approached me and provided some much-needed emotional support. He informed me that most situations like these were resolved within twenty-four hours. As the trained search and rescue members arrived on location, I also heard a comment that made a dramatic impact on me. One search member said, "Don't worry, if he's up there, we'll find him." I believed that person with all my heart because he was experienced in these matters. In retrospect, I can now interpret that statement as "The only way we're not going to find him is if he's not up there." I have been told by several people that many of the searchers believe Jaryd wasn't actually there, but not the sheriff. The sheriff said Jaryd was dead on the mountain. It's the ultimate thing an abductor would want to hear if he or she had taken Jaryd. It would all but guarantee success.

I waited around the trailhead for a while to see what was happening. I honestly believed someone was about to walk off the trail holding Jaryd's hand, and I desperately wanted to be there to experience that! I wanted to hear the talented search and rescue team say, "We told you we'd find him!"

As I waited, I watched two fishermen exit the trail. They were swarmed by deputies and questioned about the now "missing little boy." I finally decided to head back to the resort and fill part of my void with the presence of my daughter. I also realized it was time to make the dreaded phone calls to relatives. The circle of pain was about to multiply.

When I arrived at the resort, I ran up to Josallyn and gave her a big hug. I held her tightly, feeling her brother through her because they were a team, formed perhaps by sharing the same womb at different points in time. I didn't want to let go after the reality of this temporal life had confronted me. I had taken hugs for granted, and I would have given anything to be hugging Jaryd again. I was going to experience this hug from my daughter for all the gusto it could produce. As I squeezed her small body, I broke down and cried. I believe this was when Josallyn understood the magnitude of the situation, and Jaryd was actually gone. She returned my pain with tears of her own as we both realized the two of us were possibly the only family we had.

The embrace finally ended, and I slowly pulled away. I gazed deeply into the glistening brown pools of love that were fixed upon me. The eyes of small children are amazing places to become lost in, and at that moment, I found so much comfort in hers. Our children see us for much more than we actually are, as they look deep into the shadows of our souls. Her eyes took me to a place that gave me the courage not to lose hope. I could feel strength beginning to percolate from somewhere deep within me, but I could not exactly identify the location of its inner source.

After returning to the resort, I mentally inventoried the things I needed to do. With my newly found courage, I grabbed my phone and headed to the bathroom. I knew I could close the door behind me and be in the only place that assured some type of privacy. I also knew there would be no way to control my emotions while informing family members about the tragic events of the day, and I did not want anyone watching as I broke down and cried. The closed door would afford me the opportunity to shed what dignity I had. I knew the alarm was sounding to the floodgates of my heart, and a tearful rage was on the verge of being unleashed.

I decided to place the first call to my mother in El Centro, California. My hands trembled as I punched at the number pad on the phone. A dull tone in the receiver signified her phone was ringing. It caused my heart and mind to race feverishly as I searched for the proper words to deaden the impact of my news. I wanted so badly to be the child again so I could be reassured everything would be all right, but the control of this situation even escaped the command of my parents. I inhaled deeply, anticipating the voice of my mother at the other end of the line. When she answered, her voice was happy. Hearing her caused me to weep in a manner I had never experienced. With a crushed spirit, one's sobbing is birthed from a painful moan that cries out from the soul. It is a deep-rooted, groaning sensation that searches for deliverance as the pitch of its bellow increases. Its only purpose is to purge the body of the horrendous grief afflicting it.

Several seconds passed before I was able to communicate with her. I'm not sure how I did it, but I barely whispered, "Mom… Mom, my…my son is missing." I want you to close your eyes, and if you have children, remember when they were three. Now imagine this happening to one of them. Whatever you imagine, it is a thousand times worse when it is real. Each word slowly stabbed into me like a dull dagger, and the sensation created the most unbearable experience I had ever known. I dropped the phone, crouched against the wall, and cried.

My mother's voice became a faint sound, as if someone were speaking to me from a radio with its volume turned almost off. Although scarcely audible, I heard her ask, "Allyn, what's wrong?" I'm not sure she really understood what was happening, but she waited for a second and continued. "Honey, are you okay?" It took all the energy I had to reach down and retrieve the phone from the floor, but I managed to pick it up and try again.

"Mom, they lost my son in the mountains. Mom, Jaryd's missing, and I don't know what to do!" I wasn't sure she could understand me because my words seemed incoherent. We tried to speak for several minutes, but anguish continued to steal my ability to put more than three or four words together. I held the phone to my ear and listened to the silence. If nothing else, it was nice to know she was there even though my words were trapped in my throat. I finally told her I needed to call my brother, Arlyn, and hung up.

I couldn't make it through one call, so I wasn't sure how I would make it through a second. I had no desire to relive the experience I had just shared with my mother, but I dialed anyway. Again, the phone buzzed in my ear as I waited to hear a voice, knowing it could be a number of people. My nephew, Josh, who was seventeen at the time, answered the phone, and I told him I needed to speak with his dad. He told me his parents had gone to San Diego, and that they probably wouldn't be home until Sunday afternoon. I briefly told Josh about his cousin. He questioned me in a loud voice of disbelief. The news hit him pretty hard, and he promised he would do everything he could to contact his parents. Although he was never able to locate them, he called me several times during the first night.

It was time to make the call I dreaded the most. I needed to call Jaryd's mother, Angie. She had moved to San Diego about the time I relocated to Colorado. I had been teaching in the Imperial Valley, and my children and I needed a change. I had left her phone number back in my apartment in Littleton, not planning to speak with her from the resort. I wasn't sure how to contact her, so I called her mother and, for the third painful time, recounted the story of the day. Both grandmothers now had the news. I asked her for Angie's number, and then I told her I would call her later with hourly updates.

After speaking with Angie, I wasn't sure what her plans would be. I contacted my father and delivered the overwhelming news to him. It was devastating making one phone call, but making several calls tortured my soul as if I were at the doorsteps of hell.

Several hours had passed, and with each step I took, I hoped God was in control. I've been told He doesn't give us more than we can handle, but if this were the case, why was I being tortured? I would have never guessed I could survive an event like this involving one of my children. My heart goes out to all the people who have lost children to accidents and diseases, but to this day, I still don't seem any closer to knowing what actually happened or why. My faith tells me Jaryd is in God's hands, but not necessarily in heaven. I would like to think he was taken to heaven in some type of rapture. Now wouldn't that be a story!

After the phone calls, I headed back to the trailhead. My mind jumped around so much I was sure the pain was going to kill me, so I needed to be back at the site. The leader of the search and rescue unit was there when I arrived and was in the process of establishing some sort of command center. The people involved with the search were extremely concerned, and it was encouraging to learn the sheriff's department had taken charge of the entire operation.

One of the investigators continued to interview the people who had been on the trail during the day. After I spoke with the investigator myself, I questioned the sergeant in charge concerning the feasibility of having a helicopter on scene with infrared capabilities. I was told the helicopter they used had an infrared system that was inoperable and there was nowhere else to turn. I later learned, from several sources, that they would have been more than willing to use their infrared helicopters in the search for Jaryd, but they were never asked to render assistance. However, the sergeant did assure me a chopper would be in the air by morning if Jaryd had not been located by then. He also told me they were trying to get a Huey out of Warren Air Force Base in Wyoming and that they hoped it would be airborne by eight the next morning.

What a blessing it was to watch as the search and rescue members prepared themselves, as if Jaryd were their own child. The urgency displayed in their eyes was staggering as they grabbed their dogs and charged toward the trail. These people had no idea what failure meant, and their attitudes were contagious, encouraging, and full of confidence. I felt so proud they were on my team as doubt began to shrink in my heart. The challenge was theirs to overcome, and they were primed to meet all obstacles head-on. They created a healthy faith in me that my son would be back in my arms before any helicopter had the chance to get airborne.

"Go," I whispered. "Find my son."

As I waited at the trailhead, each passing second seemed to drag by at a lethargic pace. I couldn't imagine Jaryd alone in the darkness consumed by a raging fear that could only lead to delirium. It is not fair to expect a child to exist in a shroud of blackness that would cause his imagination to spring from one life-threatening apparition to another. The mental torment he was exposed to hovered above me and gnawed in to the inner places of my heart where I usually only found God's solitude. The thoughts that danced before me in a heinous cerebral waltz were crippling. The chill on my skin from the dropping temperatures was also maddening. Never had I realized the uncomfortable sensation of cold air as it encircled exposed skin the way I had that night. The cold was tolerable at first, but the longer it worked on me, the more I desired relief. If my son were out there, alive, the dark and cold had settled in as deplorable companions, and they were set on robbing him of safety and comfort. It was a fact of which I could hardly bear to think.

I tried to convince Janet to return to the resort with me, but she informed me she wasn't leaving without Jaryd. I reluctantly climbed into my Blazer and started the long journey back. I drove at a slow pace, imposed by my need to wipe the tears from my eyes.

That evening at the resort was difficult. I felt I was being born into a different person, and the labor pains were fierce. The investigator had put the hikers in my apartment, and he questioned them one at a time. I desperately wanted some privacy, and although I couldn't sleep, I was emotionally drained. I stayed out in the store away from everybody. I checked the clock every fifteen minutes or so, hoping the sun was about to make its appearance in the east, but the night dragged on. Many calls came in, and with each new ring of the phone, I hoped it was the good news I had anticipated from the rescue team, but it wasn't. I still had confidence that if they didn't find Jaryd during the night, they would find the tough little guy in the morning.

I tried to sleep that first night, but the hurt was too overwhelming. Avery, my younger brother in Nebraska, told my mother that he was going to sleep outside without a blanket until they located Jaryd. I could relate to how he felt. The comforts of home only created guilt, knowing Jaryd might be out there somewhere without the normal luxuries of the resort. Even my daughter kept waking through the night to hug me. The tenderness she showed me was good, but her actions could not take away the pain that was encompassing our lives.

I waited all night...and nothing happened.

....

The following information contains excerpts taken from the official incident report provided by the investigating deputy:

> On 10-2-99, I received a page from communications advising that they had a report of a missing five year old on the Big South hiking trail up the Poudre Canyon and that Emergency Services had also been advised. At that time I responded to the scene in emergency mode. While enroute, I heard Deputy Romero "go arrival" at the trailhead and shortly thereafter, he advised that there may be more than one person missing. By the time I arrived he had determined that there was only one person missing, that it was a three year old boy, identified as JARYD ATADERO, that JARYD had last been seen around 11:30 or 12:00 p.m., near marker No. 3 on the trail, that JARYD had been with a group of adults and his sister, and that they had been on a hike that morning.

Upon my arrival and obtaining the information from Deputy Romero, we determined that Deputy Romero would go in on the trail and attempt to locate the child. Deputy Romero had been speaking with JANET, who was seated in his patrol vehicle. We had her change vehicles to my department vehicle where I continued obtaining information from her while Deputy Romero went up the trail. Other members of the hiking party were standing around the trailhead parking lot in that immediate area.

Interview with JANET

As they went up the trailhead the last time she saw JARYD, he was behind two men and one woman, who were with their group on the trail. Behind them was JARYD, behind JARYD were two men with fishing poles. Following those two men was one man, three women, who included JANET and one child who was JOSALLYN. The other part of their party was lagging behind, that being BRUCE and two older ladies. She said she lost sight of the front group and the fishermen after they turned a corner and JANET never caught up with the front group. She said she never passed them as apparently they had gone off the trail. After JANET came back down back from the trail and was looking for JARYD, she realized that they had not found this other group and she went down to the cabin. There she encountered one of the women from the group fixing food. That woman told JANET that they had gone off the trail and that JARYD would go back with the others.

JANET told me that after she had last seen Jaryd, while on their way up she had heard what she thought was a cry at which time she thought he was still with the group ahead of her.

Interview with Kim

I next spoke with KIM. KIM told me that she, NANCY, and ANTHONY were at the front of the hiking group. She last saw JARYD before they got to the rocks on the trail. At that time JARYD was in front of them. KIM told him not to go too far ahead and he responded to her, "Okay." After that, she lost sight of him.

KIM told me that approximately twenty minutes after they last saw JARYD, they became concerned about his whereabouts and began stopping and listening to sounds. Thirty minutes after they last saw JARYD, they started back down the trail. KIM told me that they asked other people on the trail while on their way back down about anyone seeing JARYD, none had. On the way back down they talked to a fisherman and his wife.

Interview with Anthony

I next spoke to ANTHONY briefly. He gave me the times that he recalled since he had been paying some attention to the times. He told me they had started out on the trail at approximately 10:40 a.m., they last saw JARYD between 11:20 and 11:30 a.m., they turned back between 12:50 and 1:00 p.m., arrived back at the trailhead between 1:30 and 1:40 p.m., and went back and told JARYD's father of the situation.

Anthony said, "The fishermen had told them they saw Jaryd going up the trail. The fishermen caught up with Jaryd and he hung with them until they went off to go fishing. They told investigators that they have fished in that area a lot this year and have not seen any signs of bears or mountain lions.

Interview with Nancy

NANCY told me that JARYD caught up with her group or may have been with them the whole time, she wasn't sure which, but she remembers seeing him with them.

She told me that the fishermen had passed them and that JARYD was running after them. KIM yelled to JARYD to stop and stay close and NANCY said something to the others about keeping track of JARYD. She remembers thinking that they should keep a close eye on JARYD, but after KIM making her statement to JARYD to stop and stay close, the three of them went back to talking and didn't pay close attention to where JARYD was. NANCY thought he was following the fishermen and would be with them when the fishermen stopped to fish and that they would get JARYD at that time.

Information from Nolan and Arthur

The next interviews I did were with the two fishermen who had been on the trail, NOLAN and ARTHUR. I spoke briefly with them after they had been interviewed at length by Search and Rescue managers. They told me they had last seen JARYD ahead of them. They had forked to the river to fish while JARYD stayed on the trail. They knew that the group with him was approximately five to ten minutes behind him at the time they forked off to the river.

Interview with Bruce

After obtaining the names of all of the people who had been on the hike, I started interviewing the rest of them in the family room of the Poudre River Resort. The first one I spoke with was BRUCE. BRUCE told me that he did not know the time they had started the hike. He was sort of the leader for the hike, but while he was putting on his boots in the parking lot of the trailhead some of the people started out ahead. Bruce then decided to take up the rear and he did not see the first part of the group. He told me that he never really saw JARYD, he just noticed that there were two kids along with them.

They hiked in for approximately one and a half hours. BRUCE went out on a ledge looking at the river. He heard a sound that was like a kid screaming. BRUCE thought it sounded like a kid playing and JANET thought it sounded like he was scared. It sounded to BRUCE that it was close and JANET had then said that JARYD went with the fishermen or others in the group. Bruce thought some things were inconsistent at that time and was concerned.

Interview with Margaret

MARGARET thought the last seen point was approximately one hour up the trail and said that she could visualize that point on the trail very well. She said that BRUCE then went on ahead with the woman with the dog, who would have been NANCY, and they kept going. JANET, MARGARET, and JOSALLYN were going at a slow pace because of the altitude and the little girl. JANET was becoming more worried and they went down by the river a couple of times and stopped. SANDRA, BRUCE, and MARGARET then went onto the bridge where they only saw one footprint in the snow, which she described as a small footprint. She told me that she remembered hearing what MARGARET thought was a scream while coming back just past the boulder field.

Interview with Sandra

She last saw both kids approximately thirty to forty-five minutes into the hike. She told me that JARYD passed her real fast and JANET was yelling at him telling him to wait and don't hurry. SANDRA saw one person, then two people, then two fishermen ahead of her. She told me that JARYD zoomed by a couple of the people before he got to the fishermen. SANDRA thought that's where he was going was to the fishermen and she presumed that JANET knew where he was going and that he knew the people ahead.

SANDRA never saw JARYD again. She stopped and talked to JANET for a while with JOSALLYN. JANET said that she wished the others would come back with JARYD. They then went on up to campsite No. 7 and beyond. Said they saw one track in the snow at the end of the bridge and that it looked like the track of a man's hiking shoe.

Interview with Mark

MARK told me they went to Poudre Falls, and after that, they decided to go on to the trailhead and start hiking. He told me this was a spur of the moment decision, that it was unorganized...

MARK said, one time, while on a rock in the river, he heard something that sounded like keys jingling but he didn't see anyone along the bank or the trail. On the way back down the trail, MARK heard something that he thought was the same pitch as a child's voice, although he couldn't make out any words.

Group Observation

From my interviews with the group of people, it was determined that there was no specific plan as to where the group was going hiking that morning. Some of the group thought that Poudre Falls, which they were going to see was going to require a hike and when they arrived there and saw that the falls were right off the road, they decided that they would go on to the next trailhead and begin a hike. No one knew what length of hike they were going to be going on or what the terrain was like that they were going to be hiking in.

Day Two

Sunday, October 3, 1999

It is not the way I planned to spend Sunday morning in the mountains, but I was thrilled as the Colorado night slowly faded to day. One by one, the stars said their final good-byes as they were absorbed into the infinite heavens. I wondered if Jaryd were out there...somewhere...witnessing this same event, thankful and aware of the new opportunities this day held. As the sun raced for the eastern horizon, the sky seemed to be in motion as it faded from purples to grays. To nature, it was just another occasion to perform for those who enjoyed God's powerful spectacles. Patiently, I sat and waited, and without any fanfare or wilderness hoopla, the sun finally winked its first appearance from the east. I wondered how many people were actually awake to witness this remarkable show. The process of heating Colorado was underway, and I was hoping the temperature would climb into the seventies.

Surviving my first morning without Jaryd made me feel more dead than alive. The aroma of the traditional morning coffee was upon us, and my stomach was in no condition to welcome the trivial events I had taken for granted so many times before.

Wanting this experience to go away, I looked around, hoping Jaryd would dash into the store. Mentally, it was more comfortable to place myself in an imaginary world where everything would revert back to the way things were yesterday morning; but as each minute passed without him, the weight on my heart intensified. Although visions of Jaryd running through the store danced in my mind and I mentally lived through our triumphant reunion over and over, he didn't come in. Sadly, the cookie and hot chocolate went unattended. I was beginning to question and face a possible future without my son.

Each morning for the past eighteen months, my family waited for the day's newspapers to arrive. Some of those days were cold and lonely winter ones, but it was a different type of cold and loneliness I was experiencing now. Although many people view the mountains as a romantic place to escape, winter has a way of choking off our needed ties with the companionship of civilization. That winter yearning to be around people had returned, but this time, of course, it was for Jaryd. After awhile, I walked out to the newspaper stand and gave a quick glance at the Fort Collins *Coloradoan*. The paper was there, and I was astonished to read the headlines across the front page—*Boy Missing near Poudre Falls*. My god, the story of my little boy was now the story for everybody to see. I felt weak as I fumbled through my pocket for change to drop into the machine. After depositing the money in the slot, I lifted the cover, retrieved the top paper from the stand, and unfolded it. My hands trembled as I raced through the article.

Sunday, October 3, 1999

Boy missing near Poudre Falls

Rescue crew searches into night for 3-year-old lost during hiking trip

By David Ruisard

The Coloradoan

POUDRE FALLS -

Rescuers continued to search late into the night Saturday for a missing three-year-old boy here.

The Poudre Valley tot disappeared about noon Saturday while hiking with family friends along the Big South Trail, a half-mile east of the waterfalls.

The 11-person hiking party searched for the boy on its own before placing an emergency call with the Larimer County Sheriff's Department at 2:20 p.m.

The story immediately brought me to tears as I walked back in the store and continued reading. I couldn't believe my son was actually missing, and I hoped the article would provide the latest news or something positive of which I was unaware. The events surrounding his disappearance were in black and white, and as much as I wanted to deny the facts, the story had taken root and was beginning to grow into an event I could have never imagined. It seems that most days, we occupy ourselves with external affairs, reacting to them according to the impact they may have on our internal peace. I tried to withdraw to my normally small and warm, intimate world, but the true vastness of this situation was making itself known. I was lost in an immense cold and dark domain that only yesterday morning had not existed.

As I fought back tears, the need to be a strong father to Josallyn kept me from sinking into the surrounding mental catacombs that were closing in on me. I wasn't about to give in and surrender, although vultures were circling my heart in anticipation of my imminent death. I prayed silently and asked God to give me the strength to face this day. I brushed away the sorrows and received His strength, then wiped the tears from my eyes.

I wasn't sure how Jaryd's disappearance was affecting Josallyn's little mind, and I wanted to do something to keep her distracted. As I stood there, a strange sound echoed from outside. It was a hollow whooping sound that repeated over and over. I told Josallyn I thought it was a helicopter and that we should go outside to see it. She flung the front door open, and we walked into the parking lot. The two of us stood there and silently gazed eastward as we searched the sky for the aircraft. "There it is!" I shouted as I pointed back down the canyon. At 8:17 a.m., Sunday, the Huey passed directly overhead.

I cheered and yelled like a wild, out of control maniac. I leaped and pointed and screamed, "Hang in there, Jaryd. They're coming to get you!" What an awesome sight that helicopter was! Josallyn must have realized how important this was in the search, so the fact that I was making a spectacle out of myself didn't bother her in the least. She just smiled at me and gently rocked her approving shoulders back and forth. It's difficult to explain the elation that flowed through and around me as the Huey made its way west. *Whoever you are, God bless you,* I thought. They were on their way to find my son, and I concluded today was going to be a good day. I felt as though we would celebrate this afternoon with a great feast because my son would be coming home. It felt good to be alive with hope.

Josallyn and I walked back into the store, and a great feeling of comfort and confidence followed us. I held my head high, and I could actually feel somewhat of a swagger in my steps. Last night was a devilish experience that seemed to never end, but now the top of the world provided me with new visions, and I was filled with hope.

It took Josallyn fourteen years before she could pick up the book and read about her little brother. To this day, I can close my eyes and see the helicopter as it passed over us that morning. I mention this because Josallyn can remember several things about the search, but she has no recollection of the helicopter.

....

During the summer before Jaryd vanished, while my brother Arlyn was still here, we had a different retreat with the Christian Singles Association. It was an exciting experience that brought many Christians together. There were several functions on the property, and the area afforded many opportunities to those who wanted to get away and explore. Many of the men camped out by the river, and most of the women were housed in the cabins. They used our kitchen to cook for the group, and we helped by keeping fresh food available during breakfast and dinner. Most people checked out Sunday afternoon, but the remaining group gathered in our back room for church services. It was an exceptional conclusion to a special weekend.

Before summer had arrived, we had taken the bold step of placing a lighted cross in the front of the parking lot of the Poudre River Resort. It was a thrilling experience to see that cross glowing in the darkness of the Rockies. A friend and I drove down the road so we could turn around and watch the cross come into our view as we approached the resort. We had a peculiar feeling that we had started something big when that cross became a symbol of safety in the mountains. We often had stranded travelers who needed an emergency place to stay, or others who were out of gas, stop because of the cross. We believed it was our mission to help those in need, and we never charged for rendered services or rooms when people found themselves in difficult traveling situations.

During our first big month of the summer, the canyon experienced a landslide that all but closed the canyon for several weeks. We lost a lot of business during June, and it was hard to recover from the disaster. My brother once asked me if I thought the landslide happened because we were bold enough to place a lighted cross on our land. It shined like a beacon of hope, and in some ways, it did seem as though the cross marked the beginning of our problems. A minister, who was an acquaintance, suggested that we would be challenged because of our beliefs. After the Sunday morning church services, one of the Christian Singles Association men was involved in a motorcycle accident on his way out of the canyon. Tragedy continued to follow.

....

After Josallyn and I had earlier witnessed the helicopter, we knew there would once again be a church service in the back room of the resort. The weekend retreat was coming to a dramatic conclusion, and the anticipated worship service started at nine thirty. It turned into a prayer service for Jaryd.

I could never downplay the amount of pain I was going through. It was real, and no matter what I did, the agony followed with a life of its own. The ache reminded me of the summer storms that often swept through our mountain valleys, but unlike the accompanying rain I had often enjoyed, I was now faced with a downpour of depression that seemed to come in waves. As unusual as this may appear, I also felt there was a person who was feeling worse than me, but for a different reason.

During our prayer meeting, we waited for the arrival of Janet, but she failed to show. Several people were sent to her cabin to get her, but the remorse she was experiencing had trapped her in a private world that was keeping her from showing her face. I can't conceive the torment that engulfed her, but those who went to get Janet reassured her that she was loved. She needed to be comforted, and with a lot of coaxing, she finally decided to join the group.

I will never forget watching her methodically climb the back steps as though she were about to face the executioner. Upon reaching the deck, I saw that she gripped a Kleenex in her hand. Her head was down, and she appeared as though she were a lifeless body slowly floating toward the French doors of our patio.

When the doors opened, she entered the room, and everyone's eyes were fixed on her. We tried to imagine the pain she was going through, but we couldn't. The pain she felt and the pain I felt were different types of pain. Hers was born of guilt and mine of loss. The most important thing for her at that moment was that she had entered into a room filled with love, and nobody was moving to place blame on her. It was good to see her. The more I looked at her, the worse I felt as I stood there and watched the mourning unfold before me. I will always remember the joy my son brought into my life, but Janet needed to realize the joy she brought into Jaryd's was also important. Yesterday, when Jaryd left the resort for a day of fun, he did so because he loved Janet. She was a very special person to him, and I believe if he had the chance, Jaryd would choose to go hiking with her again.

I did not feel comfortable about approaching Janet. It wasn't because I was angry with her or anything like that, but sometimes, no matter how much we search, there are no words capable of communicating one's feelings. I also believe I would have done more damage than good because my pain was substantially different from hers. She was a woman who was living in hell on earth. The torment that filled her heart was far worse than what any one of us could have inflicted upon her. If I walked up to her and put my arms around her, I probably would have crushed her more. It is a terrible thing to cause pain to another person, and she could barely stand the fact that she may have done something to hurt Jaryd or me. It was a nauseating scene to observe, but I stood there and watched as our friends went to her aid. I was glad they were there for her, and even though it was my desire to look into her eyes and hold her hands, I couldn't. I would have done anything to lift the ugly veil of grief and guilt that had descended upon our lives, but as the day passed, I realized it was consuming us at a horrid pace.

On the day Jaryd vanished, my uncle Gus was at the Wailing Wall in Jerusalem. While he was there, a powerful impulse persuaded him to pray for each member of my family by name. He responded to the urge and then later departed the country for Germany. While in Frankfurt, he observed a story on the news concerning a father and his lost son in Colorado. To his dismay, the story was about his family. An acquaintance, while visiting friends in South Korea, learned of the tragedy while watching the news there. Thousands literally came together from around the world to pray for Jaryd.

....

As I anticipated an encouraging report from the search site, the morning passed with little valuable information concerning the whereabouts of my son. Jaryd's mother, Angie, had arrived from California, and I knew if we didn't find Jaryd today, he wouldn't be able to survive the elements of another night. I had not yet considered the option of life without my son because I believed it would destroy my own existence, and I was not about to give up my precious hope.

That afternoon, the sergeant in charge of the search and rescue team came to the resort to touch base with me concerning the investigation. While I was speaking with the sergeant, I received a call from a woman who owned certified Colorado search dogs. This stranger offered her services to us for no charge. I couldn't believe a person could have such a heart to call and volunteer to search for a boy she had never met, and I felt extremely blessed by her gesture. I had prayed for help and deliverance from this trial, and I questioned God's purpose for placing me in this situation. Little did I know, my private tribulation was about to multiply. As I spoke with this woman, I informed her that the sergeant in charge of the mission was actually standing right next to me. I handed the phone to the sergeant and tried to listen to his side of the conversation.

The sergeant did not speak directly in front of me, but as he turned away, I could hear every word spanning the short distance between us. The woman on the other end of the phone had taken the time to find my number and was obviously willing to help, yet I heard the sergeant tell her, "If we need you, we'll call you." I found this peculiar because as he talked, he wasn't writing down her phone number. I thought, *How are you going to call this lady if we decide to place her in the field?*

From my perspective, I didn't understand what had just taken place, and I had no idea this experience would later resurface. Disappearances create situations that test our resolve and established rules of operation. Although I know everybody was working diligently to find my son, rules are guidelines meant to channel our efforts. Deviating from them for the purpose of enhancing our odds of success would seem to be a prudent option that was being overlooked. I didn't envy anyone who had a significant role in this mystery, and each person involved would not only search the mountain, but would end up searching his or her soul many times before any likely answers would materialize.

Many professional organizations, such as hospitals, military, law enforcement, and sports, will conduct postoperative evaluations in hopes of strengthening areas of weakness. No matter how much practice is involved, perfection has a way of eluding us because we are not capable of predicting all factors in any given situation. Being the professional organization that they are, I understand the sheriff's office undertook such a task when the official search was concluded. Various issues were aired, and like any review of an event of this magnitude would expect, recommendations were offered. There was also a shift in the command structure during the search, and the experience provided an opportunity from which many could learn.

I am certain the sergeant had no idea I could hear his conversation that morning because he would have never wanted to hurt me, but it did. It was that conversation that caused me to begin to question, from a father's perspective with a lost son, what was really going on. Why would he tell a lady with perfectly good dogs that he didn't need her when I was sure we did? I have watched many search and rescue missions play out on the news, and I have always had the impression the more who are involved, the better the chances of rescue.

There was an expert tracker called Seaux (Sue) on the evening news who concluded that tracking Jaryd would be troublesome because the evidence the sheriff's office was attempting to preserve had already been trampled on and destroyed. Seaux had firsthand knowledge because he was actually on the trail searching at that moment. When initial signs had been obliterated, I believed it was time to rely on more eyes and scent, and the vision of my heart desired to see thousands of dogs.

I received many phone calls from people who were trained trackers with certified dogs, and they were eager to get involved. One of the people whom I spoke with was extremely disappointed. The sheriff's department had also told him that if they needed him, they would have already contacted him. This person's desire to become involved was incredible, and I didn't have the ability to ensure he was included. There was an outpouring of similar requests because it is not in our nature to standby and witness an event like this without being compelled to step forward to offer help. The sheriff's office was tasked with making many difficult decisions that most of us will never have to make. The people of Colorado are not comfortable with being on the sideline in situations like this, and our collective patience was being tested. I could feel their presence as the search continued to unfold.

About an hour later, a tracker named Don Bendell called me to see if he could volunteer his services. His voice was quiet but very confident, and he sounded like the most sincere person I had spoken with in a long time. His credentials were incredible. Through this ordeal, I learned there is a thriving subculture of people who train and live to aid those of us who lack the knowledge and ability to track humans. It is such a tough business that these people actually carry resumes and letters, attesting to their accomplishments, with them. There were at least two occasions when I witnessed trackers attempting to help in the search. Each time, they had to sell themselves to the sheriff. I heard things like, "Contact Sheriff So and So of Whatever County, and he'll tell you to let me in."

The people in charge of the search kept their list of participants tightly controlled. I wanted every certified person and canyon neighbor up on the trail. Obviously, if a parent is placed at the head of a search, the event would take on an entirely different appearance; and if I would have been calling the shots, the symbolic gates to the trail would have been wide open. After all, I had nothing else to lose, and time was chopping at the trunk of success. There were many pure-hearted people looking for my son, and their integrity and character wanted me to find more people like them.

While Don Bendell talked, I could feel his empathy, and I quickly realized all he wanted was to find my son and bring him back to his daddy. He didn't want any publicity; he just wanted to share his true human compassion. As he pleaded his case, he told me someone at the sheriff's office kept telling him he was not needed. A few years earlier, a couple of law enforcement officers had been shot in southwestern Colorado, and the manhunt that followed turned into one of the largest searches in US history. Covertly, Don's tracking skills and experience were utilized in the search by local and federal authorities, yet those affiliated with Jaryd's search greeted this same man with extreme suspicion. He shared with me the then familiar quote, "If we needed you, we would have called you."

I didn't have to plead my case to Don. Although he had been told not to show up, he took the initiative to make one last call, and I felt blessed. I asked him if he would come and help me find my son, and he said he would be on location the first thing in the morning. I told him if there were any problems, I would inform the authorities he was working for me. He had a search dog, a horse, and a lot of equipment he needed to load, and the drive would take him several hours. He asked me for nothing in return.

I know the sheriff was treating the search area as if it were a crime scene. He didn't have much of a choice because of the lack of any serious evidence. A crime scene would provide him with the leverage to control access to the area. However, there was also no evidence of foul play, which only worked to blur the position where we all wanted to stand. The possibility that Jaryd was the victim of the river or a wild animal also complicated the desire to focus resources on the most likely scenario. The paradox of the situation dictated that a crime scene required less participation for fear of destroying evidence, while the lack of foul play loaned itself to a search requiring a saturation of resources. Once again, I felt we were in a situation we couldn't win, and the sheriff was placed in the position of deciding which side of the fence we needed to stand on. The problem was, I did not believe he had enough information to make an adequate call. Considering Jaryd had also placed the sheriff in the national spotlight, he had to go with the flow of the moment.

As the years passed, I continued to run into people who wanted to speak with me about the search for little Jaryd. I received the following e-mail about nine years after Jaryd had vanished:

> Hello Allyn,
>
> It is such an honor to talk with you, even in an e-mail, all these years later. My late husband and I and our very loyal supporters of our canine trackers, Ben and Travis, have always been touched by Jaryd and the fact we were not allowed to help you. We never forgot you and to this day, remains a heartbreaking time in our lives.
>
> I'm sure you've learned from Casandra, that we tried so very hard to work through the politics and be allowed to work the search for Jaryd. Our dogs were experienced in crime scenes as well as lost, found and abducted children.....they were highly trained in many facets of

tracking/trailing, were in their prime and had earned an impressive service record. It was to no avail. In short, we were told that the SAR unit "in charge" of the search, would not allow anyone other than their members in the search area or take part in their search efforts. We were not strangers to the politics that are, unfortunately, still in existence today. But, that did not lessen our frustration and sadness in being shut out of a search where we could have possibly been a source of assistance.

I don't expect certain heartbreaks to go away, however, I continue to do all I can to train canines for scent specific tracking, to bring them to a high level of talent as to rival any canine doing this important work and become the unpaid professionals they are.......

On the day Jaryd vanished, my brother Arlyn had gone to San Diego. He and several of the teachers at McCabe Elementary School in El Centro had completed a language development training program. The group traveled to San Diego's Old Town as a cultural experience that culminated the training. Arlyn's wife, Robyn, who is also a childhood friend of mine, accompanied him on the trip. The two of them decided to stay in San Diego until Sunday. Saturday afternoon, Arlyn suggested to Robyn they call home and inform their son, Josh, of their location. After they discussed it, they concluded one day away from their world would hurt no one. The seclusion would be appreciated, and what were the odds something earth shattering would happen?

Arlyn and Robyn pulled into their driveway in El Centro late Sunday morning. Josh was outside with the portable phone waiting for them. My brother told me it was strange to see Josh there because he had a look of despair they had never seen. As Arlyn opened his door and stepped out of the truck, Josh walked up. His lips quivered, and his eyes watered, and I know my brother must have been pretty confused about that time.

"They can't find Jaryd. He's lost in the mountains somewhere."

"What?" It was the only response Arlyn could make. He gave Robyn a quick glance, and she immediately realized something was wrong.

"Josh," she said, "what's wrong?"

Josh fought back tears as he continued to deliver the news. "Jaryd's lost in the mountains, and Allyn can't find him. They lost him yesterday."

"Who lost Jaryd?" Arlyn demanded. My brother later explained to me how he felt when he first heard the news. He said it was as though he could feel himself retreating from reality as a strange form of tunnel vision moved in. The words were there to explain what was transpiring, but they didn't seem to make sense.

"You're *kidding!*" Robyn screamed with an angry voice of skepticism. The words she had spoken were drawn out and deliberate.

"Allyn and the kids went to the resort for the weekend. Josallyn and Jaryd went hiking with a group of adults, and they lost him."

"This can't be happening," Arlyn whispered as he headed for the house. "Please, God, don't let this be real. Don't let this be real."

Robyn exclaimed, "Arlyn, you know we have to go to Colorado."

"Hang on, Robyn, let me call Allyn and talk to him. Maybe they found him and everything's okay." Arlyn disappeared into the house and immediately headed for the kitchen phone. He later told me he had a difficult time dialing. I know he had no idea what to say to me, but I finally received his call early Sunday afternoon. Arlyn didn't say much because he was hit pretty hard with the news. We only talked for about a minute, but Arlyn lacked all composure to carry on a conversation. He told me he would call back when he could speak. I know he hung up the phone and cried in the kitchen. Robyn and Josh went in with him, and they all broke down for several minutes. Robyn continued to insist the two of them needed to drive back to San Diego and catch a plane to Colorado. My brother said the worst thing for him was knowing I was going through hell, and he couldn't do anything about it. I realize it was rough on him because he said he was aware his suffering could never compare to what I was going through, and his pain was pretty severe.

Arlyn called me back within twenty minutes. I know he was trying to develop his own plan. He had called our mother and briefly discussed options with her. He also called his superintendent, Dan Eddins, and Dan told Arlyn to take as much time as he needed. Although it was a terrible story to communicate, the reverberations of its impact had yet to sweep across the nation. Arlyn went to school, and two good friends of mine met him there as he got things ready for a substitute teacher. Jinger Myers, Betsy Enders, and my brother sat in Arlyn's class and cried. They walked to the back of campus where my mother lived and called me. It was good to hear the voices of dear friends. Even though we were miles apart, our hearts joined, and we cried together. It was during the time Arlyn was working in his class that the helicopter searching for Jaryd crashed.

Arlyn, Robyn, my aunt Katie, and my mother, Bertie, had managed to get themselves booked on an early Monday flight from San Diego to Denver. They departed El Centro that evening. Arlyn made phone calls to other family members; the prayer chain was beginning to grow. Arlyn's oldest son, Todd, was already in northern Colorado with me because he attended Colorado State University. Josh decided to remain in El Centro so he could take care of any concerns that might possibly arise. Later, as the story grew, Josh would become the incident's focal point in the Imperial Valley. It was a role he didn't want to accept, and he avoided the media as much as he could. One reporter would later track him down in a car lot as he accompanied a friend who was in the market for a used car.

Todd was instrumental in running our resort store as the rest of the family traveled back and forth from the search site to the resort or to Fort Collins. Several times, members of the media would come into the store, searching for a member of the Atadero family for a comment. Members of the Villavicencio family had graciously accepted that role for us. Gil Villavicencio was a childhood friend from the Imperil Valley who had relocated to Colorado several years before our arrival. Todd never gave his identity as he diligently labored in the background. My family's help and support through this time will always be something I could never put a price on. Their help was precious to me.

Although I know it was difficult for my brother to talk to me, it was just as painful for me to speak with him. As we spoke, the hope I held close to my heart was waning. I didn't have any positive news worth sharing, and desperation was smothering what little optimism that was clinging to my soul. It was bad enough knowing my son was missing, but it was also likely he had endured one terrifying night alone in the woods. The thought of him somewhere out there was excruciating, and as much as I didn't want to think about the possibility of a second night, horrifying visions of that very thought darted through my mind. The moments making up the day were racing by faster and faster, and the looming tide of darkness lurked a few hours away. A cold shiver was triggered by each image that propelled itself into my consciousness. How could a mountain be so stubborn as to refuse to divulge any information pertaining to Jaryd's mystery? The more I searched for answers, the more acute my awareness became to the ticking of my watch and the fading of daylight.

The strength I hoped to receive from my family would have to wait until the morning. I thought how wonderful it would be to share Jaryd's rescue with them. They would arrive at the resort and see my son in my arms and listen as he shared fantastic stories of his survival. Those thoughts delivered warmth and happiness to my internal world of frigid desperation.

It is really strange the way things affect people. As my world crumbled around me, I sort of expected everybody to rally to my aid. But they say life does go on, and it does go on regardless of whether we are ready for it or not. I kind of expected the world to pause for a second to mourn, but it didn't. As far as I was concerned, I had come to a door that revealed a peculiar truth that everything is temporary. I questioned the origin of feelings and wondered if they could actually be suppressed. What is life's purpose when the agony of such a destructive pain is allowed to invade us? We must all experience it sooner or later, and I have watched before as others on television exposed their deepest grief for the rest of us to witness. Saturday was like most quiet days for me until it had been ripped to shreds by the beast of fate. The heartache I now felt had replaced all feelings of security that had been there just hours before. Pain comes calling when we least expect. If only we could possess the wisdom to truly understand the totality of our existence, we would tolerate the temporal invasions of pain.

Those who had been on the hike with Jaryd began leaving. Their lives awaited them in Denver, and as much as they desired to stay and help, it was time for each of them to return to their real worlds. I was nothing more than a terrible accident on the side of the road of life, and people were slowing down to look, but the road ahead is what waited for them. Each of them slowly passed me by.

My point is, sooner or later, we all have to deal with grief in our own private way. There's no escaping it. No matter how bad a person may feel, there is no way for another to truly experience or share that pain. For the most part, the journey is a solo flight, and each of us should be prepared when our number is called. My closeness to God provided a peace that I was fortunate to have. In some ways, I wasn't taking this flight alone because I felt God was moving in and setting up camp with me. When my friends and acquaintances were heading back toward their lives and jobs,

I was able to accept it without resentment. Each time I dwelled on the passing events, God provided comfort because He was the only one who could truly bear my pain. Maybe everybody who headed home concluded it was only a matter of time before Jaryd would be found.

Three of my closest friends, who were not on the hike, did stick around and render the much-needed assistance I required. Brenda, Candice, and John realized the magnitude of the situation, and they decided to stay and help a brother with the fight of his life. By Sunday afternoon, members from the media made their presence known. Several entered the store to satisfy their curiosity. Their eagerness bothered me, although I know it was their job. In their perfect world, they hoped to stumble across a story or an interview that might elude the others. By having the store on the premises, it provided them with the perfect incentive to make an intrusion into my world of sadness. We were open to the public, and I did have bills to pay, so in they came, concealing their snooping by pretending to shop. At least that's how I initially felt about them, but my relationship with the media would turn into a positive experience.

Initially, it was my friend Brenda who became my spokesperson. Brenda is very professional in every undertaking she accepts, and there was no doubt she had my best interests at heart. As she fielded questions on my behalf, I found myself standing near an open window on the west side of the store. Many of the first interviews were given outside that window, and without the media realizing it, I could privately hear every question and listen to each response Brenda gave. I was at each interview without anybody knowing it, and this provided me comfort.

My son had been missing for twenty-four hours, and in my heart, I believed he was about to be found, so I really had no need for the media circus that had arrived. I didn't care about their jobs or who had the best news in the Denver market; but I can now say, from a strange perspective, most of the people who gathered in the canyon treated my family and me very well. Considering the number of people who arrived, the story I didn't want them to miss was the one where Jaryd would come home.

Survival on the Mountain

I am not sure of the events of the next part of this story, so bits of it are what I believe to be true from what I have heard. I was nowhere near the trail site when the search for Jaryd turned into a rescue mission for the brave men who had placed themselves in harm's way for the good of my son. A model UH-1N, alias "N" model Huey, tail number 69-6602, assigned to the Thirty-Seventh Helicopter Flight, F. E. Warren Air Force Base, Wyoming (about one hundred miles away from the resort if one drives, sixty miles as the crow flies) had been scouring the location during most of the day. Several sorties had been conducted over the area where Jaryd was last seen.

....

As the engines thundered, gravity loosened its grip on the helicopter, causing it to magically pull away from the asphalt of State Route 14. The shadows of the forest had been creeping easterly for some time, and conditions seemed ripe for a favorable conclusion to a search that had so far yielded nothing but frustration. The Huey UH-1N, from Warren Air Force Base in Wyoming, swooped southward with its crew of four Air Force personnel and one member of the local search team. Cameras from various news organizations were on hand to record its final ascent into the lower heavens encircling the mountains. The battle for Jaryd was intensifying, and not a soul onboard was aware their flight was doomed. The realization of the challenge was already enough to demand the total alertness of their mental faculties, but gravity would soon reclaim that which it had been cheated out of, and each man's mortality was racing toward a confrontation with the struggle between life and death.

"Okay, everybody, keep your eyes peeled," shouted the pilot. "We're gonna find Jaryd."

While the rotor blades sliced through the sky, a huge down draft rushed along the contours of the metal chamber that secured the searchers. Combined with the deafening pounding of the pistons, a constant mild vibration rattled through the craft and became part of reality's mix that is seldom experienced by a civilian searcher.

The landscape's perspective assumed a new look from above. Trees no longer seemed to reach for the sky while anchored to the ground by massive trunks. Green textured carpets of pines and shimmering fields of golden aspens blanketed the surface of the highlands. The view from the chopper was absolutely breathtaking. Enormous peaks stretched above submissive valleys while rivers and streams searched for lower elevations to rest. Tiny dirt roads scarred the backcountry below while the black ribbon of State Route 14 snaked through the Roosevelt National Forest. The splendor of the terrain was deceptive in its radiance. It was difficult to believe that something so ravishing and tranquil could consume the innocent life of a curious child who was enthralled with the environment that had drawn him there. It was even more painful to accept the fact that the Big South Trail would be so resistant in its willingness to deliver Jaryd back to the world from which he came.

The Huey approached the area where Jaryd was last seen and descended. The men knew they could see more territory at a higher elevation, but a low-flying helicopter would surely attract Jaryd's attention. As the Huey approached the tree line, all eyes remained vigilant for any sign of the missing boy. Tops of trees seemed to edge closer to the mighty craft until it was too late. The propellers clipped the trees, and the helicopter fought to gain altitude, but gravity prevailed as it pulled its victims into the pines that lined the east edge of the river. The Huey groaned as trees scraped against its metal shell. Branches snapped and popped as the rotor blade crashed against the top of the forest canopy, causing the wounded craft to roll. The top of a huge pine tree entered the left side of the helicopter and protruded through the right as the giant machine collided with the side of the mountain. Shattered tree trunks were splintered among the mangled wreckage. At that very moment, the search for Jaryd ceased. Searchers on the ground who were near the downed helicopter came rushing to the crew's aid. As they approached the twisted remains of the Huey, urgency became more paramount as one of the engines continued to roar. Everyone needed to be evacuated from the helicopter and the area just in case the downed chopper exploded.

It had been about forty-five minutes since several of my friends had departed the resort for Denver when the phone rang. Each ring brought new hope as I anticipated the good news that was surely imminent. I really expected to hear a voice exclaiming the news of Jaryd's discovery, followed by a request for me to go and pick him up. When I answered the phone, that's exactly what I heard. There was an extremely excited voice on the other end, and it made my skin crawl with anticipation. I thought, *Oh, God, please tell me they found him.* The person on the line was my friend Leanne, and she was at the bottom of the mountain at a Conoco gas station called Ted's Place. It's located at the part of Highway

14 that enters Poudre Canyon. Leanne was very excited as she asked, "Did they find Jaryd?"

My heart pounded with excitement because I concluded she had news that had yet reached me. "What do you mean?" I asked. Leanne told me an ambulance and a second emergency vehicle had just raced by her heading up the canyon. From the looks of things, she figured all the fuss had to be about Jaryd. I told her we hadn't heard anything at the resort, but I would check into it. One can imagine the emotions that overwhelmed me for the hundredth time. I sat down and patiently waited for the phone call I thought I was about to receive. The hope that my prayers had been answered swirled through my mind as I replayed the day's events in my head. The incredible thought that it was probably all over was soothing to my troubled soul. I felt I was about to collapse from exhaustion.

I nearly jumped out of my skin when the phone rang again about fifteen minutes later. This time, it was one of my friends who lived in the canyon below me, and I was greeted with the same question, "Did they find Jaryd?" Blind faith was stirring up the canyon's optimism all because a speeding ambulance was heading toward the Big South Trail.

Something had to be happening, and I figured the sheriff's office would be the source of my next call, so I waited. Five minutes crawled to ten, then to fifteen, but still no news had arrived from the authorities. I feverishly paced about as the wild carrot of hope dangled before me. *Why aren't they calling me? Somebody should have called me by now!* I questioned my sanity as I heard the faint sound of a siren in the distance. As it quickly got louder and louder, my eyes filled with tears as I tried to cry the remnants of the intense pain away. My heart was in the process of preparing itself for the amazing joy it was about to experience.

Could this be true? The anticipation of seeing my son was driving every sense in my body crazy. As the frequency of the sound waves from the siren tightened, I ran outside to see the ambulance race by as if it were yelling, "Don't worry, Jaryd, we are coming to get you!" It was the best sight I had seen since the helicopter had flown over earlier in the morning. As I looked around, I noticed four different neighbors running toward me with excitement glowing from their faces. They all wanted the answer to the same reverberating question, "Did they find Jaryd?"

I looked at them and gave them the answer they least expected. "I don't know!"

They looked at me with disbelief as one of my neighbors said, "They haven't told you anything yet?"

I hesitantly answered back, "Nothing, not a thing."

The momentary excitement of the situation faded when Josallyn and her mom came outside to ask me if there was some place close they could go and buy a coloring book. I told them Glen Echo Resort was about a mile back down the road, and they probably had something there for Josallyn. They both jumped into the car to venture down the road to share a little privacy with each other, not knowing they would be back a lot sooner than they realized. They were gone for about ten minutes when the car flew back into the driveway and skidded to an abrupt stop.

Things were happening too fast, but they were the wrong things. I was confused when they returned so quickly, not to mention the expression I saw on their faces. The way they pulled into the parking lot also caused me to wonder what was going on, and the looming question of why the sheriff's office had not contacted me was very troublesome. Angie ran up to me and shouted, "You're never going to believe what I just heard from some people shopping at Glen Echo!"

She was right. I would never believe what she had heard, but more important was the question of why others were hearing things and I wasn't. I still believed good news was in the wind, and people were catching its scent, but the expression on her face didn't communicate happiness. Rage brewed inside me as I waited for her response. She said, "They told me the helicopter that was searching for Jaryd crashed into the mountain."

I stared back in disbelief and whispered, "No, no, no, this can't possibly be true." My mumbling got louder and louder until I exclaimed, "They would have called to let us know. This can't be true...it just can't be true!" I shook my head and felt betrayed, fully believing that if anything happened concerning Jaryd's search, I would be one of the first people contacted. Was it possible someone at the search site concluded the relevance of this substantial incident would have no impact on my family or me? Emergency crews had rushed up the canyon, signifying to the local residents and me that something had happened. Regardless of whether it was positive or negative, the initial incident responsible for the chain of events was the disappearance of Jaryd, and yet no communication was warranted? They must have known the emergency response team would pass directly in front of my business. How could communication with me be overlooked? I stopped and collected my thoughts. There had to be some way I could confirm what I had just heard.

My mind went into a frenzy as I searched for someone to call. I didn't want to contact the sheriff's office because the trust I had placed in communicating with them was gradually fading. They had to know the ambulance that drove by me had false hope as its main passenger. When it passed, that hope leaped from the vehicle and made itself an unwelcome guest at the resort. It only took one person to say, "Someone should call Jaryd's family and let them know what happened." It was evident that that one person did not exist because I was never contacted until I took the initiative.

I started looking for phone numbers from media personnel, thinking they would be able to give me the information I needed. Nothing. I could not find a thing. Fury tore through my body as I threw papers around hoping to find a phone number to anyone who would communicate with me, but I didn't want it to be the sheriff's office. My mind began to swim. *Nothing! Somebody call me and put a stop to this pain. Somebody please call me!*

The more I searched, the more desperate I became. I finally found the number to the sheriff's dispatch. I held it close to my eyes and again wondered why they hadn't called. As I gazed at the card, I remembered being told that if I needed anything, all I had to do was place a call to dispatch, and they would have somebody involved with the search contact me right away. However, if dispatch knew what was going on, somebody should have taken the initiative to make contact with me before this.

I had no choice. I picked up the phone and dialed dispatch. As the father of Jaryd Atadero, I had expected all channels of communication to be open and flowing with information. I was at a delicate place in my life that required courtesy, especially if it curtailed a false onslaught of hope and emotion. There wasn't a person in the world who would stand in the shoes I was now standing in. Was it possible that I had been momentarily overlooked? How had the shoppers at Glen Echo learned of this potential accident? Questions flooded my mind as the sheriff's office dispatch answered the phone. "This is the sheriff's office." The female voice on the other end of the line was pleasant, and I again felt hope swelling within me.

I told the woman working in dispatch that I didn't know whom to call, and I was hoping she could answer a question for me. I informed her that I had heard the helicopter looking for the little boy had crashed into the mountain. It was an easy question requiring a simple answer, and I expected a response of, "Yes, it did," or, "No, it did not," but I didn't get either. She said, "Let me transfer you to somebody who can answer that question."

I responded without any hesitation. "No, please don't. I'm the father of the boy who is missing, and many of my friends and I have heard rumors concerning the search helicopter. All I want to know is, are they true?"

The other side of the phone became silent as this person tried to digest what I had said. The voice came back. "Yes, sir, it did."

I asked her, "How long ago?"

"About an hour."

I hung up the phone in disbelief. Bad was getting worse, and I needed to find a quiet place where I could retreat. With my head hung low, I walked back into the game room to search for clues that would confirm I was experiencing a bad dream—but there were none. I approached the couch and eased my fragile body down onto it. Tears filled my eyes as I brought my hands up to my face in a feeble attempt to hold myself together. I whispered, "Please, God, don't let anyone die. I don't want anybody sacrificing his life for the sake of my son." I cried for the safety of those who went down with the helicopter.

My depression grew deeper and deeper. All I knew was the helicopter had crashed, but I did not know the extent of any of the injuries or if anyone had perished. My imagination was already running rampant as visions of Jaryd continued to invade each and every moment of my conscious existence, and now more tragedy was being heaped upon the raging inferno that burned within my heart. And still no answers. My mind dabbled with conclusions to events that only left me room to ponder what may have happened. The more my mind mingled with the unknown, the greater my soul was pierced by the desire for factual information pertaining to the entire rescue effort for Jaryd. I couldn't handle not knowing the condition of the men aboard the helicopter.

The official report about the crash came out two months later, and it indicated the helicopter was flying too low to maintain any lift. All five people aboard the helicopter survived the crash, but they all suffered from some sort of injury. Three of the injured were taken by a Flight for Life helicopter to the local hospital.

From the Field Incident Report

The helicopter crashed at 1530 hours on the trail approximately a quarter mile north of campsite #1. Search teams in the area quickly went to the aid of the passengers. Two specialists began organizing the treatment and the evacuation of the injured. The Recourse Officer made notifications to communications, asking them to contact Warren Air Force Base and to have an air ambulance stand by. I received enough information that we had at least two people that were serious and would need transportation by helicopter. I requested an air ambulance from Greeley, but was advised that they were busy and that one would be coming from Denver. At that time, I also asked communications to contact Warren Air Force Base about using Army helicopters with winch capabilities to help with the rescue.

To further complicate things, the crashed helicopter's turbines were still operating and blocking access to the trail for quick and easy evacuation. I was advised of patient conditions and that they believed that they could get by the helicopter safely and that it would take about one to one and a half hours to get the most serious patient to the trail head. The air ambulance arrived at the trail-head and was staged on the highway until the first patient was there. A land ambulance from Poudre Valley Hospital and off duty paramedics from the same hospital and Glacier View Fire arrived and went in to assist with treatment of patients. It was soon determined that three patients would need to be flown to a hospital and I coordinated the helicopters arrival and departure. The last two patients were transported by land ambulance. All patients involved in the crash were removed from the site by 1830 hours and the scene was secured for the Air Force investigators, who started to arrive around 2200 hours. At approximately 1800 hours, an Army helicopter from Fort Carson arrived in the area, but was released as they were no longer needed. We also received information that an Army National

Guard helicopter from Cheyenne, Wyoming was also en route. They were also cancelled.

Due to the crash, all efforts to find the missing child were halted until the crash victims were taken care of. Additional resources from Rocky Mountain National Park were requested to help with the helicopter crash, but did not arrive until after we had completed the evacuation. They were available to assist with the search. They were then assigned the shift and briefed on their assignment. They were to act as trail blocks and to search areas that had not been completed.

Up on the mountain, the search for my son had stopped, and a rescue mission was underway to save those who had gone down with the Huey. The search for the lost little boy had evolved into an entirely different operation, which would ultimately, and rightfully so, tap the limited resources already in place. I understood this fact, yet it was difficult to accept that something out there seemed to be doing all it could to disrupt the efforts of the compassionate men and women involved with the search for my boy.

The magical twenty-four-hour window of hope was upon us, yet there was no trace of my missing son. I was not sure what my next step would be, but I knew I was not going back to Littleton without Jaryd. I paced back and forth when I suddenly realized there was a world out there, and I was part of it. I had to go to work the next day, and I needed to call someone who could inform my school about my situation. I had no idea who to call because I was a new teacher in the district, and most of the people I knew had unlisted numbers. I thought, *Who do I know who might have his or her number listed?* Then it came to me! *Christy Cooper. She gave her number to me, and it's in my truck!*

I ran outside and looked in my glove box only to find a mess. *Come on, Allyn. It's got to be in here somewhere. Try the center console.*

There's a lot of junk in there. I threw papers everywhere until I came across her phone number. I thought out loud, "Cool, here it is. Now go call Christy!"

I ran back to the front door of the store and quickly pulled it open and then searched for the cordless phone that wasn't hanging where it was supposed to be. My mind was gone, so I couldn't remember where I placed the phone each time I got off it. In a frustrated voice, I said, "Come on, where's the phone? You guys need to put it up after you use it!"

Butch politely reminded me, "You used it last." As we searched for the phone, it started ringing, so all we had to do was follow the signal until we located it. *It is so simple*, I thought. *If only Jaryd had a phone, I could call him.*

Butch saw the phone first, and he a made a mad dash to pick it up. Before the person on the other end could hang up, he grabbed it with his right hand and clicked it on. "Poudre River Resort, can I help you?" I could hear a small voice in the receiver speaking to him. He gave me a quick glance and said, "Allyn, yes, he's right here." As he handed me the phone, he announced, "Allyn, it's the sergeant from the sheriff's office."

I reached for the phone and held it to my ear. "This is Allyn… Yes…Was anybody hurt? Thank you." I hung up the phone. It was that simple, and it was all I needed at that moment.

Butch questioned, "What did he want?" I could tell he was also irritated with the lack of communication on the part of the sheriff's office. Butch had gotten his hope up as the emergency vehicles raced by the front of the store.

I replied, "He wanted to know if I had called dispatch then he told me the helicopter crashed."

Butch bellowed, "Did you tell him you already knew."

I explained, "No, but he wanted to let me know there were no life-threatening injuries, and he promised he would stay in touch."

I was still in disbelief and was having a hard time accepting all the things that had unfolded during the last twenty-four hours.

My son was lost, he might have spent the night alone in the mountains, and now a helicopter crashed. What next?

Before the phone rang, I was in the process of calling Christy. I dialed her number and waited for her to answer the phone. I was impatient because the phone seemed to ring forever. Finally, a voice came on and said, "Hi, you've reached…" Making contact with an answering machine may be mildly frustrating at times, but it was especially annoying today. Even the minor things didn't go my way.

How could I leave a message to tell a friend my son was missing in the mountains? I attempted to compose myself as I humbly spoke into the phone, "Hi, Christy, this is Allyn. I'm up at the resort, and I need you to call me as soon as possible. Jaryd is missing, and I need Rick's number. Thanks, Christy." Rick is the principal at Deer Creek Middle School where I taught in Littleton.

I hung up the phone, hoping Christy would call back soon. I was very nervous because I didn't have any control of the events taking place in my life, and I felt I was at the mercy of the world. I sat down and prayed, knowing God could take my pain and bring me comfort. It was time to reach deep into the spiritual world and take hold of what I knew was mine. I am not defeated now nor was I defeated then. I had to refocus and meditate on God's promise to be there in time of need.

April Pergal, a friend of mine whom I had taught with in Calexico, California, arrived at the resort. She had relocated to Fort Collins to peruse her master's degree at Colorado State University. Many of my friends were beginning to learn about my son, and those who were close enough came running. April had been around Jaryd a lot during the past summer, and she was taking things pretty hard. Two other teacher friends from Calexico, Will Slater and Judson Hickman, wanted to come to Colorado to help me. They are the type of men who go out of their way to achieve results, and Will is a misplaced mountain man stuck in the wrong time period of American history. Brent Kunzler, an Army Special Forces veteran who works with my sister-in-law at Pioneers Memorial Hospital in Brawley, was also ready to pack up and head to Colorado. Other friends, Steve and Brenda Scaroni of El Centro, offered us the use of their plane. The offers that poured in made my head spin.

....

A car pulled into the parking lot, and a lady with a sheriff's jacket got out and walked into the store through the front door. She looked around then walked up to the counter and introduced herself. "Hi, I'm Susan, and I'm with the sheriff's Victim Response Team." I never thought of myself as a victim, but I was willing to talk to her. She was extremely nice, and she wanted everyone to know she was there for our comfort. She would be the person who would keep us informed from that point on. I guess in some ways, she was actually assigned directly to me. I appreciated the sheriff for making this move.

We talked, and I really liked her because her feelings seemed genuine. She made it her objective to become close to our family. She asked me if I had talked to any of the media yet, and I told her I hadn't. She informed me that there were a lot of media personnel on the mountain, and they were requesting an interview with me. I'm not sure where she was receiving her information, but I had a funny feeling it was Susan's job to protect my family and me from them. When a father is propelled into an unpleasant situation that involves becoming the spokesperson for his family, the natural response may be to shy away from the media and their cameras. Privacy can be such a premium in cases like this, and once the line is crossed, it is difficult, if not impossible, to get it back. My gut reaction was to stay away from them.

Butch listened to our conversation and said, "Allyn, one by one, they will hunt you down, or you can ask them to come down here at seven tonight and get it all over with."

I finally gave in to what I really did not want to do. I asked Susan to go to the search site and inform the media I was holding a press conference at 7:00 p.m. in the store of the Poudre River Resort.

Susan was gone for about ten minutes when the phone rang again. I picked it up, and the voice on the other end belonged to Christy. She was breathing hard and she asked, "Allyn, what's going on? What do you mean Jaryd is missing?" I had a hard time talking, but I tried to explain to her what had happened. Christy told me she would call Rick and then she would head up to see me.

Shortly after I spoke with Christy, I received a call from Rick Myles, my principal. He was very apologetic, and he reassured me that the entire staff at Deer Creek would support me with anything I needed. The next thing he said really surprised me. "Allyn, I'll be up either tonight or tomorrow." I didn't expect Rick to come and be by my side because I knew he was needed at school. Our resort was also a good two-hour drive from Littleton. Littleton is an amazing place. I was lucky to be working with a group of people who knew what it was like to deal with tragedy. My new teaching assignment was only three miles from Columbine High School, and they were eager to show me their true humanistic compassion. The tenderness from the community and my school was overwhelming. I could write a book on the wonderful experiences that followed me after I returned home to the streets of Littleton.

At 4:00 p.m., my little boy was still gone. I stayed at the resort because my family and I were not allowed on the trail, and I felt useless. I wanted to help with the search, but I knew those involved would do a better job. It was rough. Sitting and waiting was hard work, and it was taking a toll on me. I wasn't thinking about food or anything else that my body surreptitiously craved. I just wanted to hold my son.

As I impatiently paced the premises, food flowed into the resort. My neighbors, and many of the people from around the canyon whom I didn't really know, made it their responsibility to feed us. At first, I didn't really know how to accept this gesture of kindness, but it was reassuring to know food would be one less worry for us to be concerned with. Brenda kept trying to get me to eat, but I had a difficult time looking at food. If I were to eat something, it would only be a matter of minutes before it would come back up. I also felt a sense of guilt thinking about food. How could I eat and enjoy the pleasures of satisfying the physical pangs of hunger when it was possible Jaryd was wandering around, searching for provisions to fulfill his own little needs?

I went outside and watched the sun slip behind the horizon, crushed by the thought that I had assumed my son would be back in my arms by this time. Once again, the pit in my stomach began to grow. No matter how I tried, I couldn't face the thought of going another night without Jaryd. The immediate question consuming me was, *Will this nightmare ever end?*

I thought back to the night before when my hopes were high because of the faith I had put into the search and rescue team. My previous night's anticipation and anxiety had turned into a sickness most people will never experience or imagine. My strong faith in God continued, but the reality of the situation strangled the hope of finding my son that day. I know we will be tested, but I never imagined the tests to be so enormous and consuming.

When the chips are down, most people fall to their knees to ask God for his divine intervention. I knew God was the medicine that would take my pain away, and I not only asked for his intervention, but I thanked him for allowing me the opportunity to have my son for the nearly four years we enjoyed together. I didn't want my son to be a fleeting memory, but if he was, I would always thank God for blessing me with my son. If

Jaryd was gone from this earth forever, what an awesome thought to know that God was holding him safely in His arms right now. I know God trusted me because He searched the earth and found me worthy of receiving the privilege of accompanying Jaryd on his very short journey here.

My body was tired, but my mind was alert as it continued to bring up every memory I had of Jaryd. My life was slowly turning into a nasty rerun because everything I looked at conjured up a special memory of my son. I couldn't look at anything without seeing Jaryd. If I closed my eyes, he was there. When I walked into the store, I could see him sneaking around by the candy and donuts. When I entered the game room, I could see him trying to play pool. When I looked outside, I could see him chasing his sister and having a good time. When I touched his toys, I could feel his energy and excitement. When I picked up his pillow, I could smell him as though he were right next to me. I took his sleeping bag and put it away because I never wanted to wash his presence out of it. His clothes were like gold to me. Every spot on his shirts called out, asking me if I remembered how they got there. Each memory deepened the pain I was experiencing with the loss of my son, and I was beginning to question my own purpose.

My heart was broken because I wanted to hold my son so badly. Not a moment went by that I didn't want to see him looking up at me and hear him say, "I love you, Daddy!" I wanted to hold his hand, kiss his face, and see his smile and dimples. I realized my life would never be the same without him, and my pain would be long and everlasting.

It was around six that evening when Christy arrived at the resort. She walked up to me, and we shared a long awkward embrace. It was good to see her. If the roles would have been reversed, I am not sure what I would have said to her. She has two children, and all anyone had to do was mentally trade places with me for a minute and they would be filled with empathy. The more a person could place him or herself in my shoes, the more real the horrible rush of fear would become as it pricked at one's senses. A quick shake of the head for anyone else and the fear was gone, but the more I fought, the worse its presence became. Christy was there for moral support, and she volunteered to do whatever it took to help find Jaryd. It was good to see her.

As Christy and I talked, the 7:00 p.m. press conference slowly approached. I wasn't sure how I would behave with all of the cameras in my face because the lack of rest had pushed my emotional state to the point of crumbling. While facing tragedy, most people are never pushed into the spotlight to stand before lighted cameras. There is nothing anyone can do to prepare for that situation. What would the reporters ask, and how would they react to what I had to say? I did not realize it at the time, but I was getting ready to show the world my excruciating pain. Through it all, maybe I could share my faith too.

When the reporters arrived, they reacted differently than I had expected. They were very quiet and somewhat apologetic. They put microphones on my shirt and ran wires underneath my clothing down to a transmitter that was connected to the back of my pants. Thankfully, while they were performing their jobs, they continued to handle me as if I were a tightly sealed container of nitroglycerin waiting to go off. I appreciated their tenderness. As they quietly did their jobs, I thought about the unusual situation I found myself in. My entire world had been turned upside down a little over a day ago, and its weight seemed to rest on my shoulders. When I woke yesterday morning, there was absolutely no way I could have predicted the swirling current of reality that was pulling me down.

Susan, the victim's advocate, approached me and asked if I wanted her by my side during the interview. I accepted her offer because I was uncomfortable about what the reporters might ask.

She stood to the right of me when the interview started. Most of the questions pertained to what had happened and how I was holding up. I attempted to respond to each question the best I could as I watched the recording of my image from the front side of a camera. My son's picture was being transmitted everywhere, and all it took was a few minutes and some insight from me. If he had been abducted, he was about to become the most publicized little boy in some time, and it would be difficult for whoever had taken him to hide. From that moment on, I would talk to any reporter who desired an interview. I realized it was a great opportunity for me to keep Jaryd's picture fresh in the minds of everyone in our country. Sightings of Jaryd were about to inundate the sheriff's office, but which ones would be taken seriously? In a sea of hoaxes, would a tiny life preserver materialize? The sheriff's resources were also about to undergo a new series of challenges as they hoped to respond to any credible reports.

I felt I was doing as well as could be expected until one question ripped out my heart. "What was the last thing you said to your son when he was leaving?"

I tried to share with them what I said, but I broke down. I turned to the right where Susan was, put my head on her shoulder, and cried. I tried to calm my emotions so I could finish answering the question. When I gathered myself, I turned back to the camera; and with tears running down my face, I replied, "I told Jaryd to roll down the window, and I put my head into the car and kissed him. I told him I loved him. Then he answered back, 'I love you more.' His eyes were full of joy, and neither of us could have imagined it would be the last time we would see each other."

Susan held me again and tried to give me some comforting advice. I think she would have stayed, but she had her own family waiting for her at home. She said she had to leave, but she would be back up the mountain the first thing in the morning. My first of many interviews was over.

When I think about the entire situation, it makes me feel as though I've been poisoned and sentenced to a slow and torturous death. There was a time much later when Jaryd's body would have been good enough for me. I had concluded that all I wanted was to hold him again. I didn't care if he was dead or alive; I just wanted to feel the body of my son in my arms one last time and to have rest and closure for us both.

I left the interview area and walked back into the apartment to prepare myself for another lonely night, as if a person can really do something to get ready for the hellish night that awaited me. I was glad Jaryd's mom was there because she made the night a little easier for my daughter, Josallyn.

Monday, October 4, 1999

I tried my hardest to get some sleep last night, but not knowing the whereabouts of my son kept me awake. I was sitting there looking around, thinking Jaryd was sleeping with me. There was one problem—last night was like a replay of the one before. No matter how hard I tried to reach out and hold his little hand, he wasn't there.

Again, the darkness of the night seemed to last forever. When I went to lie down, I had a hard time comprehending my son was possibly spending another night in the cold. Once more, I asked myself, *How can this be happening? Can Jaryd actually be walking around during the day, and is he finding a place to sleep at night? If he is up there, why are they having such a hard time finding him?*

Halfway through the night, I thought about the helicopter crash, and I reflected on something I had said to one of my friends concerning Jaryd and the crash. I made the comment, "Jaryd must be afraid of all the people looking for him. He probably thinks he's in trouble for shooting down the helicopter." I could see Jaryd standing there with a stick, pretending it was a rifle, pointing it at the helicopter and shooting at it. When the helicopter came crashing to the ground, Jaryd probably thought he shot it down.

My poor little guy probably panicked when he saw the soldiers running up the mountain carrying real guns.

I lay there all night long. *Jaryd, where are you?* I couldn't believe someone or something was trying to steal my joy and destroy my family. Did I do something wrong, and was I somehow being punished? How could I sleep when I had more questions than answers? The more my mind wandered, the more confused I became. Maybe some questions would always be left unanswered, but the questions that could not be answered were growing exponentially.

I got up and walked over to the window several times to look outside, hoping to see the sun peak back over the eastern horizon. I felt as if I were being tortured by whatever it was that caused Jaryd to disappear. I knew the trail had been searched several times, but why was there no trace of Jaryd? Another unanswered question!

I tried to lie down and get some sleep, but I was nervous. It was about 4:00 a.m. when I got up for good. I walked into the store, and like every other morning, I made some coffee. I stood there, with a chill in the air, and tried to understand what Jaryd was going through.

I walked back into the apartment area and looked at my daughter and her mother sleeping. I was happy Josallyn was getting some sleep.

I went back into the store, walked over to the counter in the fishing area, stood there, and stared at the emptiness as if I were in a mystical trance. The more I thought about my son, the more the tears welled from my eyes. The tears slowly grew into a river that flowed down my face as my crying tried to purge the pain that had seized my body. The second night without my son once again brought on the uncontrollable urge to vomit.

I tried to hold myself together because I had this strange feeling today would be the day they would find Jaryd. At the same time, I knew the rest of my family would be arriving around noon, and hopefully, they would somehow ease my pain.

....

About 9:30 a.m., my principal, Rick Myles, walked in the front door of the resort. He approached me with grief and sorrow written all over his face. He looked at me and said with sadness, "Allyn, I'm really sorry. If there's anything I can do, just tell me." I learned you didn't have to ask Rick to do a thing. He took the bull by the horns and jumped right in.

There were a lot of people hanging around the resort, and the task of making breakfast was enormous. People slowly meandered in for a bite to eat, but when it came to doing the dishes, not many people were sticking around to volunteer.

I could hear the water running in the kitchen, so I decided to walk into the apartment to see what was going on. It was Rick. He was standing there with his hands buried in the water, and he was quietly doing the dishes. I jokingly thought, *What a man.* I said, "Rick, your wife is a lucky woman!"

About that time, Chris, a friend of mine, walked into the apartment. He was very animated, and he wanted to know if I knew of anybody with a set of waders. Chris was bound and determined to get a search party together to walk the river below the area where the searchers were looking. He was trying to grab anyone who walked by. Christy Cooper walked in, and Chris tried his hardest to get her to accompany him on his desperate river search. I knew Christy had other things she had to do, and she needed to get back to Littleton to be with her own family. Chris was determined, and he wasn't going to take no for an answer. Christy was trying her hardest to be polite, so I stepped in and told Chris, "Christy really needs to get back down the mountain."

Chris reluctantly said, "Okay," then continued his mad search for waders and volunteers. If Jaryd was in the river below the search area, Chris was going to find him.

It was around ten in the morning when members from the media showed up with more questions. They were all searching for a picture of the little boy who had vanished off the face of the earth.

It was kind of strange, but for some reason, I was getting this bizarre feeling that I was the focus of this story. I thought, *Wait a second, my son is missing, not me!* I was not really sure why they wanted to talk to me. Was it because the longer Jaryd was missing, the greater my pain became, and my pain was the item that needed to be exploited? I really didn't care what the reason was; I wanted them to keep flashing my son's picture around the world. Who knows, if he was kidnapped, maybe it would be a viewer who would find him.

The media personnel were turning into an army of ants, and each one of them searched for a different angle to the story. One reporter asked, "What was Jaryd's favorite activity up here?" I told him he liked to throw rocks out into the river, but he knew he wasn't allowed to go near the water by himself. He then asked me if I would be willing to go down to the river and take a few pictures while we discussed some memories about Jaryd. I agreed and then grabbed a bunch of pictures of Jaryd to take with me.

It was hard, but I stood at the river's edge and talked to the reporter about all the wonderful memories I had of Jaryd throwing his perfect skipper rocks across the top of the water and how he loved to fish with Daddy. After the short interview, I walked back up to the store and saw several vans with different call letters of television and radio stations on their sides. People were standing outside, drinking coffee, and hoping to be in the right place at the right time if and when Jaryd was to be found.

As I tried to walk into the store, a TV journalist approached me and asked a few questions. His main question was, "What do you think about the press conference the sheriff called for this afternoon at the trailhead?"

I replied, "Excuse me, what press conference? Nobody told me about a press conference. Where did you hear that?"

I thought, *Wow, the sheriff called a press conference, and he didn't invite me.* At this point, this seemed like an event that should include me. My family and I were, once again, the last to be told. I was beginning to learn that the greatest source of information for the Atadero family would be the media.

Shortly after this incident, another media person asked me how I felt about a gentleman in New York who had offered a fifteen-thousand-dollar reward to the person who would find my son alive.

I learned later the reward was only valid for persons who were not members of the official search and rescue team. The reward was the carrot to motivate concerned citizens into action. Again, I had no idea what they were talking about, and I asked them where they got their information. The answer was just like the first reporter's, "Somebody from the sheriff's office told us!"

Later that day, I questioned some of the members of the sheriff's department and asked them about the fifteen-thousand-dollar reward I had heard about. They said they told the man not to do it because it would cause too many problems in the search area.

I asked, "How would this cause a problem?" The answer I got went completely against their philosophy about what they thought may have happened to Jaryd. The sheriff kept telling everyone there was no way Jaryd could have been abducted, but the reason they didn't want a lot of people on the mountain searching for Jaryd was just in case he was abducted. That didn't make sense to me. Once again, the lack of any credible evidence didn't leave us a place to drop our anchor.

Here's what I was told: "There are a lot of crazy people in this world, and you never know what may have happened to Jaryd. A fifteen-thousand-dollar reward could cause a lot of problems, especially if Jaryd is still alive. What if a crazy person has your son, but they could use the money? He or she might kill Jaryd, stuff him into a backpack, and go up the trail as if they were one of the concerned citizens searching for him. As they're walking up the trail, they find the perfect spot to pull Jaryd's body out of the backpack, and they lay it on the ground. They begin yelling, 'I found the little boy's body!' This person would not only get the reward, they would also get the recognition of finding Jaryd."

Although the sheriff's department was somewhat convinced Jaryd wasn't abducted, the precaution had to be taken to ensure this possible scenario was not exploited by a potential perpetrator. Sadly, we found ourselves in a situation where we had to turn down a stranger's generosity. As Jaryd's father, this was a tough pill to swallow, and I truly believed we were missing out on an opportunity to get more people involved. I understood the logic involved concerning the decision, but considering the lack of positive results so far, I believed it was an option worthy of thought.

I remember when a man pulled in to get some gas at the resort. He was telling us he wanted to go up the trail and help with the search for my son. He said his backpack was loaded, and he was ready to go. One of the staff members from the sheriff's department asked him if he could look into his backpack, and the man agreed. Although abduction seemed to be the least likely of incidents, there was activity to suggest that it hadn't been ruled out either.

There was also the theory that if Jaryd was abducted, the parties involved would have been observed by someone, but Janet removed Josallyn from the mountain and nobody noticed! She was able to accomplish the feat of turning the impossible into the possible with my daughter, but when it came to the events surrounding my son, the duplication of his disappearance wasn't given much weight. Remember, when I arrived on the scene, everybody told me Janet was still up looking for Jaryd and that my daughter was with her, but that wasn't true. When I stepped off the trail, Janet had already taken Josallyn back to the resort and returned, and not a single ounce of concern had been raised. I'm not suggesting that Janet knows what happened to Jaryd, because she's a good, honest woman. But if she could have taken Josallyn off the mountain without anyone noticing, why couldn't someone else have done the same with Jaryd?

As I continued my investigation, answers to other provoking questions also eluded me. We were told there were only two ways onto the trail—from the road where the parking lot was and from the other end of the trail near Peterson Lake. The river was low the day Jaryd vanished, and it could easily have been crossed in several locations. When the Air Force moved in, they settled in a parking area approximately one hundred yards west of where the hiking party had originally stopped. From the hikers' vantage point, cars that may have been parked there were out of view. A person could have abducted Jaryd, crossed the river, and been gone before anybody knew he was missing. I know this was in the back of the minds of some of the deputies because I watched as one searched the bed of a pickup truck, hoping to find clues of Jaryd's whereabouts.

Susan arrived shortly after I had talked to the media, and my first question to her was, "Do you know anything about the press conference the sheriff called for later this afternoon?"

She said, "Yes."

When I heard this, I politely questioned why I had not been informed. Although I was not allowed up the trail to search for myself, I felt I should be kept current on all matters concerning Jaryd's search. Just in case the authorities released information concerning any leads on Jaryd, I wanted to hear them firsthand. I was sure the media would keep me informed, and they would also seek my reactions to any news.

To me, Susan was an obvious asset to the sheriff's department, and the public was fortunate to have her employed as a civil servant. She truly wanted to ensure my needs were met, and I think Susan could sense Jaryd's mom was somewhat uncomfortable being at the crowded resort, so she came up with a game plan that would both help Angie and Josallyn avoid a lot of the problems we were facing on the mountain.

Susan asked me if it would be okay for Josallyn and Angie to go down the mountain each night and stay with her at her house. Susan had a daughter the same age as Josallyn, and she thought this would help everyone with the tension of Jaryd's disappearance. I thought it was a great idea because it gave Josallyn a chance to be with her mom, and it would keep her away from the chaos happening here at ground zero.

....

It was around noon when some of my relatives arrived at the resort. My brother Arlyn, sister-in-law, Robyn, my mom, Bertie, and my aunt Katie came from the Imperial Valley to hopefully be by my side when Jaryd walked off the Big South Trail.

It was strange seeing Arlyn because he had just left Colorado about six weeks earlier, and I did not think I would be seeing any of my family until the following summer. We got our hellos and tears out of the way then everyone wanted to know what was going on with the search. I told them I had not been to the search area because I wanted to stay out of the way of the searchers, and the authorities would not let me go up anyway. My mom told me she planned to go up the trail to look for her grandson. She hoped a grieving grandmother would be afforded this opportunity.

It wasn't long before the three ladies were driving up to the search area. They did not realize what they were in for. My brother and I were getting ready to head up to the trail because we wanted to see what the press conference was all about. The sheriff still hadn't officially invited me, but I knew I wasn't going to miss it. The phone rang, and it was one of the officials on the mountain wanting to speak to Susan. When she got off the phone, she said we needed to get up to the trail. We had family members causing a scene, and they did not want to have to arrest anyone.

My family was causing a scene? They were faced with being arrested? My mother's grandson was missing, and she was acting like any other caring grandmother would have acted. My sister-in-law, Robyn, was probably the voice of reason, but I am sure she made a huge push to get on the trail also. All they wanted to do was walk up the trail and have a look for themselves. I can't imagine what it would have been like if Jaryd's other grandmother, Irma, would have been there. That would have been a show for all the cameras. It must have been difficult to have to tell the ladies the trail was off limits to them.

My brother and I got into our car and raced up the mountain to stop the ladies from doing what comes naturally. Josallyn and her mom got into Susan's car and followed us up the road. The entire family would somehow be by Jaryd's side, missing or not.

On the way up the mountain, we saw my mom drive by us, heading back down to the resort. I thought, *Wait a second, wasn't she one of the three ladies causing problems up at the search site?* She must have been irate if they threatened to arrest her. That would have been great for the primetime newscast, "Grandmother of missing little boy was arrested because she wanted to help."

We reached the trailhead and got out of our car. I couldn't believe what I was seeing. The quiet mountain had turned into a media convention, and the parking lot was totally full. Where had all of these people come from?

We barely had a chance to take a few steps when the media realized we were there and came running up to question us. Wow! I was overwhelmed! Last week, my son and I were holding hands watching football, and now the entire world wanted to know what happened to my little Jaryd.

My family tried to avoid the media circus as we waited for the sheriff to show up to conduct his press conference. What was he going to say? I was hoping to hear some good news about Jaryd.

Right before the press conference started, my mom, Aunt Katie, and Robyn showed up again. We asked them what had happened because we were told they were causing a problem. They said it wasn't true, and they never caused a problem. They wanted to know if they could go up the trail, and they were told no. They decided to go back to the resort for warmer clothes and pick up some supplies for a few of the guys in the Air Force.

I am not sure why the press conference was called. There wasn't any new information released, so I was back to my waiting game. When the press conference ended, a lot of the networks wanted their own exclusive footage of my daughter and me trying to survive. One person asked if I would be willing to cross the street to get away from all the commotion. This reporter was very nice and wanted to get some footage of us walking close to the river. After her interview was over, she wanted me to walk and talk with my daughter to get some footage of us being a family. It's a technique each and every one of the reporters used. Everybody wanted a video of my daughter and me interacting.

It wasn't long after the news conference when the sun began to dip below the horizon again. My nauseous feeling would rise as the sun would set. I guess it was because I had a hard time dealing with the fact that my son was spending another cold night out in the woods. It was a little different this time. This was the third night without my son, and I was starting to question his survival. If he was alive, he was cold, hungry, and terrified. And if he was alive on the mountain, why hadn't he been located?

We went back to the resort, and for the first time, I seriously asked myself if somebody could have taken Jaryd. It was not a pleasant thought, but it was a hopeful wish. Maybe if someone took my son, they were taking good care of him. At least he may still be alive.

It was about 7:30 p.m. when the phone rang. Butch answered it and then asked me if I knew someone named Nikki. I took the phone because I thought it was my cousin Nichole. It was a call I'll remember for as long as I live. It wasn't my cousin; it was Jaryd's babysitter, Nikki Tiburcio.

I picked up the phone, and I could hear a woman screaming and crying with the pain only a mother could have. She yelled, "Allyn, please tell me it's not our Jaryd! Allyn, please, it's not our Jaryd, is it?" I was frozen with pain, and I did not know what to say. My son was part of her family, and in return, her family was part of ours.

I tearfully replied, "Yes, Nikki, it's our Jaryd."

I could hear her deranged voice, saying, "No, Allyn, it can't be our Jaryd!"

Nikki and I were both trying to communicate, but we were having a hard time talking to each other. She told me she had some recent photos of Jaryd that were taken at the birthday party for her son, Ethen. Her husband, Jeff, would get them developed and e-mailed to us the next day.

I hung up the phone and realized the impact Jaryd had on my friends. He was the kid who was easy to like. My hell was painful, but my pain reverberated through all those who knew him.

I was starting to calm down when my brother Avery called. He asked me if I wanted him to come to Colorado. I told him no because he had a new job as a football coach at Doane College in Nebraska. He was finally living out his dream, and I didn't want him to put his job in jeopardy. At the same time, if Avery were here, he would have been in everybody's face, and I know somehow he probably would have been arrested. He could have been a problem, and I didn't want him to interfere with any of the search officials. He's one of those types of guys who go above and beyond the call of duty. If there was anything I wanted, he would have done it.

That night, my pain was somewhat eased with my family being there. It was also strange because Josallyn had gone down the mountain with her mother to stay at Susan's house, and I was alone. My son was missing, and my daughter was gone.

I went to bed expecting to get the one hour of sleep that was normal for the past two nights. My hope was slowly turning into the unthinkable. Would I ever see my son again? I had been sleeping for thirty minutes when someone began banging on the front door. The voice on the other end was yelling. "Allyn, are you in there?"

I quickly got up and raced to see what the commotion was. I opened the door, and three members of the search and rescue team were standing there moving back and forth with excitement. One of them had tears running down his face as he shouted, "Allyn, we found him!"

I looked down, and Jaryd was standing between, what I believed to be, his guardian angels. He looked up and ecstatically said, "Hi, Daddy!"

The joy coming from Jaryd's eyes was full of peace. It was obvious he was also thankful for this wonderful reunion, and it was a private moment only the two of us could share. Sure, my heart was bruised form the agony of the ordeal, but my spirits were floating higher than what I could have ever imagined. I reached down and pulled Jaryd off of his feet, and the two of us hugged. I held him tightly and squeezed to the point I was sure he would object, but he returned my embrace with a firmness of his own. I could feel life surging through me again. Each breath that he took seemed to bathe me in a profound serenity that became more intense with each beat of his heart. It felt good to be alive.

That night, the two of us must have talked for hours. There was so much for us to share, and I was amazed at the clarity he had in his recollection of the events surrounding those dark days of his disappearance. Jaryd could vividly recall the details of the trail, the first night alone in the frigid woods and the thought of bears following him. When the sun came up, he knew I was looking for him. He saw the helicopter and often heard voices. The searchers had come near a couple of times, and he said he had yelled, but he was thirsty, and his throat was sore.

After several days had passed, we were becoming accustomed to being a family again. The excitement made it difficult to sleep, and the attention given to Jaryd's search had been refocused on our reunion. I felt I had a reason to live again, and I was astonished at the difference between the depths and heights I was currently experiencing. The gap between the two emotions is seldom experienced by anybody, yet there I was, looking back at the unimaginable distance between the two. The thought of returning to those emotional valleys created a harsh apprehension I couldn't shake, and although things were going well, life no longer possessed the innocence most families expected. I was determined to make the best of things and appreciate not just the days we now shared, but each moment as they were a lifetime unto themselves. Knowing me, I also knew one thing was bound to happen. We were going to return to the Big South Trail.

The day arrived when we found ourselves standing alone in the parking lot of the Big South Trail. Being there brought back a host of terrible memories, and although I needed answers, I was a little anxious. The first thing I became aware of was the absolute stillness of the place. It seemed as though the entirety of nature was waiting and watching for us to move. There wasn't a stir of a single leaf, and the river seemed to have lost its voice. The normal chatter of the local birds had evaporated somewhere into the hills and the sun, perched high above, failed to bend the resting shadows.

Jaryd and I stood anchored to the ground while taking in the vastness that had become our witness. I wanted to move so badly, but to move forward was to possibly step back into the nightmare that the two of us had recently emerged from. The answers were out there beyond the first gentle climb, and we had come too far not to proceed. I also knew that nothing could happen to Jaryd as long as I was with him. I was his protector.

With my first step forward, the wilderness spell snapped as a small gust from behind us urged us along the trail. Strangely, there was almost a politeness in the breeze as if the trail was apologizing for Jaryd's prior concealment by the forest. We moved along the path while cautiously discussing the events of Jaryd's hike. I was amazed as Jaryd shared his story the only way a three-year-old boy could. I'm not sure he understood the impact this event had on my life and I appreciated his innocence surrounding the retelling of those days.

To the south, a bank of clouds lazily drifted northward toward us, gradually billowing into a spectacle worthy of our attention. They seemed to emphasize the harmony of nature we had become part of as their edges swelled and rotated beyond the mountain tops. Jaryd and I moved farther along the trail, and as the distance between us and the trailhead expanded, the more active the clouds became. I was sure the secrets to Jaryd's journey were about to be revealed, but the clouds began to evolve into a far-off storm. Strangely, the sun began to set in the south, turning the day to a dull gray. The clouds quickly filled the sky and rolled toward us like a charging army. It was as if we had done something to stir the anger of the mountain as the entire area became alive with fury. The plan must have been to lure us deeper into the mountain prior to setting the trap.

Things were happening so fast. A torrential wind tore at our clothes while it peppered us with gravel. We turned toward the trailhead as a bright flash instantly blinded us. A clap of thunder caused the ground to shake while a distant roar moved up the river valley toward us. I fought to regain my vision, then a second flash struck. The sides of the hills shuddered as the thunder reverberated through us. The distant rumble moved closer, then I realized it was massive sheets of rain sweeping through the canyon. It was difficult to see Jaryd, but he tightly gripped my hand while we struggled to get back to the trailhead. I could also hear the river to my left, its flow intensifying as it washed trees and boulders toward the parking lot. I gathered my bearings and knew I could get the two of us to safety because adrenaline was pumping through me the way it had when I was first told Jaryd was missing. Then the rain hit. It hammered against us with such force that I felt I was under attack by a swarm of bees. We had to get back to the car as quickly as we could.

Water streamed down the side of the mountain past us toward the river. Soaked and shivering, we ran along the trail splashing through mud, but moving was becoming more difficult. Small tributaries gathered momentum as their flows rushed past us. I felt as though we were racing against a giant who had targeted us with a fire hose, and things were turning alarmingly dangerous. A wall of water crashed down the side of the mountain, and I realized there was no way for us to avoid it. It slammed into Jaryd and me, knocking Jaryd off his balance. Jaryd pleaded for me to hold on as I fought to pull him toward me. More determined to rebuke us, the wind grew stronger, and the wash we were in flowed faster. Jaryd struggled but couldn't regain his balance, and I could feel his fingers slipping through mine. The fear etched across his face was sickening as our eyes met in a final embrace. I'm sure he realized it was over as he slipped away from me. I stood there and watched in horror as the water carried him to the river below. Full of dwindling hope, he never took his frantic eyes off me. Paralyzed in my efforts, I couldn't breathe as he disappeared beneath the river. I closed my eyes and screamed. When I opened them, I was trembling in my bed. It was another cruel dream.

The mountain was mocking me. It had won again.

I've seen Jaryd many times, and the encounters were as real as the pages in this book. At least that's what my mind was telling me. I can't count how many times I've closed my eyes at night and Jaryd would show up.

The worst dreams are the ones that start with a tease then end with staggering disappointment.

The Mystery Thickens

Tuesday, October 5, 1999

It was Tuesday morning, and Jaryd had finished spending his third night out in the cold. If he was out there, could he have survived? If not, what happened to him? I know I asked myself these questions several times, but I didn't have an answer. My frustrations grew as each minute passed, and I would find out later in the day the frustrations of everyone involved were beginning to magnify. Long hours and failure can bring out the worse in people, regardless of how nice they are.

When I got up and walked around, I could tell there was something different. I wasn't eating much, and I probably had a total of three hours of sleep in the past three nights. My arms were tingling, and I was feeling somewhat light-headed. I was experiencing something I had never experienced in my life. My body was telling me it was going to shut down if I didn't eat and get some sleep. Since I wasn't tired or hungry, I knew my mind had taken control of my body.

We waited around all morning hoping to hear some information, and I was back at that point where I needed to hold my son again. I hinted to my brother that I didn't care if Jaryd was dead; I just needed to hold him. I needed to know where he was. I imagined I was holding my son's body as I kissed him and told him I loved him. I didn't want to see him dead, but if he was, I desperately needed to hold him.

The morning was quickly passing, so my brother and I decided to head up the mountain to see if there was any chance we could take my family up the trail to help with the search. When we arrived at the search area, we walked over to the trailer designated as the command center. There were two gentlemen in suits standing there, looking at us with curiosity. The older of the two approached us and introduced himself.

"Hi, I'm Captain Newhard. I'm in charge of the actual investigation of the disappearance of Jaryd." He was a pleasant man with hope written all over his face. He told me he and his wife were on the mountain on Sunday, searching for Jaryd, and that he would do anything it took to bring him home. He was one of the most sincere men I had met in a long time.

While talking about the investigation that was taking place, Captain Newhard and his partner revealed some interesting information that would be very controversial in future days as we tried to figure out what actually happened to Jaryd. As we talked, Captain Newhard told us about some of the phone calls they received concerning Jaryd. You have to remember, at this point, most minds believed Jaryd was lost on the mountain. Captain Newhard and his partner told us about a psychic who had called with information that would break the case wide open.

The psychic told them where to look for Jaryd's body. She said we would find him under a tree, next to a lot of rocks. We all laughed because there were a lot of rocks and trees in the Rocky Mountains. I made the comment, "Did she say what state he was in?"

The captain reassured us every lead in the case was being checked. He continued with a few other stories, "Heck, Jaryd was spotted by a couple in Florida at a McDonald's." I knew

McDonald's was Jaryd's favorite place to eat, but I didn't believe he was in Florida.

The other gentleman standing with Captain Newhard jumped in and said, "I've got one more for you! There is a ranger at Mesa Verde National Park who swears he saw Jaryd there on Sunday. Can you believe that?"

Once again, the captain reassured us, "All leads are being checked." I'm convinced that as far as he knew, his statement was accurate.

I couldn't believe there were so many sightings of Jaryd, but for some reason, the sheriff was adamant about Jaryd's whereabouts. The sheriff was sold on the fact that Jaryd was on the mountain. What kind of story would this turn into if his hunch was wrong, and would the search for Jaryd ever end?

I didn't think much about the Mesa Verde incident until three weeks later. Mesa Verde is about five hundred miles from where Jaryd disappeared, and it would take about ten hours to drive there. If someone had left the mountain with Jaryd around 2:00 p.m. on Saturday, they would have arrived at Mesa Verde about midnight that night or early Sunday morning. That's about twelve hours before Jaryd was spotted on Sunday. With this knowledge, it's possible Jaryd never spent a night on the mountain.

About three days after Jaryd's disappearance, a lady named Kelly contacted me, hoping to help me find my missing son. She sounded sincere, and I was a desperate man. She tried to show me her actions were admirable by dedicating a lot of time and energy in the search to find the truth about Jaryd.

Kelly called me every other day to see if there was any new information she could investigate. One day, I was telling her about the Mesa Verde story when she abruptly stopped me and said, "You never told me about Mesa Verde. How come?" This conversation was about four weeks after the disappearance of Jaryd, and I thought I had told her in one of our earlier conversations.

I was wrong. When our discussion ended, Kelly made it her goal to find the ranger who thought he had spotted Jaryd.

Kelly called me three days later and asked me if I wanted to talk to the mysterious ranger who thought he saw Jaryd. My skin crawled and I questioned, "You have his name and number?"

Kelly innocently said, "Yep!"

I could not believe what I was hearing because I had already told Congressman Tancredo's assistant about the story. He said he was going to find out who this person was, but they could never come up with the right information. How did Kelly do it? She had actually talked to the ranger's boss, and he explained everything to her.

Kelly gave me the ranger station's phone number, and I called them to get in touch with a ranger named Craig. The person I talked to told me Craig was a seasonal employee, but he remembered the day Craig thought he had seen Jaryd. I asked the person I was talking to what he thought of the incident. He told me he never had the chance to see Jaryd, but Craig was very adamant and was sticking to his story. He said Craig was a very honest person and someone I could trust.

I had Craig's home phone number, so I decided to call and ask him a few questions. When I made the call, there was no answer, but I was lucky because Craig had an answering machine. I said, "Hi, my name is Allyn Atadero, and I'm the father of the little boy who disappeared in the Colorado Mountains on October second. I heard you might have seen him the next day. Can you please give me a call?" I left my phone number, thinking Craig would never return my call.

About an hour later, my phone rang. When I answered it, the person on the other end said, "Mr. Atadero, this is Craig." Briefly, my entire body stopped functioning because I was extremely excited to be talking with the man who may have seen my son last.

I responded, "Hi, Craig, I heard you may have seen my son?"

His response was something that upsets me even today. "I'm really glad to be talking to you, but at the same time, I'm very mad. Do you know you're the first person to get in touch with me? Not one person responded to my report, and they blew it off like it never happened. I can't believe nobody contacted me!"

We were having this conversation on November 5, 1999. Jaryd had been missing just over a month, and law enforcement officials never responded to this report.

Craig continued, "I noticed the young boy was very friendly but thought it was odd he wanted to hold my hand." Everybody who ever knew Jaryd would tell you he liked holding hands.

Craig said he never gave it a lot of thought until he was watching the Denver news that night and saw Jaryd's picture and heard his name. He told me the picture looked just like the little boy he had seen, and the man was calling him something that sounded like "Jerald."

The next day, Craig saw the man and little boy drive by him in what looked to be a 1998 or 1999 silver Geo Tracker or Suzuki Sidekick, but he never had the chance to get the license plate number. This incident made Craig realize the man and the little boy must have spent the night in the park.

Craig said he was so sure it was Jaryd that he notified Chief Ranger Robert Johnson. Mr. Johnson had some of the rangers look all over the park for the vehicle, but they found nothing. Craig told me they faxed his report to the sheriff's office and contacted the FBI. He said nobody responded.

About three days after I had talked to Craig, I went to the sheriff's office to talk to the lead investigator on Jaryd's case. I asked him about Craig and if he had made contact with him. He said he had. He produced the same report that Craig's office had faxed me. The report was handwritten, and I recognized it.

I asked the investigator, "Are you sure you talked to him? He swears I'm the first person to get in contact with him."

The investigator replied, "Yes, I write down the names of everyone I talk to in my report. Here, I'll show you."

I waited for about a minute as the investigator searched his notes for Craig's name. He quietly said, "I can't find his name here."

"I know why you can't. You never talked to him. I talked to him a few days ago, and Craig told me I was the first person to get in touch with him."

The next response was, "I thought I talked to him."

When I got home, I called Chris Schauble from KCNC-TV in Denver and told him about Craig. Chris had been covering the story from the mountains, and I felt comfortable contacting him. Chris was totally blown away and wanted to know if Craig was willing to talk to the media. I told him Craig was so upset that he said he would talk to anybody.

Chris was on a mission. He contacted Craig and recorded his conversation with him. I remember one question Chris had for Craig. He asked, "Craig, on a scale of one to ten, how would you rate this sighting as possibly being Jaryd Atadero?"

Craig said, "A seven. I'm pretty sure it was him."

Chris Schauble had to interview the sheriff to get his response. The sheriff never addressed the fact that no one had actually talked to Craig, but he had an interesting response. He said, "I've never heard of anybody abducting someone and then parading him around in a tour group." It's amazing how the Elizabeth Smart case would later challenge this reasoning. Every time I questioned a reasonable event, I didn't seem to get any closer to the truth about Jaryd. Although it had been discussed before, I am also surprised the word *probability* didn't come up again.

The one question I wished the sheriff could have answered was, "Why didn't your office respond to Craig's report?" It may have been a detail that was overlooked on a different mountain—a mountain of sightings that continued to grow.

My family and I wanted desperately to go up the trail and see for ourselves what was going on. We wanted to look for Jaryd. Each time we asked, we were told no! The deputies on the mountain told my family they would be arrested if they tried to get in the way. We continued asking as the day went on.

Finally, one of the deputies approached us. "I am not promising you anything, but I am trying to talk them into letting you go up the trail this afternoon."

Was it really too much for a family to ask? My son had been missing for seventy-two hours, and they couldn't find a trace of him. How could we be a problem for them? I didn't believe we were, but for some reason, it must have been important for them to keep us off the trail.

A couple of hours later, a sergeant from the sheriff's office told my brother and I that he had received approval to take us up the trail to the point where Jaryd was last seen. There was one problem: he said my mom was too old to go. He didn't want to get himself into a situation where someone had to go up the trail to rescue her.

Who was this guy? He didn't know what kind of shape my mother was in, and he had no idea that he had just insulted the grandmother of the missing little boy. I watched my mother walk off and sit on a huge boulder. I could tell she was totally dejected. My brother said, "We can't go up that trail without Mom. That's not right!"

I went to the sergeant. "My mom has to go with us. There's no way we can go up that trail without her." He reluctantly gave in and said we would be leaving in five minutes.

Arlyn, Robyn, Mom, and I were the only family members they allowed to go up the trail. Since the media was not allowed on the trail, my brother decided to bring along his camera so he could take pictures of the area where Jaryd was last seen. The sergeant escorted us along with about four of the search and rescue members. We were about nine strong, and our group was only slightly smaller than the one Jaryd and Josallyn had gone hiking with. We stayed together, and if Jaryd had been with us, I couldn't see any way we could have lost him.

As we headed up the trail, it began to wind and gradually climb up the mountain. The river was to the right of us, but it didn't present any danger at that point. I tried to imagine both of my kids walking up the trail three days earlier, and I kept looking off in the distance hoping to see a sign of Jaryd.

We were on the trail for about one hundred yards when some of the searchers behind us yelled, "Jaryd! Jaryd!" Tears welled from my eyes as I listened to them calling out my son's name.

The sergeant asked me if their yelling was bothering me. I thought, *It's not bothering me. It's tearing my heart out and beating it against the rocks of reality.* But I said, "No, not at all."

They continued their unsuccessful calling out to Jaryd as we continued our military march up a now-narrowing trail. The trail was so narrow that we had to walk in single file. To the left of the trail, the mountain climbed quickly to the sky. To the right of the trail, there was a deep drop that ended in the river. I couldn't believe an adult would take a child on this trail without holding onto his hand.

Everywhere I looked, Jaryd could have been hiding in a hundred places. Where was my baby? My only son was left here on the mountain so that Mother Nature could take advantage of him. I could feel death all over the mountain—my own. I wasn't sure how I was going to live without my son.

There were quite a few different colored markers on the trail that indicated certain things about the search. There was a bush with an orange marker on it with a walking stick leaning against a huge rock. The sergeant said, "I'm not sure why that marker is here, but that walking stick might be the one Jaryd was using."

I grabbed it and held it as if Jaryd and I were holding hands. I wanted to feel his touch, and I was willing to do whatever it took to quench my desire to hold my son. I continued up the trail using the same stick that was believed to be Jaryd's. The stick now rests against the wall, next to the fireplace in my home.

As we approached the sight where the helicopter had crashed, the sergeant stopped us to inform us that we needed to respect the military's wishes. We continued, and the helicopter slowly came into view. The sergeant asked the military personnel for permission to bring the family farther up the trail. The Air Force sergeant granted us permission and presented us a clipboard to sign, and then he allowed us to continue on our journey.

The wreckage area was guarded by members of the Air Force's 790th Security Forces Squadron out of Wyoming. They had set up a camp away from the public's eye to run their operations, and media exposure had no place in their mission. When they discovered that Arlyn had been a sergeant in the Security Police and was one of them, they presented him with a medal from their squadron that says, "Defenders of the Force." Arlyn gave the medal to me to keep for Jaryd. Butch, our resort manager, had also been a sergeant in the Air Force's Security Police.

As we passed the crashed helicopter, I looked at my brother and said, "I can't believe nobody died here." The main section of the chopper had trees that had ripped through its body, and the tail rudder was torn completely away and landed with one of its blades almost touching the trail. We were told one of the engines continued to run for almost three hours before it shut down. Some of the men on board actually thought the chopper was going to explode.

We continued up the trail until we came to the point where Jaryd was thought to have been seen last. I took my water bottle and emptied it. I walked over to the river and filled the bottle with water. I sluggishly put the cap on the bottle and reached down to retrieve a few small rocks from the same area. I put the rocks in my pocket, thinking the water and the rocks were the only two things I would be able to hold on to that would give me some type of spiritual connection to Jaryd.

I walked over to a big rock that was overhanging the river, and I climbed on top of it. I stood up and looked out over the river and talked to Jaryd as if he could hear me. I said, "Jaryd, it's Daddy. I love you, and I'm sorry. I promised you I would never let you down. Jaryd, if you're dead, I hope you can hear me and see me. I'm here with you right now, son." Then I violently cried.

This was it. There was no reason to continue up the trail. God gave me some peace, and I knew Jaryd realized Daddy didn't give up on him. I had talked to my son; now I wanted to go back down the trail.

I climbed off the rock and the sergeant asked, "Do you want to continue up the trail?"

Before I had a chance to answer, the lady who was told she was too old to go up the mountain said, "Yes, we came here to look for Jaryd!"

I looked at my mom and replied, "No, this is good enough. I got to see the place where my son disappeared." I was emotionally drained, and I didn't think Jaryd was up there anyway. I looked at my mom. "They've been up this mountain several times, and they haven't found a trace of him. He's not up here."

My mom reluctantly agreed and said, "Whatever you want, babe."

We gathered together and started our trek back down the trail. As we walked, we continued looking for Jaryd and tried to figure out where he could be.

When we approached the helicopter crash sight, I told my brother I wanted to be the last one to go through the area because I had something I wanted to do. As soon as everybody had exited to the other side, I walked up to the sergeant to ask him a question. The sergeant was standing at attention, and I looked him in the eye and said, "I know this is going to be a dumb question, and I probably know the answer to it, but I'm going to ask it anyway. Is there any way I can have something from the helicopter to give to my son when he returns? I don't care if it's a screw. I just want to hang it on his wall to remind him of the heroes who did everything to find him."

The sergeant remained at attention, and with a tear coming out of his eye, he said, "Yes, sir, I'll make sure you get something." I was expecting him to say, "I'm sorry, but there's no way we can do that."

I respectfully replied, "Thank you."

I was home for about five weeks when an officer in the Air Force came to my school and presented me the American Flag decal that was on the helicopter. They cut it off the downed chopper and gave it to me for my son. Thank you, gentlemen. That flag is something I cherish with all my heart.

On the way down the trail, we passed Don Bendell, the tracker who wanted to volunteer his time with the search. As he walked passed us, he told the sergeant with the sheriff's department he wished they would have let him bring his horse up the trail. He was hoping they would allow it the next day. The sergeant responded like he was upset they allowed Don up the trail. He made some comment like, "Don't count on it!"

My brother looked at me and asked, "Did you see the way the sergeant treated him? I wish they would just work together to find Jaryd."

As we approached the parking lot that was connected to the trailhead, the sergeant stopped us. "The media is probably waiting for you guys to get off the trail so they can ask you a few questions. Before we get down there, I want to let you know one thing. You have caused us a lot of problems by wanting to come up this trail."

I couldn't believe what I was hearing. This guy was actually reprimanding us for wanting to see where my son was lost. He was letting us know we were a problem! I don't believe he realized he was part of a special gift the sheriff had given us. The time we spent on the trail may end up being one of the highlights of my life, and I am thankful for his efforts, as well as those of the others involved in the search.

We continued down the trail, and the irony of the hike was that my mom was the first person to reach the top and the first to the bottom. The lady they were worried about was probably in better shape than the rest of us!

As we got to the bottom, it seemed as if every camera in the world was waiting for us. The reporters asked the typical questions, and we gave them our time.

CNN quoted one of the deputies, saying, "It might have been better if the parents had been taken sooner to see the trail. We had kept them out of the area, thinking that that was best."

Since my brother had taken pictures while we were on the trail, he held up a roll of film and said, "I took these pictures of Allyn on the trail and of the area where Jaryd was last seen. I have no plans of going to Fort Collins and having them processed. However, you are welcome to the film as along as your bring me back a copy of the prints." The film was taken by Major King, a cameraman with KMGH-TV out of Denver. He and his reporter, Rhonda Scholting, became friends of ours. Major said he would get the film developed for us, and he would bring the pictures back to us the next day.

It was strange. My son was a national story, but most of the people who were reporting his disappearance were becoming our friends. The ones both behind and in front of the cameras had emotions that were truly hard to hide. I remember seeing several cameramen with tears running down their faces as their counterparts questioned me.

After we were questioned by the media, a different sergeant asked me to go into the trailer designated as the debriefing room.

Let me try and explain what was going on. The sergeant who took us up the trail was the one originally in charge of the search. Two days after Jaryd vanished, he relinquished his duties. I'm not sure why, but the official report indicates he was having problems dealing with the search. Because of this, a new sergeant took over the search, and he was the one who asked me to go into the trailer with him.

There were four of us there, two from the sheriff's department and my friend Kimberly and me. The new sergeant laid out the agenda for the next couple of days. The first thing he told me made my blood boil. He said, "If we don't find Jaryd by Thursday (this was Tuesday), we are going to bring up another thirty searchers."

That was it! My frustration had reached a boiling point, and I needed to vent. I slammed my fist on the table and I yelled, "What do you mean you're going to wait another two days before you bring thirty more searchers up the mountain? My son is missing! You should have brought them up two days ago!"

I went off like a madman. "I don't understand any of this. If I were going to war, I wouldn't take five or six people with me. I'd never win! If I go to war, I'm bringing my family, friends, and anyone else who wants to help me win my battle. The greater the numbers, the greater the chance I have for success. We're no longer going to be successful with a handful of people. You haven't found my son, but you realize you need more people, so you're going to wait two more days to bring them up. Why? So they can help you find his body? Let's face it, in two more days, you will be looking for a body."

I paused and tried to regain my composure. I was getting pumped up and was ready to shove anybody who got in my way, and I didn't care if they arrested me. That would have been a very interesting side story of which no one wanted to become a part.

Although I tried to stay calm, my voice raised again as I said, "I have another problem with you guys. There was a lady who called my resort, and she told me she had certified search dogs and was willing to bring them up to help with the search. I let her talk to one of your fellow employees from the sheriff's office, and the person was told, 'If we need you, we'll call you.' I'm not sure how your math works, but I think twenty dogs are a lot better than four."

I was fuming by this time. The sergeant looked at me and answered in a hostile voice, "I wouldn't change a thing if I had to do it all over."

I snapped back, "Are you trying to tell me you think four dogs are better than twenty?"

He screamed back, "Yes, I think four dogs are better than twenty dogs!"

I thought, *I can't believe this!* I looked him in the eyes and calmly said, "That is the most asinine thing I've ever heard." Trying to keep myself under control, I asked him one last question, "You don't have any kids, do you?"

His response was obvious. "No, I don't."

I had him. I stared him down and said, "No wonder it's easy for you to make ridiculous statements. Now I know from where all of these crazy decisions are coming. You're not thinking like a parent. I'll make a deal with you. Let's go outside and interview everyone on the mountain, and let's ask them what they would rather have, four or twenty dogs. If anyone answers four, I'll get off the mountain and let you do your job."

The sergeant responded, "We can call this search off any time."

I thought, *Go ahead. Prove my point.*

I was ready to ask the sergeant to step outside because I thought he no longer had my best interest in mind. He was going to call the search off because he was mad at me? Try and put yourself in my situation. As a parent, you want as many people as possible looking for your child. He was missing for three days, and it was time to quit messing around, forget about egos, find my son, dead or alive.

We got up and went outside, and I was still pretty hot. I looked at Kimberly and said, "I hope I didn't get carried away in there."

She replied, "No, I think you handled yourself pretty well."

I walked over to where the sergeant was standing, and I apologized for my behavior, but I wanted him to realize I was acting like a father, not a bystander. He said he understood and did not hold anything against me. If a person finds himself in a situation like this, emotions will become raw, and tempers will rise. As hard as the sheriff's office was working, we all had reasons to become frustrated. They entered this challenge totally expecting the same outcome as I did. We were on the same team, and we were either going to win together or lose together. We just happened to be losing.

I ran over to where my family was, and I told them what had happened. They told me not to worry because I had some viable questions that needed to be answered.

I was getting cold, and Nate Hier of the Air Force walked over to me to volunteer one of the warmest jackets I have ever put on. Nate and members of the Air Force treated my family with the greatest respect, and they were our only buffer from the circus that was taking place on the mountain. Our family was allowed into their private camp, and if we walked toward their tents and somebody followed us, the Air Force personnel would step between us and not let them approach my family. It was nice to see them taking care of us like we were part of their family. Because of Arlyn and Butch, they actually felt we were.

My family and I continued to hang around, hoping the searchers would find a clue to Jaryd's whereabouts. I was frustrated with the thought of waiting two more days to bring up thirty more searchers when Arlyn approached me. He was kind of surprised and said, "There is a lady over there, and she wanted me to ask you if you would consider being on *Good Morning America* tomorrow. We'll have to get up pretty early, and I know you're tired. What should I tell her?"

I thought, *No way, I can't believe this.* I couldn't believe Jaryd's story became something the nation was watching with great concern. I looked at my brother and voiced my thoughts. "If she can pull it off, why not? Now everyone will know what my son looks like." If somebody took him, it would be hard to hide his face.

Josallyn and her mom got into Susan's car and prepared for the long trip back down the mountain to Susan's house. I was glad Josallyn was getting a chance to get off the mountain, but for me, it had been a long time since I had gone to bed without any of my children.

As my daughter entered the car, she said, "I love you, Daddy. I'll see you early in the morning."

I was alone in a world that wanted to destroy my desire to continue living. Even though I was facing the worst challenge of my life, the greatest reason to live had just smiled and told me she loved me.

My family and I arrived back at the resort, and we tried to settle in as comfortably as the situation would allow. I was looking ambivalence right in the face because I was enjoying my family, but the loss of Jaryd was eating me up.

We were about to close the store to the resort when a tall man named Seaux entered and looked for something to drink. He walked up to the counter to pay for his merchandise, and he candidly talked about what was going on with the search for the missing little boy.

He shared a lot of information, and I listened with great curiosity. As he continued his story, I looked him in the eyes and said, "I want to thank you from the bottom of my heart for helping in the search for my son."

He paused and said, "I'm sorry, I didn't know you were the father."

With his new information about whom he was talking to, his conversation got more serious, and he told me what was going on and what he thought the searchers should do.

He drew me a map of the section of the trail that was being searched, and he labeled all the campsites for me. He said he thought they were searching in the wrong place, but nobody would listen to him. He wanted them to go back to one of the campsites where Jaryd was last seen, and he wanted them to take the search east. He told me he had found information that indicated Jaryd might have wandered off in that direction.

I took his map and promised him I would ask the authorities to consider his advice and look in the area he was talking about. I didn't know it at the time, but this map would come into play several years later.

When Seaux left, I went back into the apartment area of the resort's main building to find comfort with my family.

Wednesday, October 6, 1999

I went to bed about twelve thirty in the morning, knowing I needed to get up in less than an hour and a half. I figured that amount of sleep was longer than I had been normally getting the past few nights, and an extra half an hour meant I was sleeping in.

Two in the morning came quickly. The alarm went off, and I appreciated the fact that I had actually been sleeping. I tried to get up, but my body felt like a thousand-pound rock, and I was having a difficult time lifting it.

Finally, I was up, and I was trying to figure out why I had said yes to *Good Morning America*. I reminded myself that if there was a chance Jaryd was taken, he needed his picture plastered all over the country. That thought woke me like someone had injected caffeine directly into my veins.

After I took a shower, I woke Arlyn so he could get ready. While he was trying to make himself look presentable, I was thinking about the long slow drive ahead of us. I thought, *God, please don't let me fall asleep while I'm driving*. What a tale that would be—searchers find missing little boy but father perishes while driving down the mountain to tell his story on *Good Morning America*. With that thought in mind, I made sure the coffee was primed and ready to go.

My brother and I climbed into my blazer, and we took it slow because there were a lot of deer out on the road at this time of night. We were tired, but our conversations made the trip fly by. We were talking and listening to the radio when a quick news brief came on about the missing little boy. The man on the radio talked about two fishermen who were in the river fly fishing. The news man said Jaryd had yelled out to the fishermen, asking if they had seen any bears in the area. They yelled back to him, urging him to rejoin his group.

I thought, *Wait a minute. These two men had a chance to save my son, and they didn't?* I looked at my brother and asked, "Why hasn't anybody told us about this?"

As we continued down the mountain, we tried visualizing Jaryd yelling at a couple of fishermen and asking them about bears. If this kid was concerned enough about the wildlife in the area, then why weren't the two men concerned enough about the little boy's safety? It is a question that will never be answered.

Finally, we pulled into the sheriff's department parking lot. We saw a large truck with a cable running out of it that led to an office located upstairs. A few minutes later, we walked into the office area and watched the network people prepare for the morning interview.

Shortly after we arrived, Josallyn and her mother, Angie, walked in. I could tell my daughter was tired, but there was no way she was going to be left behind and not see her daddy. She slowly walked over and asked me to pick her up. As I accommodated her wishes, I questioned if she was okay.

As a child, I'm not sure how I would have handled the situation Josallyn was in, but I knew my daughter was keeping all her emotions to herself. I was afraid I was going to physically lose one child and psychologically lose the other.

About a half hour had gone by when the technicians asked us to have a seat so they could wire us for sound. They hooked a microphone onto the front of my shirt and ran the wire down the inside of my clothing and plugged it into a device that was hooked to the back of my pants. They brought an earpiece up my back so that it couldn't be seen, and they had me plug it into my ear.

When I put the earpiece into my ear, I thought, *This thing is loud.* One of the technicians saw the look on my face, and he informed me there was a volume control on the box that was hooked up to the back of my pants.

I could hear the entire show live from New York. A producer jumped on the line and said, "Allyn, can you hear me?"

I gave a quick, "Yes."

She informed me we would be on shortly, and she wanted to let me know that Charlie Gibson would be doing the interview.

We waited, and then I heard Charlie talking about a little boy who was missing in Colorado. As Charlie was talking, I watched a monitor that showed the actual program as it was taking place.

While Charlie was doing the opening to the story, the TV screen flashed several different pictures of Jaryd. Tears welled from my eyes as I pleaded with God to give me the strength to continue with the interview.

Charlie was very gentle with his questions, and he was a lot different than I had expected. Charlie asked the sheriff the question of the day. "Sheriff, how does a little boy just get up and disappear? Do you think there could be any foul play involved?"

The sheriff answered back quickly, "Oh no, we've all but ruled out any type of abduction. There's only one way in and one way off the trail. If somebody took Jaryd, they would have had to walk past everybody on the trail, and that never happened."

Since Jaryd's disappearance, I purchased topographical software that displayed the trails in the area. To my frustration, I found numerous ways off the Big South Trail. I thought maybe the sheriff didn't want to expose any leads his department was working on because of the many access points. I told myself it was a "keep your cards close to your chest" type of maneuver. While we talked, his department continued its dedicated search for the country's missing little boy. Although we came from different perspectives, we had each become the national spokesperson for our respective positions.

When the interview was over, I heard the network break away to a commercial. I was getting ready to remove my earpiece when Charlie came back on and said, "Allyn, are you still with us?"

I said, "Yes, Charlie, I can hear you."

Charlie replied, "I'm so sorry to hear about what happened to your son. This is a situation no parent should ever have to go through. I'll keep you in my prayers, and I wish you all of the luck in finding Jaryd."

I was very impressed with Mr. Gibson because it was his duty to report the story, but he took time to communicate his sorrow to Jaryd's mom and me. The part that never hit the airwaves meant more to me than what our nation saw. Mr. Charles Gibson, thank you for being the consummate and compassionate journalist you are.

After we finished the interview, we went to breakfast and then headed over to Colorado State University. My nephew, Todd, was living in one of the dorms while studying electrical engineering. My dad had flown in from Las Vegas the night before, and he was waiting for us there.

When we arrived at Colorado State, we went into Todd's dorm room to watch *Good Morning America*. I was standing toward the back of the room because each time they showed Jaryd's picture, my tears flowed like rain. It was hard watching, but it was nice knowing his picture was being seen all over our country. Actually, seeing myself on *Good Morning America* seemed more like an out-of-body experience than anything else. Not only had I become part of the curious crowd of onlookers and well-wishers who made *GMA* part of their daily morning ritual, I was an unwilling player desperately seeking help from anybody who would hear my story. I could hear my voice and see my image, and there was nothing about the event that made sense. A few days earlier, I was looking forward to watching college football, but now I found myself being shoved into the glare of the national spotlight. My voice spoke to me from the corner of the room, and little did I realize this was only the beginning of what was to come. The night before, while watching *NBC Nightly News with Tom Brokaw*, I observed my family and myself walking up the trail to search for Jaryd. Today, I was on ABC sharing my story. Things were moving fast, and I was unprepared for the storm I was in.

We left CSU and drove back up the mountain. To my surprise, I was wide-awake and looking forward to taking my dad up to the trail that took my son. As we arrived at the resort, I realized my son had just spent his fourth night away from me. This was the first time I told myself to face the truth, whatever it may be.

I thought, *Allyn, will you ever see your son again?* That thought caused me to freeze in my footsteps, and my body reacted as if it were quickly thrown into a room with no air. My chest became very heavy as I labored to extract any oxygen I could find in the room.

My mind yelled in pain, *My God, what if I never see my son again?* It was a thought that caused my stomach to churn as it tried to heave the breakfast I had just put into it.

I cried with an anguish I had never experienced in my life. When I was nineteen, my best friend, Robert Romero, was killed in a car accident. I had already lost all four of my grandparents, my uncle Nolan, and my aunt Shirley, but I'd never felt like this. Each one of my family members brought me great pain, but this was far worse than all of them put together. This was the ultimate pain and suffering life had to offer.

I tried to shake my head to clear the devastating thoughts that floated through my mind. I wasn't sure how deep the pain could cut, but I knew I had to pull out of this mind-provoking tailspin.

With tears in my eyes, I desperately tried to find one of my family members. I was looking around, hoping to find any reason to smile and break the spell of horror that was slowly taking me to my grave.

....

Wednesday morning, Arlyn had gone back to the trail without me. He said I needed some rest, and he wanted to see if there was anything new happening. Since we looked alike, he was often confused for being me. When the reporters realized we were twins, they worked different angles. He shared some stories with me, and through his experience, he met the lady who ultimately led to my *Good Morning America* appearance. One lady from MSNBC questioned him about being a twin. She then confided in him that she was a twin, and as twins, they could trust each other. Another one called out his name, "Arlyn, Arlyn, Arlyn... There are only two men in the United States I know named Arlyn, and I'm married to the other one." That was their connection.

Another female reporter pulled my brother aside and told him he had a duty to report any breaking news to her first. He asked her why, and she responded, "Well, I'm with CNN."

Major King, the cameraman who had taken Arlyn's film, spotted him and gave him a folder of photos he had blown up from yesterday's hike. As Major shared the pictures with him, Arlyn looked up and noticed all kinds of cameras and reporters running toward him. Before he realized it, he was in the middle of an impromptu national press conference. Understanding that he couldn't just walk away, he held up the photos he had taken of me while we were on the trail and attempted to explain the details of each. They asked him where I was and what I was doing. He told them I would be up later, but that I needed some valuable rest.

Wednesday, about 1:00 p.m., the rest of my family and I headed back up to the search area. This was the first time my dad had been to the area, and he was astonished with the carnival-type atmosphere that had developed in the parking lot at the head of the Big South Trail.

There were television cameras, the Air Force, newspaper media, search and rescue, deputies, the Salvation Army food trailer, and numerous onlookers hanging around the area. There were so many people they had to mark off the area with crime tape to keep them out!

Across Highway 14, there were three Native Americans sitting against a side rail beating some type of drum and chanting. They brought comfort to my heart as I listened to them methodically call out to the mountain. I was very grateful to see our Native Americans contributing what they could to the search.

My family and I walked around and spoke to different people in the parking lot. The scene was so congested that the Salvation Army had stationed one of its disaster response units on-site. It looked like a snack bar on wheels, and it fed the people who had assembled to either search or cover the story. Of course, our family also had access to their provisions. As time passed, my hunger asked me to visit the Salvation Army trailer, where I grabbed a hotdog and a hot chocolate, and then I walked back to where my family was standing. I had not anticipated the value of the service the Salvation Army was providing until after they arrived. In an event like the one that was taking place, feeding people is one of the details that is easily overlooked until it is too late. I was happy the Salvation Army had taken the initiative to help in the way they were. Through their efforts, I realized one did not have to be up on the trail to ensure this operation continued to move forward.

My relatives were talking to the Native Americans who had crossed over to our side of the street. These people provided a unique degree of peace that touched my heart because they acted as if they were our long-lost family. I hurried over because I wanted to thank them for their efforts. It was strange because we were standing on the inside of the crime tape, and they were standing on the outside of the sectioned-off area.

I invited our new friends to step over the tape, but they responded that they were not allowed in the restricted area. I asked, "Why?"

The leader, Tom Many Wounds, replied, "We are here to ask the spirits of the mountain to give up your son. We would like to volunteer our expertise in tracking, but the deputies said they would arrest us if we crossed into the yellow-taped area."

Their response really frustrated me. I didn't want to insult the actions and beliefs of their culture because they may have conflicted with the rules of the ongoing search. For generations, this land had belonged to the Indians. If the trees could speak, they would have been able to share a rich history of Native American interaction and respect. To me, there was nothing negative about their presence, and standing in the company of Tom Many Wounds and his friends was very inspirational. To insist they could not cross the yellow tape of inclusion did not sit well with me, and although I wasn't in charge of this situation, I knew I had the power to make a little difference. They also knew they were standing with a grateful father who appreciated their effort.

My great grandmother, Arizona Plunk, was from the Cherokee Nation in Oklahoma, and her great grandfather was a chief in the Cherokee Nation. Considering my son has Native American roots, I would do anything to make these fellows comfortable.

I asked our newfound friends if they were hungry. They said, "Yes, but we can't approach the food trailer." The food trailer was about ten yards inside of the marked-off area.

When I heard this, I felt another piece of my heart break. All they wanted was something to eat and a warm cup of coffee. I said, as my voice got louder the more I talked, "If you guys want something to eat and something to drink, I'll get it for you!"

My brother and I walked over to the food trailer and got food and drinks for those who were not allowed to sit up front with the rest of us.

They thanked us, and Tom Many Wounds offered me a prayer wheel he had been rubbing on. He said, "As you pray, rub the prayer wheel, and your prayers will be answered." I was honored as I reached over and took the prayer wheel from his hand.

I didn't have it long, because I quickly found out the prayer wheel meant more to my mother than I had first realized. She took it from my hands and rubbed it. I asked for it back because I wanted to keep it with the water and rocks I had collected on the trail the day earlier. My mom gave me a look as if she were trying to say, "Please, let me have it for a while." She now has it hanging on the wall in her office.

We said our good-byes to our Native American family and walked over to where a small group of people were gathering. There was a little commotion, and I wondered what was going on. The closer I got, the more I recognized some of the people in the small but rambunctious crowd.

As I got closer to the group, I heard someone say something about a cougar or mountain lion to the sheriff. My blood raced as I listened to the conversation about small shoeprints crossing an area that intersected with mountain lion prints. As this conversation continued, I saw some of the people involved with the search talking to the media about a possible tragic conclusion to Jaryd's life.

The sheriff walked away from Seaux, the man who had given me the map a few nights earlier. Seaux stood there, all alone, as if he were analyzing everything he had just mentioned to the sheriff. I slowly walked up to him and asked if he could repeat his story to me. He looked me in the eyes and said, "I need to talk to you anyway." I could care less what he had to say; I just wanted to know if he found my son.

Seaux said, "I was on the east side of the trail, and I was following the prints of a small shoe, which could be your son's. As I followed the trail, the shoeprints disappeared at the intersection of mountain lion prints."

As Seaux continued, I could see the media off in the distance scampering to get set up because the sheriff was getting ready to release some new information in the case.

Seaux said with frustration, "I wish the sheriff would have stayed and listened to the rest of the story about what I found. I followed the tracks of the mountain lion for a long distance, and that cat never saw your son. There was no blood, clothes, dragging marks, or any sign of a struggle. I guarantee you, that cat never saw your son."

I thanked Seaux, and a smile of relief crossed my face. I couldn't wait to tell everyone the part of the story the sheriff didn't hear.

I looked off in the distance, and I could see the media feverishly trying to set up for the emergency press conference the sheriff had just called. I quickened my pace as I hurried toward the cameras because I wanted everyone to hear the truth about the mountain lion tracks.

I walked up and stood next to the sheriff and waited for everyone to get into position. When the press conference started, the sheriff told everyone a tracker had found a little boy's tracks that mysteriously disappeared when they intersected with those of a mountain lion. There was a quiet rumble of disbelief that echoed throughout the media as they patiently waited to ask me about this new theory the sheriff had just laid out before them. As the sheriff finished, questions flew uncontrollably in my direction.

It was my turn. "Before I answer any questions about a mountain lion attack, I want you to know I just talked to the tracker who spotted the tracks, and he has reassured me the mountain lion never saw my son." I continued, telling them the story that was just told to me, and I paused, waiting to field any new questions.

"Allyn, how does this new information make you feel about what may have happened to your son?"

"Do you feel a sense of relief and comfort knowing a mountain lion may have attacked your son?"

I thought, *That is a stupid question. He should have asked, "Do you feel a sense of relief knowing that you might have an answer to the whereabouts of your son?"*

I tried to answer the second question. "No, I don't have any relief nor have I experienced any comfort thinking a mountain lion could have killed my son. In fact, it makes me sick to think a theory like this could be true. About twelve years ago, I was chased by a mountain lion, and to think my son experienced the same thing I did, but with a different outcome, is hard to comprehend."

As the sheriff and I walked away, he tapped me on the back and said, "I hope you're right about the mountain lion."

As I relived the chase I had experienced twelve years earlier, I thought, *I do too.*

It was about nine o'clock on a dark June evening in the summer of 1987 at Camp Wolahi when I was sitting with a friend by the counselor-in-training cabins right across from the archery range. We were informed earlier in the week about a mountain lion that was displaying abnormal behavior, and we were told to keep an eye out for it. As Diane and I talked, we heard something fairly large running back and forth, making a lot of noise just beyond the archery range. During our conversation, the question came up, "Do you think the noise up there could be the mountain lion?" We nervously laughed it off because we thought no one would believe us.

About ten minutes later, a friend named Donna walked up the trail just east of us. She was a free spirit minding her own business while using her flashlight to brighten up the trail just ahead of her. She had no idea Diane and I were watching her and laughing.

As Donna got closer to us, we heard the loud noise of dead pine needles crunching as something very heavy moved back and forth again. This time, Donna heard it and froze like a deer on the trail. She did not move, but she slowly lifted her flashlight and searched the dark night for the answer of the question Diane and I had already asked. Could this be what we were warned about earlier?

About a minute went by before Donna decided it was safe enough to move on. She quickly scampered another thirty yards up the trail to where the older girls were camping. There were about twenty girls from the ages of eleven to fourteen camping outside. Their sleeping bags were thrown on the dirt so the girls could look up through the trees and see every star that passed that night.

Diane and I were still sitting on the log, listening for more loud noises. We heard nothing and laughed when we talked about how Donna had reacted to the loud, disturbing noise in the night. We decided to go up to where Donna was and let her know we had watched the entire incident. When we arrived at the camping area, we told Donna how we had seen her deer impersonation, and we all laughed loudly like three drunks in a bar. The laughter was short-lived, because it was as if our excitement had once again awakened the beast that was making all the noise.

Eileen Schultz was the unit director in charge of the girls camping in that area. She informed us that she had heard the noise all along and was somewhat concerned for the safety of the people in the general area. We decided someone needed to go down to the director's cabin to inform her about the mysterious noise.

Donna and I volunteered to go down because our cabins were back in that general area. As Donna and I got about ten yards down the trail, we heard a noise that indicated something was running straight toward us. It was as if we were a target the enemy had locked on to and there was no escape. We both froze and pointed our flashlights in the direction from which the noise was coming. It sounded as though an out-of-control horse was galloping straight toward us, and what we saw terrified us beyond any fear we had ever experienced in our lifetimes.

Our flashlight beams made contact with the eyes of the animal that was quickly approaching us. The eyes were a beautiful gold, bobbing up and down with every stride the animal took. We could see its claws reaching out, knowing it would only be a few more seconds before they would tear into our flesh and take us down like a lost fawn. Our pounding hearts ripped the silence away from the night as we watched the mountain lion get closer and closer. It stopped, jumped off the trail, and quietly hid behind a bush five yards away from us. Why did it stop, and where did it go? The lion quietly watched and prepared for its next move.

Donna and I stood there shaking with fear, and I thanked God for the chance to experience another breath of air. Yes, this was the animal we were all warned about. There's a lot more to this story, but I never realized this would be the first, but not the last time, a mountain lion would try to destroy my life.

I thought about the question, *Do you have any comfort knowing your son may have been attacked by a mountain lion?* If the person who had asked this question could have only experience the fear I felt the night I was chased, that ridiculous question would not have been asked. Comfort never entered the situation.

Later that afternoon, the sheriff placed a call to the Department of Wildlife. He wanted more information concerning the type of animal prints that intersected those that were thought to be Jaryd's, and he was hoping they could use some dogs to track the animal and capture it. If they could find the mountain lion, they would put it to sleep, attach a transmitting collar, and then follow it back to a den hoping to find Jaryd's body.

As we waited for the Department of Wildlife to arrive on the scene, my brother approached me with a question from a person representing one of the networks. He said, "Patty Burke wanted me to ask you if you would be willing to be on the *Today Show* in the morning?"

I was very tired, and I told him, "No, I don't think I can get up early in the morning and do this entire thing over again. Not this time."

My brother informed Patty of my decision. A few minutes later, Patty approached me and asked again if I would consider doing the *Today Show*. I told her I was too tired to get up and go down the mountain at two o'clock in the morning. She was very persistent and replied, "What if they get you a room in town for the night?"

I said, "I'll think about it."

About ten minutes had passed when Patty was back, telling me they had a room at the Marriott for me. I thought, *Maybe I need to get away from this nightmare, and a night off the mountain might do me some good.* I said okay then went back to waiting for the Department of Wildlife to arrive.

As we waited for the mountain lion dogs, the sergeant who was originally in charge asked me to go into their war room so they could show me what they had been doing in the search. Once I sat down, he told me how the dogs were utilized and where they had been on the trail.

As the conversation continued, he also explained how the dogs would use the scent from clothing to help find the missing person for which they were searching. One of the search and rescue members, sitting to my right, picked up a bag of Jaryd's clothes and passed them over my head to the sergeant who was standing to the left of me.

As the clothes crossed over my head, my heart stopped, and I yelled, "Wait! Are those the clothes the dogs have been sniffing to find my son?"

The search and rescue person responded, "We only used the clothing for the first two nights. After that, we let the dogs loose, telling them to go find somebody. There are two techniques we can use: one technique is they use a person's scent and another technique is we tell them someone is missing and we send them off without a given scent."

"I understand that, but I want you to look into the bag at the clothing you're using." They slowly opened the bag and pulled out a pair of shorts.

I looked at them and said, "You can't tell by looking at those shorts that they're too big for a three-year-old? Those are my shorts! You mean to tell me your dogs have been searching for my son using my scent? No wonder they can't find him!"

I was pretty upset when I told my brother what had happened. I was trying to calm down when I looked my brother in the eye and said, "I was wondering why each time I walk by a dog, they want to put their nose up my crotch."

While talking to my brother, one of the sergeants approached me and asked if I had any more of Jaryd's clothing at the resort. I said, "Sure, I have his jacket and a couple of pairs of shoes." The sergeant wanted to know if he could follow me back down the mountain to get some fresh items that contained Jaryd's scent. When we arrived at the resort, I went into my Blazer and gave the sergeant the articles of clothing he needed.

It was about 8:00 p.m., and I was getting tired. I told my brother to stay at the resort because my friend Kimberly was going to take me down the mountain and hang there with me for the night. Kimberly was a blessing in disguise. She followed me around because she was genuinely concerned about my health and my heart-piercing pain.

Kimberly and I packed up a few of my clothes and headed for the Marriott. I wasn't sure what to expect; all I knew was I had a quiet place to lay my head down and a dry pillow that would catch my tears as I slept.

We arrived at the front desk, and I gave them my name and told them we had a room reserved for the night. They went through their paperwork and handed me a card key for a room on the sixth floor.

Kimberly and I got into the elevator. I pushed the number six and waited for the elevator to move. Nothing happened. Kimberly laughed, and I pushed the number six again. We waited, but again, nothing happened. We were both tired and thought someone was playing a cruel joke on us.

I took a hard look at the number six, and I noticed a small opening right below the number. I took our room key and slid it into the slot, and it activated the number six. I pushed the number again, and the elevator moved upward. I thought, *Wow, a private floor!*

We got off the elevator and searched for our room. I moved quickly because I was exhausted and wanted to get into the room and sleep. Finally, I inserted the card, and the door opened to reveal a suite with two large beds and an office surrounded by windows that allowed for a perfect view of Fort Collins.

About five minutes after we arrived, someone knocked at the front door and said, "Room service!" When I opened the door, there was a man standing there with a huge plate covered with all types of fruit, cheese, meat, and crackers. It was from the management of the Marriott.

I sat down on my bed and watched the local news for the first time. My body was tired, but I didn't go to bed until one o'clock in the morning. I had slept a total of six hours the previous four nights, and my body, again, was trying to communicate with me. The tingling sensation returned, and my nervous system was acting like it was about to shut down. I laid my head on the pillow, and a few seconds later, my body dropped into a deep sleep.

I opened my eyes. I was standing on the trail where Jaryd had disappeared. I looked around, and there he was, about five yards away from me. He had his shirt off, his arms were crossed in front of his chest, and he slowly looked up at me. His hair was wet and combed back as if he had just gotten out of a swimming pool. He looked at me, and then he smiled.

My son was okay! I was so excited to see him. I cried and ran to him.

I abruptly sat up in bed and looked around the dark room, searching for Jaryd. I thought, *Where are you? Where did you go?* This was the second of many dreams I had about my son. I loved them because they were so real, yet I hated them because they were mean tricks my mind was playing on me.

I sat there. I cried and wanted to go back to sleep so I could see him again. *Why did I wake up?* I thought, *Please, God, let me go back to sleep so I can see my son again. Please, God! Please, God!*

I couldn't sleep for the rest of the night because the reality of my world had hit me again. Did I see my son, or was it a dream? What was it? Where is he? I couldn't believe I'd *never* see him again. It was only four nights ago that I was playing catch with him, and we were giving each other high fives. This can't be true! My life with my son was just starting. What's going on! I can't sleep, and I hate it!

The Final Day of the Search

Thursday, October 7, 1999

The alarm went off at three fifteen in the morning, and I was still reeling from the dream I had only a couple of hours earlier. Physically, Jaryd was missing; but mentally, he was right there with me. I was happy because I knew my mind would never let go of the special person I called my son.

I got out of bed and took a shower and wondered how long this nightmare would last. Everything around me seemed surreal, and I hoped someone would pinch me and bring me back to reality. I thought back to Saturday. It was very simple; this situation should have never changed my life. I can still see Jaryd standing in front of me as I said, "Yes, Janet can take you on a hike." I was having a hard time believing that trust was making an effort to destroy my life.

I tried to shake off the funk I was in as I walked over to Kimberly to wake her. I knew we had to be down in the lobby by 4:00 a.m. to meet our ride to the sheriff's office, and we were running short on time. It was strange, but the day was turning into a repeat of the one before.

We arrived in the lobby. Our ride wasn't there. I was getting nervous because I knew we only had a few minutes to get to our destination. I went to the front desk and asked the person there if anyone had called. He told me a driver had just called to get the directions to the Marriott and should arrive in a few minutes.

We patiently waited. After five minutes had passed, a man dressed in a suit walked in and asked, "Are you Allyn?" Our ride was here.

We went outside, and a beautiful limousine was waiting for us. The driver opened the door, and I could see Josallyn and her mother sitting inside, waiting for us to enter. As I got into the limousine, my daughter jumped into my lap and said, "I love you, Daddy." She reminded me what it was like to have a beautiful child in my life. I had mixed emotions because Josallyn brought me the warmest feelings, but Jaryd was still missing. I looked at Josallyn and said, "Jaryd sent this car for us." I am not sure if that was the right thing to say, but I didn't want to leave Jaryd out of any part of our life.

We arrived at the sheriff's office and went upstairs to the room we were in the morning before. Again, it seemed as if we were going through a time warp, because today was taking on the resemblance of the one that had just passed. It kind of reminded me of the movie *Ground Hog Day*.

As we entered the room, we were confronted with two questions about the programming that was planned for the rest of the morning. "Allyn, would you mind waiting around and doing the *Later Today Show* then the *Ted Koppel* show?"

The three shows would take all morning, and I would not get back up to the search area until about 2:00 p.m. I did not want to wait, but the thought of getting Jaryd's picture out was very tempting. I said, "Why not? I'm already here, so let's do it."

Once again, we sat down and were wired for sound as we prepared to do another morning show. As we waited, the producer talked into my earpiece to let me know we would be talking to Katie Couric.

After the interview, we waited in the sheriff's office for about an hour and a half to get rewired for the *Later Today Show*. All the questions were the same, just different people asking them. I didn't really care; my son's face was being plastered all over the nation. I wanted the world to recognize him because I thought there was a chance he could be out there, and if he was, hopefully, somebody would find him.

When the interview was over, we were told to meet back at the victim advocate's house in two hours to film the *Ted Koppel* show for later that night.

I didn't want to sit around, so I had the limousine driver drop Kimberly and me off at the Marriott so we could freshen up and gather our things. Kimberly was tired, so she decided to lie down and take a nap. I was pretty wired, so I decided to take a walk down to the lobby to purchase a newspaper to check the latest information concerning my son. I was still under the impression that most of the information I was receiving was coming from the media.

I looked at the front page of *The Coloradoan*, and the picture I saw put a knot in my stomach. My sister-in-law, Robyn, was sitting on the ground with tears on her face, and you could feel the pain she was going through. That picture was on the front page of newspapers across the country. We are very close, and she is the only aunt Jaryd really knew. She even insisted on going up the trail the day before to the place where he was last seen. The picture caused Robyn to guard her emotions while in public because she felt her grief was private.

I looked at the headlines and could not believe what I was reading. The information being portrayed was true, but I understood it differently. I started reading.

> Thursday, October 7, 1999
>
> Tracks may be boy's
>
> Searchers find lion's markings nearby
>
> By Jenn Farrell
>
> *The Coloradoan*
>
> RUSTIC- Tracks heading up a hill one mile into the Big South Trail may have been left by 3-year-old Jaryd Atadero as he scrambled up the mountain. Those tracks are near some left by a mountain lion, giving searchers their first clue as to what might have happened to the missing boy.
>
> But while one tracker says he is 90 percent sure Jaryd left those markings, a Colorado Division of Wildlife tracker believes they were left by a bear...

I continued reading, hoping to find the information that said the mountain lion never saw Jaryd. I was disappointed because everyone was making a big deal out of the fact that Jaryd may have been taken by this cat. There were no headlines in any paper that would lead the reader to believe this never happened.

I have talked to a lot of people since Jaryd disappeared, and they tell me the little boy was taken by a mountain lion. These people are extremely adamant about how they feel because the information they received was spoon-fed to them through specific headlines or the news media. People have argued with me as if they were on the scene of Jaryd's disappearance from the beginning to the end of the search. I always end my conversation with, "I'm Jaryd's dad, and I think I know a little more about what happened than you."

It is strange, but some people read the title of the story and think they have read the entire story. If they would have continued reading the article, they may have learned more about what really happened. I read on, as I wanted to find out if they would ever discount the theory about a mountain lion dragging my son off to a den.

I turned the newspaper to page A5 and saw a picture of my dad sitting there. I could tell he was pondering something, but what? By the look on his face, I didn't think he was buying into the mountain lion thing. I continued reading.

> The mood lightened some when Seaux Larreau, a tracker with United Tracking Services, said that, after following the tracks, he had not been able to find evidence of a struggle or any other indications that Jaryd had fallen prey to a mountain lion.

Finally, there was something that discredited the fact that a mountain lion took my son. It's a theory that most people I have talked to won't believe.

There was a silent whisper going around the mountain that continues today. "He's not up there." Was Jaryd abducted? There's no evidence that supports any theory, and those involved knew Jaryd had passed all of the people on the hike and was heading toward Peterson Lake. The sheriff keeps saying there is only one way in and one way out. Most of us on the mountain know you can park at Peterson Lake and walk down the trail. That means there is more than one way in and one way out.

I continued reading the article and came across something that really disturbed me. One of the employees of the sheriff's department was quoted as saying, "About eight search and rescue personnel will begin looking about eight miles from the trailhead at Peterson Lake and work their way back to the area. The searchers believe that is the only area in which their coverage has been weak."

I thought, *Wait a minute, the sheriff keeps saying there is only one way in and one way out. Then why do the search and rescue members feel they have been weak in searching this area?*

I was frustrated because there was a chance someone could have taken Jaryd off the mountain by leaving through Peterson Lake, and they waited almost five days to search this area.

I closed the paper and went and sat by myself at the bar. For the millionth time, I could feel the tears welled from my eyes as I thought about my missing son. I tried to grab my composure because I could hear the TV, and they were about to come back from a commercial to the story about the missing little boy in the Colorado Mountains.

Jaryd's picture flashed across the screen, and tears flowed down my face again. I thought, *Jaryd, I love you so much! I'd do anything to see you again.* I was in my own little world while I thought about my son and how much I missed him.

I was minding my own business when a lady approached me and asked, "Are you Mr. Atadero?"

I looked up, wiped the tears from my eyes. "Yes."

"Our staff is very sorry about your son, and if there's anything we can do for you, please let us know."

I smiled and said, "Thank you. I appreciate that very much."

She walked away and left me all alone, sitting at the bar. I couldn't believe how nice people could be when someone is going through the trial of a lifetime.

I sat there for about five minutes when a gentleman approached me and asked, "Mr. Atadero, are you alone, or is someone staying with you in your room?"

I replied, "No, I'm not alone. My friend Kimberly is up in our room right now."

The man responded, "Can we buy you and your friend breakfast? We have a wonderful restaurant and would love to treat you this morning."

I had been up for about five hours now, and breakfast sounded great. It didn't take long for me to reply, "Thank you, I'd love breakfast."

I went up to my room to ask Kimberly if she would like to join me for breakfast. Since our time was short, we decided to pack our clothes and take them down to her truck before we sat down to eat.

I looked at the menu and chose something rather simple because I am not the type of person who takes advantage of a situation. I was pleasantly surprised when the waiter questioned, "That's all you want? Our steak and eggs are excellent. You ought to consider it."

I replied, "No, thanks, I think this will be fine."

After breakfast, I wanted to go back up the mountain. I felt guilty, and I needed to be with my family. I thought, *I don't want to do this anymore. Why did I agree to stay down here when my son needs me up on the mountain?* I had a strong desire to leave, but I had given my word, and I knew there was no way out of this time-consuming situation.

Kimberly and I drove to the house that was to be used as the backdrop for the last national interview I would give. I was getting tired, and I wanted my life back. I asked myself, *When does a reporter cross the line in the story he is pursuing?* In the beginning, the story was about my missing son. As the days passed, some appeared to be more concerned with plastering my family's pain all over the screen.

Jaryd's mom and I sat and talked to the reporter for about a half hour. The questions were more personal, and the prodding was a little deeper.

We finished the interview around noon and headed back up the mountain. It was a long arduous drive, but I desperately wanted to get back to the Big South Trailhead. I had no idea what was taking place up there, but I knew my level of frustration was getting deeper as each minute passed.

When I arrived at the search area, my brother Arlyn approached me, and he was very upset. He told me he didn't feel communication with the authorities was adequate, and he felt there was little effort being made to share information with him and my dad concerning current search operations.

I was mad. I headed off to find the deputy who was in charge. When I found him, I exploded like a volcano, and I no longer cared who was watching me. I let him know that I was tired of finding out information from the media. When any important decisions were being made, the media would approach me and ask me how I felt about what was going on. I would always reply, "Who told you that? I have no idea what you're talking about." The circumventing treatment made me feel as though the officials in charge were purposely restricting the flow of information my family desperately needed. They didn't understand the effect this would have on a grieving family because if they could truly experience empathy, they would ensure we remained at the forefront of information.

We went at it for about a minute until I noticed the reporters with TV cameras running to get a picture of me losing it. I said my piece and tried to walk away. I wanted no part of the media this time. As I walked away, they rushed up to me and asked what had happened. Out of respect for those who were searching, I played it off and said it was nothing.

I went to the person I had yelled at and apologized to him. I was mad, but I did not want to make anyone look stupid. We walked off to a peaceful area behind a truck, and we hugged each other. I knew we were in a losing situation. My son was lost, and they couldn't find him. Neither one of us had a reason to celebrate.

About a half hour later, there was a press conference to update the media about the day's events. I watched as a multitude of cameramen and reporters gathered in front of us. My brother, who stood next to me during the conference, leaned over and whispered in my ear, "You're a stronger man than I'll ever be."

I leaned over and whispered back, "Oh yeah…you should have seen me on Saturday."

The questions flew back and forth, and then there was a question that surprised me and caused me to laugh. "Allyn, is it true you earlier said, 'Oh well, life goes on. The Broncos are 0 and 4?'"

Everyone was shocked when I said, "Yes, that's true. That's exactly what I said." Then I went on to explain myself. I let them know I had the chance to get off the mountain the night before. It was the first time I had the opportunity to see the local news, and it frustrated me. As I watched, the lead story was about my son. As soon as it was over, the reporter said, "Up next, the Broncos are 0 and 4." I was frustrated because my son was just a story to them. They really didn't care. Heck, life goes on, the Broncos are 0 and 4, *at least according to the media.*

Once again, I said, "Yes, that's what I said. But I was talking about you guys and how you treat my son." I think they understood how I was feeling because it was never brought up again.

As I answered questions, I was amazed to see all the tears rolling down the faces of reporters, cameramen, sound technicians, and other bystanders. Many of us had gotten to know each other fairly well, and the lack of anything positive to report impacted them at a level I would have never anticipated. Jaryd became our nation's son. I believe those present wanted to see him appear on the trail as badly as I did. They could sense the end of the search was near, and many of us had developed a genuine bond because we had lived this experience together.

The press conference ended as the sun began to set for another night. The reporters packed their camera equipment, and people walked over to me to wish my family the best. The deputy in charge of the search slowly approached me with information that was inevitable. He said there would be a meeting at the sheriff's office in the morning to decide the direction the search needed to go. I was politely warned there was a possibility they would call off the search, but they would wait until the meeting to make that decision. I told him I understood and thanked him.

My family and I decided to go back to the resort to plan our next move. I wanted my family to know I was going home to Littleton if the search was called off the next day. I had to open my eyes and face the truth. The possibility of leaving the mountain without Jaryd was now a legitimate concern.

We gathered our belongings and walked to our vehicles in order to leave the search area. At that moment, people carrying cameras came running up to me with one more question for the night. "Allyn, how do you feel about the sheriff calling off the search tonight?"

I think my reply surprised them. Again, I said, "Where did you hear that? The deputy told me fifteen minutes ago they wouldn't make any decision until tomorrow morning's meeting."

One of the reporters said, "The person you talked to just called us over and informed us the search was called off tonight."

I thought, *Nothing has changed. They tell us one thing, and then the media is provided with a different story.* I had mixed emotions about what was transpiring, and I would never want to be in the situation of telling a family we had come to the end of the trail. Although this person may have had this information when he spoke with me, he knew I would put up a fight if he told me. He was probably as worn out as I was, and he figured somebody else could be the messenger with the bad news. We all wanted this nightmare to end. One way for this to happen was to run away from it as fast as possible. Nobody wants to hang around and answer questions after they lost the Super Bowl, and although we weren't football players, the lights were beginning to dim on our field, and we had nothing to celebrate.

We were extremely disappointed with the latest news. I let the media know that if the search was called off, I was going home. We were already told we could not go up the trail for at least a week because the military was going to shut down the trail to remove their helicopter. I was not going to stand up here and wait for my son to walk off the mountain when I believed he may be off walking someplace else.

I got into my Blazer and slowly drove down to the resort because I knew it would be the last time I would be up that way for a long time. Winter was coming, and it wouldn't be long before the trail would be covered with snow.

When we got back to the resort, I was terrified with the thought of going home without my son. It was a painful thought that continues daily. It is rough because people look at me, and they forget the living hell I'm going through. I smile at my friends, and I enjoy my students; but when I get behind closed doors, I face my situation with a sadness that slowly eats away at my body every day.

It was about 7:00 p.m. when Seaux, the tracker who found the tracks going up the side of the mountain, walked into the store with more information concerning Jaryd. He was upset because the sheriff's office had ignored his conclusion. He said he was driving home when he heard on the radio that a Department of Wildlife official had dismissed his findings because what he thought were Jaryd's footprints were actually bear prints. Seaux continues to swear by his findings and believes the prints were Jaryd's.

That wasn't the only reason Seaux drove back up the mountain. He said the search was in the wrong place, and they needed to move the search up into the area that he indicated on the map. Seaux believed Jaryd was trying to go over the mountain to find his way home, and if they looked there, they would find him.

Seaux asked Jaryd's mom and me if we would call the sheriff and ask him to helicopter some dogs onto the top of the mountain and search in the direction he thought Jaryd was headed. He said, "Once you get to the top of the mountain, it flattens out, and it's an easy trail to walk on."

Jaryd's mom bought into the idea, and she pleaded with me to call the sheriff and make the request Seaux had come up with. I told her, "No, I won't do it. You don't understand. I have learned they tell you what you want to hear, and then they do something else." She got upset with me and I told her, "You're his mother, call the sheriff yourself and see what happens. Don't get upset when they tell you one thing and then they do something else. You heard the reporters. They've already made up their mind, and they're done searching."

Jaryd's mom was upset, but she decided she would call the sheriff and plead her case. She talked to the sheriff for several minutes and tried to convince him to continue searching in the area Seaux had indicated. When she got off the phone, she told me the sheriff promised her they would discuss her request, and he would call her in the morning after the meeting to let her know their decision.

I laughed at her and said, "I told you he'd tell you what you wanted to hear. He only said it to get you off the phone because this thing has gotten everybody down. He'll call you in the morning and give you the bad news."

She wasn't excited, but she knew she had tried.

We Leave the Mountain

Friday, October 8, 1999

My family got up early Friday morning and prepared to drive back to Littleton. They were running out of time because most of my family was flying home the next day. They had originally flown to Colorado to be by my side when Jaryd was found. It was a trip that started with hope but ended with the same pain with which they had arrived.

Jaryd's mom was up, patiently waiting for the sheriff to call her with his decision about searching the area that was now a spot on a map. For some reason, she actually thought the sheriff would consider her request and send a team to the area in question. I knew she was setting herself up for a huge disappointment because he had already terminated the search. I didn't see any way he would reverse his decision. The news was out, and the story was over. Maybe.

The phone rang, and Jaryd's mom ran to answer it. It was the call she had been waiting for. I watched her face as I tried to read her emotions. She talked to the sheriff for about a minute and then hung up. Still looking for a clue in her eyes, I finally asked, "Well, what did he tell you?"

She shook her head back and forth. "They said no, they aren't going to search anymore."

I could sense her frustration and pain, and I didn't want to see her get hurt by the letdown that she had received. It was like she was the only girl without a date to the prom. She mumbled, "I can't believe they said no."

She went on to say the sheriff wanted the family to meet him at his office at 11:00 a.m. We would also meet with everyone from the sheriff's department that was involved in the search. It was the first time they had actually called us all together. They wanted to debrief us on what had happened and discuss what options we had. Actually, we didn't have many options. They had been calling the shots, and the official search was history.

We loaded our cars and prepared to head down the mountain. I was having a tremendous problem because, under a different circumstance, I would have never left Jaryd here by himself. It was painful to breathe when I thought about him. *How could I be leaving without my son?*

We piled into two cars and headed to town. I drove in a trance as I headed down the mountain. It was a strange feeling because it was like I had left my heart and soul back on the Big South Trail. I constantly thought about Jaryd. I cried for most of my trip down, and the tears clouded my vision. It was tough! Why was I leaving? I prayed, *Please, God, let me see my son again.*

When we entered Fort Collins, we stopped at a convenience store to get something to drink and stretch out our legs. I looked at the entrance to the store, and there was a flyer that my brother had made with Jaryd's picture on it, hanging on the front door. Every person who entered the store could see it. The flyer had information about his disappearance and phone numbers to call if someone had any information concerning his whereabouts.

When we paid for our drinks, the cashier looked at us and said, "Can you please look at the flyer of the missing little boy on your way out?"

I asked him, "Do you say that to all of the customers as they pay?"

"Yes, we hope someone can help find the little boy."

He was very surprised when I thanked him and said, "We hope someone can help find him too. That little boy is my son."

We walked out of the store and noticed several people staring at us. You could hear the whispering as people walked by us, "Hey, they're the parents of the missing little boy." It was sad, but I was glad people were aware of the situation.

We drove to the sheriff's office and prepared for the meeting with those involved with the search. There were only seven of us because my dad wanted to stay on the mountain for another day. It wasn't time for him to let go.

We went upstairs to the sheriff's office and were led into a conference room. It was strange because there was no one there to meet with us. We waited for a few minutes, and four people walked in: the victim's advocate, Captain Newhard, the main investigator, and a person with search and rescue whom I'd never met.

Where were the rest of the people who were supposed to meet with us? Neither the sheriff nor the sergeants who were in charge of the search were there. My brother leaned over to me and whispered, "I thought this meeting was going to include a lot more people than what are here."

I couldn't believe it. The sheriff asked us to drive down and meet with him, but he was not here. Where was the deputy who told me that four dogs are better than twenty? Where was the other deputy who told us we caused a lot of problems because we wanted to go up the trail?

During the scaled-down meeting, Captain Newhard cried with frustration because Jaryd was never found. He got up and left the room and went to his office. My heart went out to him because his feelings were genuine, and I was thankful to meet a man with his character.

I got up and left the room and walked over to Newhard's office. He was standing there facing the back wall as he tried to dry the tears that were flowing down his face. I said, "Captain Newhard, I'm sorry. I know you gave it your best shot."

I walked over to him and we hugged each other. He said, "I'm going to find Jaryd if it's the last thing I do. I'd die right now to have that boy standing here."

In my heart, Captain Newhard is one of the greatest men I have ever met. He is honest and full of integrity.

We walked back to the meeting room and said our good-byes. The meeting wasn't a total loss; God let me interact with a man who reflected the meaning of what a true angel should be. I am very grateful to Captain Newhard.

We left the sheriff's office and headed to the Loveland Airport so my brother could rent a car to continue our trip to Littleton. My friend Debbie was acting like a chauffeur as she drove my family around. She loved us, but she wanted to head back up the mountain to stay with my father and friends.

My brother went into the office to get his car. On his way out, he turned and went back inside to give them one of the flyers with Jaryd's picture. As he walked up to the front door, everybody scampered back behind their counter because they had been standing behind the tinted windows, staring at us. This is when I realized my life was getting weird.

We continued our hour-long drive into Littleton, and I was still having a hard time believing Jaryd was not with us. How was I going to walk into my apartment without my son? I wasn't sure I was going to be able to handle the quiet atmosphere of what was once graced with Jaryd's laughing and playing. I was hoping his voice would be echoing off the walls and he would come running out of his room to ask me, "Daddy, can I hold your hand?" I knew I needed to face the hardest part of my life, my existence without my son.

I arrived at my apartment, grabbed my luggage, and climbed to the third floor. I stood in front of my apartment door, key in hand, and hated what I needed to do next. I placed the key into the door knob and then removed my hand quickly as if I had been shocked. My brother reached over and opened the door for me. He knew I wasn't prepared to enter a place where I could see Jaryd everywhere I looked.

We slowly walked into a place that was screaming my son's name. Some of his clothes and a few of his toys were sitting in the living room. I walked into my bathroom, and my heart exploded with pain. Jaryd had taken a bath the day we left, and his soldiers and tanks were still sitting next to the bathtub. I did not want to touch them because they were all I had left. I fell to my knees and broke down.

After several moments passed, I slowly got up and walked into my closet. Jaryd's clean clothes were in a basket, and they needed to be folded. I sat down and folded them and held each and every article as if it were Jaryd himself.

My mom walked into the closet and asked, "Are you okay, honey?"

I didn't respond to her because I couldn't stop crying long enough to talk. I just sat there with tears in my eyes as I continued caressing and folding my son's precious clothing.

When I was done folding and putting away Jaryd's clothes, I walked over and checked my answering machine. I could not believe it—I had about fifty messages. I never realized having a listed phone number could generate so many calls from concerned people I had never met. It was amazing; Jaryd's story had affected so many people.

As I listened to my messages, the phone rang as if the person on the other side knew I was standing there. It was a reporter from one of the TV stations, and they wanted to know if they could come over and film my family as we tried to get back to our lives in the city. I didn't care anymore; just help me find my son.

The reporter showed up and talked with me for a while and then filmed us as we ate dinner. When they left, they told us it would be on the nine o'clock news.

Not long after they left, the phone rang again. It was my cousins Ruben and Robert Atadero. They had come to town and wanted to know how to get to my place. As we talked, I realized they were only five minutes away. I was looking forward to seeing them.

There were nine people staying in my two-bedroom apartment, and even though I just got home, I desperately needed to get away. It had nothing to do with my family; I just needed to be alone. It was eight thirty, and I decided to go for a little drive. When I walked out the door, my aunt reminded me the news was going to be on in a half hour. I did not have the heart to tell her I didn't care. I had already decided I wasn't going to be back in time to watch it.

I got into my Blazer, but I didn't know which way to go. I pulled out of the parking lot and drove to a couple of car dealerships on Wadsworth Boulevard. I knew I could walk around the cars, and nobody would bother me. It was my way of escaping the reality that was chasing me.

When I was done meandering through a couple of car lots, I decided to stop at a convenience store and get myself something to drink. I looked at the newspaper on the shelf and I noticed my picture was on the front page. I picked it up and walked over to the counter to pay for my merchandise. The cashier looked at the paper and said in a voice where everyone in the store could hear, "Hey, isn't that you on the front page?"

I said yes, gave him my money, and walked out as everyone in the store stared at me. I just wanted to be alone.

I slowly drove home and arrived there about a quarter after eleven. When I walked in, everyone told me about the news and how they had done a good job presenting the story.

I was tired and wanted to go to bed. I was hoping there was a chance I would wake up in the morning, and my nightmare would be over.

I climbed into bed, reached out and grabbed my daughter's hand, and closed my eyes. As I began to dream, Josallyn's hand slowly turned into Jaryd's. I was in my own little world as I fell into a deep sleep caressing my son's hand. We were together again.

The Following Information Contains Excerpts Taken from the Official Field Incident Report

Report form deputy number 1:

Cadaver dog–At campsite 3 the tracking dog turned straight east and took us up drainage to a boulder field. The boulders in the particular area are at least 15—50 feet in diameter and the dog alerted indicating that the scent was extremely strong and pooled in that area. The tracker, handler indicated this would be caused by the child they were searching for spending a lot of time in this area.

On the way out to the trail head with the tracking dog the handler gave the dog instructions to scent the river in the cadaver mode. Twice at two separate locations the dog indicated an alert on the river. The track was terminated at the trail head....

Report from deputy number 2:

It appears that the last two people to see Jaryd were the two fishermen around campsites one and two.

Tuesday evening, they advised us they had found Jaryd's tracks on the opposite side of the river in the area of campsites one and two. The tracks indicated to them that Jaryd had crossed the river, walked along the bank to the remains of an old cabin, then went up a game trail and back down the river. The trackers had gotten from the family a more accurate shoe pattern than the one we had been given on the second day of the search.

Report from deputy number 3:

East of the trail, the terrain is rugged and steep and would not seem a likely route easily taken by a three-year-old. If Jaryd were lost on the east side of the trail, any downhill course would bring him back to the area of the trail where he could be found.

Monday, October 4th—The family and friends of the Ataderos had shown up in force and were becoming difficult. They were making accusations that the search efforts were not being handled to their satisfaction.

Tuesday, October 5th—The day had been uneventful until late afternoon when a tracking team found what they believed to be footprints of a small person intersecting with a mountain lion on a steep hillside, east of the trail (downstream from the crash site). This tracking team...followed what they believed to be tracks of a mountain lion traveling down slope, intersecting the small prints and then head back up slope. The tracker said the small, child size tracks disappeared at this location. This suggested to them that the mountain lion had intersected the child and had carried him up hill.

Wednesday, October 6th—I elected to go into the field and catch up with the tracking team. Our intent was to locate and examine the prints found late Tuesday evening. The route to this location was exceptionally steep (65% slope). It required hiking up loose soil and rock that slid with every step. It was very tough going and required a commitment to continue. It did not appear to be the sort of place that would attract a child and with an elevation gain of 350 feet in less than a quarter mile, it would have been an exhausting journey....

The tracker was convinced that he had found footprints made by a child...Neither Johnson nor myself could agree with the trackers findings. There was definitely sign of animal presence; I was not convinced of a child's presence in the area.

I definitely did not believe the area to be an attack zone. Other than tracks, there was no disturbance of soil or vegetation that would support that theory. While I was not willing to discount the trackers findings, I did not believe them to be definite in any way.

I left...and hiked on up the hillside in the direction where the smell of decay had been noticed the previous evening. I encountered the dog team working in the area. We searched but found nothing more and smelled nothing on this day. I did locate the den of a large animal, possibly that of a bear, but there was no hair, scat or litter in the area to provide any clues.

3:10 Department of Wildlife (DOW) officers arrived bringing an individual experienced in tracking mountain lions. I was asked to accompany them back to examine the area again. This time the opinion of the DOW tracker contrasted drastically from the scenario postulated by the UTS tracker.

The DOW tracker said that in his opinion, neither human nor mountain lion tracks were present at this site. He said that these were a series of tracks made by a 300 pound black bear going up and down the slope several times in this area. He said that no attack had occurred here. After a lengthy search further up the hillside he did locate mountain lion tracks. They belonged to a 90 pound female but these tracks had no association with the previous site where the UTS tracker said an encounter had occurred. The DOW tracker spent some time hiking further up the Big South Trail to look for other signs and agreed to return Thursday with his dogs trained to locate fresh animal kill and track lion if necessary.

Thursday, October 7th—The morning provided time to reflect and discuss the mission status. The DOW returned with their tracker and his dogs. In order to allow the DOW dogs to work without distraction, no other teams were fielded between the Incident Command Post and May Creek Bridge. One search and rescue dog team was fielded at Peterson Lake with an assignment to work north to the Big South Trail and the Incident Command Post. This will take all day and by the time they crossed May Creek Bridge the DOW team was out of the field. I spent some of the morning in interviews with the media.

Friday, October 8th—I did not return to the search area on this day but instead participated in an operational planning meeting with Emergency Services staff. I spent a great deal of the day fielding phone calls and logging calls from psychics.

Saturday, October 9th—I spent several hours this day on the phone dealing with civilian volunteers trying to gain access into the restricted search area, more psychic reports and Atadero family issues.

Sunday October 10th–I was paged to call Todd Atadero who resides in the dorms on the CSU campus. I later went to the dorms to obtain a sent article from him. He gave me one pair of children's underwear in a zip-lock bag given to him by Jaryd's father. I accepted them, although I have no knowledge as to how the article was collected.

Wednesday, October 13th—I returned to the Big South Trail with Emergency Services .... We hiked in to examine an area on the west side of the river near campsite number two. On Tuesday (10-12-99) a tracking team from New Jersey believes to have found Jaryd's prints in this area. Unable to contact the trackers to debrief their activities, we hiked in to investigate on our own.

We located the tracks flagged on the far side of the river in an area previously searched by field teams and dog teams. There was evidence of searcher footprints everywhere. This area is thick with tree cover and some downfall but easy to traverse. It is a flat, crescent-shaped flood plain adjacent to the river about five acres in size. It's a relatively small area with fairly restrictive boundaries. There are rock bands that come down to the river to create a north and south boundary and there is a steep east-facing slope on the west side of the flat, flood plain. Assuming Jaryd did travel here,

I feel that these natural features would tend to contain our subject in this small area.

The sign identified as Jaryd's track was located in this area next to the river. Although the tracks seem likely to be human made, they are not absolutely identifiable. The tracks occurred in an area that had a thick needle layer and only minor depressions in the duff layer could be found. There were no definable prints that could confirm that Jaryd made them. The spacing suggests a human gate but not necessarily a small child. I did not take any measurements. In my opinion, it is possible that they were made by one of the female searchers on a previous day.

Another deputy and I met with the trackers affiliated with T. B. who hiked in with the sheriff.... We collectively examined the tracks believed left by Jaryd.

Although the trackers were convinced that these prints belonged to Jaryd, they were unable to locate where he had come across the river and lost them again within a short span of distance. They were unable to follow the prints more than about 50 yards before losing them. All parties on scene admitted that it was unlikely for Jaryd to have crossed the river without getting wet. What may have prompted Jaryd to make a river crossing remains unclear. The river itself provides a good barrier for travel and I do not believe he would have chosen to cross.

Friday, October 15th—In an effort to follow up on the information developed by T.B. and his trackers, I hiked into the search area with a dog and handler out of Jefferson County Sheriff's Office. This was the second trip into the search area for the handler and his dog. He had been brought in to use his tracking dog to assist with the search efforts the previous week. The dog is also trained for cadaver search. A dog team with four search and rescue members was also fielded in an attempt to help verify and support the findings of the Jefferson County dog.... We initially concentrated our efforts on the west side area as designated by the New Jersey tracking team (across from campsite number two). Neither dog indicated significant interest on this side of the river. Three searchers (myself included) did detect an occasional odor that had a faint smell of decay but we were unable to locate the source.

To make the most use of resources on scene, I next instructed the handler and cadaver dog to work the east side. The dog showed no real interest on the east side either but did return to a cliff band near campsite number four. The dog went to this area last week when they had first searched for Jaryd. I hiked up to this area with two others to re-examine some of these cliff bands. Everywhere we searched we found tracks left by our search teams. This confirmed that the area had already been well covered by searchers.

Report from deputy number 4:

We also learned that the scent articles that we had been using were probably contaminated by other family member's scent. The scent articles had been removed from a clothes hamper, which contained clothing from the father and sister. It was also discovered that a pair of underwear that we had been using was actually that of the father. At approximately 0200 hours, I was given urine soaked clothes, one boot and a jacket that belonged to the missing boy. These items were placed in clean plastic bags and relayed to the incident command post for use by future dogs ....

Our Frustrations Continue at Home

I woke Saturday morning knowing it had been a week since my son had disappeared. This was the first time I had awakened in my apartment without Jaryd lying next to me, and I wasn't sure I wanted to get up. I looked down at Josallyn, and she was snuggled up next to me. It brought back a memory of what it was like before Jaryd was born.

It was a sad morning because I knew Josallyn's mom would be flying out that night, and the next day, there would be no more Grandma Bertie, Grandpa Al, Uncle Arlyn, Aunt Robyn, or Aunt Katie. Josallyn and I would have to get used to the fact that we were the only two left and we needed to count on each other.

It was hard to comprehend, but the chaos that surrounded our lives was almost over, and it was time for the loneliness to begin. The headlines in the newspapers would change, and the top story on the evening news would be different, but we still wouldn't have our little Jaryd. The world would move forward, even though ours had stopped.

It was hard for me to move on because I was spinning in circles, looking for something that wasn't there. When should I give up and move on? There were people wanting me to give a memorial service for Jaryd. They said, "Maybe it could be a way to bring some type of closure to your family."

Right! What they were asking me to do was give up. Jaryd is my son, and I wasn't going to give up on him. I don't care how small the chance might be that he is still alive, I will keep looking every day until there is a reason not to. My response to the memorial service was, "What if Jaryd is alive, and he sees his daddy on the news telling everyone he is dead? I'll never give my son a reason to believe I gave up on him."

My mind was wandering all over, so I decided to get up and sneak out of the room and make some coffee. I had to negotiate the network of sleeping bodies strewn throughout my living room in order to get to the kitchen. I tried to be quiet, but to my surprise, everyone was awake.

After coffee, we came together as a family and discussed the agenda for the day. The ladies wanted to go to the mall to buy clothes for Josallyn, but the guys wanted to hang out and discuss in detail what had happened during the past week. One of my cousins was an officer in the Coast Guard, and the other was a federal agent with US Customs. They both had a lot of questions, and they were wondering why the FBI wasn't involved.

As noon approached, we decided to get something to eat before the ladies did their shopping. I drove everyone to Columbine High School because we could somehow relate to their pain. The people at Columbine had sent food over to my school, Deer Creek, and some of the staff from my school brought it up to our resort. After our small detour, we went up the block to eat at Carl's Jr. The place was loud and crowded, and we weren't sure if we were going to stay or not. While conversing amongst ourselves, a group of people got up, leaving a table big enough where we could all sit. As we moved toward the table, the loud roar slowly turned into an atmosphere that was similar to one in a church environment. I could see people surreptitiously looking out of the corner of their eyes and whispering to each other.

This whispering seemed to last the entire time we were eating, but when we got up to leave, the whispering got lower, and the gazing started. I didn't know what they were saying, but I could tell their hearts were full of concern and pain. Most people who tried to look me in the eyes couldn't do it without shedding a tear. It was strange, but it was as if I had an angel following me, trying to hold me up. I couldn't see him but others could.

The ladies took off, and the guys tried to figure out how Jaryd could have disappeared. We tossed around several ideas of what could have happened to Jaryd and where he could be if he were alive.

Arlyn and I needed to take a break from everything that was happening, so we went to K-mart to get our minds off Jaryd. Our efforts were somewhat futile because our conversation always turned back to Jaryd and how confused I was. I missed my little guy, and I couldn't believe there was a chance I would never see him again.

We walked aimlessly down each aisle as if we were trying to find our way out of a maze. As we walked down one of the aisles, a stack of paper towels fell off the highest part of a shelf and landed upon us. We both stood there, looking at each other, thinking the same thing. This had nothing to do with the fact that we are identical twins; it was because we both knew Jaryd very well. My brother looked at me and said, "I think Jaryd is messing with us."

I replied, "That's the same thing I was thinking!"

Jaryd had a way of messing around with his uncle Arlyn and me. I believe he knew we would figure out his practical joke, and he thought it would bring comfort to Daddy. Jaryd wasn't a dummy; he knew a stack of pans would have caused severe pain if he would have tossed those at us.

We laughed and continued walking through K-Mart aimlessly, looking at different items. We entered the video area of the store and looked through the different movies, hoping to encounter the illusive moment of peace I so desperately yearned for, but the stark reality of what I was experiencing once again jerked my thoughts back to Jaryd. The video of *The Mummy* seemed to glare back at me as I stared at it for a brief second. With a heavy heart, I reached out and removed it from the aisle display. Holding the video in front of my eyes, I said, "Hey, Arlyn, I gotta buy this. I promised Jaryd we would watch this movie together once we returned from the resort." I then shared the story with Arlyn about Jaryd wanting me to buy the movie on our way up the mountain. We had stopped at a King Soopers grocery store in Fort Collins to purchase weekend supplies when Jaryd had spotted it. Although he wanted me to buy it then, he agreed to put the purchase off until we returned home. I intended to keep my promise.

About a half hour into our trip, I wanted to go home because I could feel people watching every step I made. We got in one of several open lines to pay for the video. The activity was normal, and the interactions between customers and employees who were working the registers were what one would expect. As we worked our way to the front of our line, all activity in the front of the store slowly came to a stop. As I paid for Jaryd's new video, I noticed that all the cashiers had stopped ringing up merchandise. They, as well as the customers standing in line, had paused to observe my purchase. What was left was an eerie silence that was periodically broken by a few faint sobs. Several people wiped at tears, and I could tell they were sharing my pain. On the way out, a lady approached me and asked if she could give me a big hug. I had no idea who she was, but she put her arms around me and cried. She said, "I know you are Jaryd's father, and we have been praying for you." I was truly touched, and I thanked her.

About three in the afternoon, my nephew Todd brought my dad to my apartment. I was glad to see him, but we only had a couple of hours together because he had to fly back to Las Vegas that night.

An hour after my dad had arrived, everyone packed up to go to the airport. I was getting sick to my stomach because I didn't want anyone to leave. I wasn't sure how my daughter and I would react to the silence that was about to engulf our home. I told my brother I didn't want to go because the airport was about fifty-five miles away; I needed to stay home and try to get a hold of myself. Actually, if they had to leave, I wanted it to be quick because my heart couldn't handle anymore strife. He understood and told me not to worry.

I hated it when my family drove off because Josallyn was crying at the thought of being alone. What could I say to her? There was nothing to say because we both knew we were sharing the same part of hell. Every time we looked into each other's eyes, we could see the hole that existed deep down in a place that Jaryd touched and filled every day. It was easy to retreat into the bedroom where we could cry and hold each other with our eyes closed. We talked to each other like the other was Jaryd, and as long as we didn't open our eyes to reality, we were okay.

I did not want the day to end because I did not want my family to go home. It was like everyone else had a place to go, but I had nowhere to hide. This was it. I would soon be alone, and there was nothing I could do about it. I hated it, but it was a road I would have to travel.

That night, my two cousins stayed, and I was grateful they were there. I think it would have been too painful to go into our first night without loved ones around. My cousins were perfect because they softened the pain Josallyn and I were going through. They will never realize how happy I was when I learned they were staying one more night.

The evening was quiet, and the silence that now occupied my home was hurtful and destructive. I sat on my couch and tried to comprehend that a week had gone by since I had held my son. I wanted one more opportunity to kiss Jaryd and see his beautiful, big, brown eyes. I thought, *Jaryd, you will never understand what you mean to me and how much I miss you.*

Josallyn and I eventually retreated into my bedroom to get some sleep. She did not want to sleep alone in her room, and neither did I. We held each other's hands, closed our eyes, and tried to drift off into a land that had no pain. It wasn't long before I could hear Josallyn breathing as if she were in a deep sleep. I, myself, did not believe I would ever have the chance to enjoy a good night's sleep again. I would fall to sleep not counting sheep but counting the minutes that had gone by without my son.

When I got up Sunday morning, my cousins were gone, and I had no idea where they were. I thought they had gone home without saying good-bye.

I walked over to the coffee pot to make some coffee, and the phone abruptly rang. When I answered it, Kelly was on the other end acting hysterical. She told me she had just talked to two officers with the National Guard, and they said they were willing to call out their troops and go up the mountain to search for Jaryd, but there was one problem: they couldn't do it without the sheriff's signature.

I was thrilled, and I told Kelly I would call her back because I needed to call the sheriff and let him know the good news. When we hung up, I frantically looked for the sheriff's business card. My heart was racing, and I couldn't wait to get more people on the mountain looking for my son.

When I found the sheriff's card, I dialed his number and anticipated hearing his voice. The person on the other end of the phone answered, "Dispatch, can I help you?" I told her who I was and I desperately needed to speak with the sheriff. I told her the National Guard was willing to move, but we needed the sheriff's signature. She assured me she would pass on the message.

I hung up the phone and anxiously waited for the sheriff to call me back. I waited for fifteen minutes, and then my level of frustration began to rise. Finally, after about a half hour had passed, the phone rang.

I raced over to pick it up, knowing it would be the sheriff. A quick conversation with him and the battle for my son would swing back into full throttle. This was the chance we both needed so that victory would be ours.

I picked up the phone and said, "Hello?"

The voice on the other end wasn't the sheriff. Who was it? I recognized the voice, but I was having a hard time placing it to a face. Then it hit me. It was the sergeant who had told me four dogs were better than twenty, the same guy who had promised me he would wait until Thursday to double his searchers.

I didn't want to talk to him! Why was he calling me? What did he want? I wanted to hang up because I was waiting for the head honcho to call me.

The voice on the other end said, "The sheriff called me and asked me to give you a call concerning the National Guard." I got excited; maybe the sergeant was going to provide the ray of hope I needed.

He said, "Allyn, I've recommended to the sheriff not to call in the National Guard because it would cost too much to utilize their expertise. It would cost the county anywhere from two thousand dollars to five thousand dollars an hour. He wanted me to inform you of our decision."

I couldn't believe what I was hearing and from whom I was hearing it. The guy who had no children was given the authority to tell a father with a missing child that although the National Guard was willing, authorization could not be granted. I believed he was mad at me because of our exchange at the trailhead, but I hadn't expected this type of reaction. Not only that, why didn't the sheriff call me? He was a good man, and I was sure he understood my position. There are parts of every story that will always remain mysteries, and this was one.

I pleaded like a child wanting his parents to buy him a new toy. I totally humiliated myself and begged him to change his mind. I was crying as I pleaded my case. "Please call in the National Guard. You have to. This is my son we are talking about. You don't understand. Please call them in."

I must have pleaded with the sergeant for about five minutes. When I think back about that day, I don't think anybody could have told me no. He did. All I kept hearing was, "No, we have already made our decision. There's nothing else we can do."

I hung up the phone and called Kelly. When I told her what had happened, she was in shock and could not believe they would not do whatever it took to help me find Jaryd. Regardless of how I feel about the sergeant, if he were in my situation, I would help him in an instant. There had to be more to this than what I was seeing, but I didn't know what it was.

Before I got off the phone with Kelly, we both vowed to search for a way to have the National Guard help. My child was missing, and even though the officials on the search felt it was time to give up, I didn't. I believe any parent in my situation would have done the same.

I wasn't sure where the sheriff came up with the amount of two thousand dollars to five thousand dollars an hour to have the National Guard get involved, but I was sure he had his sources. I was content with his figures, but as each day passed, the figures changed.

The sheriff and I were both interviewed on one of the local radio stations in the Denver, Colorado, area. During the interview, the sheriff said the National Guard would cost about five thousand an hour. It was no longer two thousand dollars to five thousand dollars an hour now that the public was getting the chance to hear the story. The lower amount was dropped, and the higher amount was the only figure being used. Later, I complained to a reporter from a newspaper in the Fort Collins area. When they interviewed the sheriff to get his side of the story, the amount changed again.

The sheriff is quoted as saying, "To bring in the Guard would have cost the sheriff's department six thousand dollars an hour." He then added, "The department could not afford such an expense when it would only be for show." I understand he has a responsibility to fiscally manage his department's budget, and I realize he has to make difficult calls that are often unpopular with the public he serves. I harbor no ill will toward him. We were just coming from two distinct positions, and our desires were converging with the National Guard.

I do not know where the sheriff was getting his figures because when I called the National Guard, they told me they remembered the story, and they would have done a search for free. The person I talked to actually laughed when I said it would cost six thousand dollars. Their next comment made me laugh. She said they would never charge anyone six thousand dollars a day because we were taxpayers, and that was their job.

I stopped laughing when I told this person, "Not six thousand dollars a day, the sheriff said six thousand an hour."

She about choked and said, "Never!" She then went on to say that they would have searched for Jaryd for free. I have no doubt the sheriff was being given his figures from a reliable source, and from his perspective, this would have cost his county an additional sixty thousand to one hundred thousand dollars each day the Guard was involved. However, from my position, this was far from the case. I wondered why there was such a huge gap between the figures the two of us were working with.

I know the sheriff had access to information and resources that I didn't. Was there something in the statement, "The Guard would only be for show," that he wasn't able to share? Something had taken him to that conclusion, and I didn't know what it was. Could it be that he didn't believe Jaryd was in the search area? I'm not sure about the sheriff, but the Mesa Verde incident bothered me. From what I knew, that sighting was never investigated. Why? All decisions were rooted in one motivation or another, and I could only speculate as to their origins. This wasn't good for either of us because, like a bad cold, a wounded parent has a way of just hanging around.

I sat around for the rest of the day, contemplating the facts as I understood them. It was one of those days that if I would have had a punching bag, I would have destroyed it.

Later that night, my cousins returned to my apartment, and I was surprised because I thought they had gone home. They told me they drove up to the trail where Jaryd was last seen and tried to go up the mountain to see if they could find anything.

They were told the trail was closed, but all three agencies (Air Force, Sheriff, and Forestry) that were there denied being responsible for the trail's closure. They were not going to allow my cousins access to the trail until they discovered my cousins were family. The person who took them up the trail spilled the beans on a lot of things. Although a person could argue that I was being suckered by frivolous hearsay, I found the information to be rather provoking. This person told them the reason infrared equipment wasn't used during the initial search was because there are a lot of squatters and militia type in the area that could have possibly been confronted. They were also told about a missing boy back in the late seventies or early eighties. This person told them the reason this child was never found was because it was all set up. The family of this child was involved in some sort of child molestation case, and the entire event was staged. The alleged missing person is alive today in Oregon, and it seems many locals are aware of this.

My cousins were then told about a cadaver dog that was brought up Friday to find Jaryd's remains. This person said the cadaver dog is one of the best he had ever seen because on the way back down the mountain on Pingree Park Road, the dogs found a body in a mining shaft that was part of a sixteen-year murder mystery. He said, "If Jaryd's body was up there, this dog would have found it."

These were stories that legends are made of, and Jaryd's tale was sure to generate a horde of its own. In the pursuit of becoming part of this story, there were things people had to say, and validating them would prove to be a difficult task. I didn't have the patience or time to do this, but each story had a way of tickling my curiosity. My cousins wanted to stay and chase some of these phantom rumors, but their time in Colorado was about to expire. My house of mirrors was under construction.

A couple of days later, I went to Sam's Club to buy a small TV for my daughter. She was lonely, and I was trying everything I could to keep her spirits up. When I approached the register, the two employees working that area recognized me, and I could see them talking and looking at me. When I gave them my membership card, they recognized my last name and told me how sorry they were about the loss of my son. One of the ladies said her church had been praying for my family. I thanked her as the tears welled from my eyes, and then I tried to find my way back to my car as quickly as I could.

Later that day, I went to pay my cable bill, and the lady behind the counter broke down in tears as I wrote her a check. My first two weeks at home produced a lot of these incidents.

Going out into the community was painful, and I prepared myself for anything that could happen while I was in public. I was always glad to get home because I could be by myself, and I could go into my room and cry if I needed to. It is hard to realize, but I spent more time with tears in my eyes than I did without.

I didn't know at the time, but there were a lot of people who had searched for Jaryd going through the same things I was experiencing. I talked to several people after I got home concerning my frustration. One person was Craig, the Mesa Verde park ranger, who was sure he had seen Jaryd the day after he went missing. I also spoke with one of the deputies at the sheriff's office, and he was as confused as I was concerning the search operation.

Quietly, people were asking how Jaryd could be on the mountain when there was no trace of him. I even called the sheriff and asked him man-to-man, "What do you think happened to my son?"

He said he did not believe an animal took Jaryd. He truly believed Jaryd fell into the river and drowned, and it would take about five years for his body to surface because the water is too cold. We all had our theories, and who was to say which one was right? The mountain lion scenario also continued to get a lot of support. Privately, I questioned why the area on Seaux's map wasn't checked. An event becomes ripe to questions when solutions fail to appear. Questions give birth to others, and sooner or later, it seems as if we're chasing our own tails. People often become challenged when attempting to make a positive impact on their surroundings. The sheriff was a brave man because he had stepped up to the plate to make a difference, and I respected him for his convictions. This doesn't mean I always have to agree with him.

I can buy into his river theory, but I wanted him to consider mine. Was Jaryd somewhere out there waiting to be rescued?

The new information presented to me by my cousins contributed to the frustrations I had with Jaryd's disappearance. I'm not convinced the stories they were told are true, but they caused my frustration to grow. I didn't know where to turn, so I decided to call upon Congressman Tancredo.

I sat down and wrote him a letter addressing all of my frustrations, but I didn't really expect to hear from him as quickly as I did. Five days later, Congressman Tancredo put out a press release concerning his actions on the behalf of my son, Jaryd.

The following is his press release:

Tancredo Releases Statement on

Search for Jaryd Atadero

WASHINGTON, DC—U.S. Representative Tom Tancredo (R-CO) released the following statement regarding the search for missing three-year-old Jaryd Atadero in Colorado:

"Let me first say that my heart and prayers go out to the family and friends of Jaryd Atadero. Being a father and grandfather, I cannot imagine how devastating and frustrating this must be for his loved ones.

"I received a letter on October 9, 1999, and have since spoken with Mr. Allyn Atadero, Jaryd's father, regarding his frustrations over the search for his missing three-year-old son. After reading and listening to Mr. Atadero's plight, and at his request as a constituent of mine, I have asked for federal assistance in the search for Jaryd.

"I wrote letters to Attorney General Janet Reno, Secretary of Agriculture Dan Glickman, Director of the United States Forest Service Mike Dombeck, and Director of the Federal Bureau of Investigation Louis J. Freeh, citing that the disappearance of young Jaryd happened on federal property, and am currently awaiting replies as to what each agency can do to facilitate a conclusion to this case.

"While I recognize that many tragedies of this nature never reach closure, by knowing that we exhausted every avenue and resource at our disposal, it is my hope that the Atadero family may find some peace of mind as they continue on with their lives." (Greg Meyer)

I was excited to get the help Congressman Tancredo was providing. However, I quietly continued to question why federal law enforcement agencies were not recruited by the sheriff considering the disappearance of Jaryd did take place on federal property. Ultimately, it was the leadership of the congressman that brought about a brighter ray of hope.

What Is, What Was, What Will Be

Scenarios

There are a number of theories that have floated through the law enforcement and rescue communities, as well as other theories from countless people who watched the Jaryd Atadero debacle on the news or read about it in the papers, but the one theory that seems to offer any hope is the one involving abduction. Of all the scenarios considered to have merit by the sheriff's department, each was given a probability. The greater the probability, the more likely the situation happened. The scenario with the lowest probability was automatically given a low, or zero, priority. I taught math for several years, and I understand probability and how it works. Depending on the event, and regardless of the odds involved in any given situation, things with low probability do happen in rare circumstances. People win lotteries, and people die in accidents all the time. What are the odds you or I will die today? The odds may be low, but they are there, and people do die from low probability circumstances every day. To surmise that poor feasibility equates to zero probability is ludicrous. That is the same as saying that because something probably didn't happen means it actually didn't. I realize miracles have low probability. That's what makes them miraculous. Some people reason that miracles never have and never will take place because of their meager ranking on the probability scale. Regardless, I know low probability does not mean never.

When my son first disappeared, everyone had the same mindset, a general sense of hope with the promise everything would work out in the end. We knew what trail he had been hiking, and if he was still there, this entire nightmare could come to an end by nightfall. It was a very simple situation, a little boy wandering off from a group of adults. We hoped he would be located that same night. There were no other scenarios to explore; Jaryd was a lost little boy who needed to be found. It was that simple.

When the search and rescue team arrived, everyone believed it was only a matter of time before I would have my son back in my arms. This *wasn't* going to be another story about a lost little boy who died. It was going to be another story about a successful search and rescue team and how they utilized their expertise to bring a family back together. I had complete faith that I would see Jaryd again and soon.

As the team began searching, I was amazed at how they attacked the mountain with confidence, knowing failure was not an option. It was strange, because I knew these warriors had never met my son, yet they acted as if Jaryd was their own child.

When I look back, I remember the tears I saw flowing from the eyes of the searchers as they passed me on their way back to the base of the trail. I know I shed a lot of tears for my son, but I did not realize the tears shed by those who were searching were equal to those flowing down my own grieving face. Part of my pain was their pain, and because of our agonizing connection, I was quoted in several newspapers as saying, "They have put their hearts and souls into this. My loss is their loss!"

We knew Jaryd was gone, but each day produced never-ending questions that took on a life of their own. These questions slowly evolved into different scenarios, and each one in turn produced new questions. As the search continued, no evidence was found that could prove or disprove any given scenario concerning Jaryd's disappearance. Was he alive or was he dead somewhere on the mountain? If he was dead, how did he die, and where was his body? If he was alive, where did he go, and who was with him?

These questions played with my mind, and I believed each and every scenario could be true. If he did die, what happened?

As you continue reading Jaryd's story, you will understand the frustration and pain I experienced on that dreadful October day. Each person had his or her own belief as to what events actually transpired, and the following five scenarios are just a few of the many I had heard.

Scenario One

To Sleep! Perchance to dream...

—Shakespeare, *Hamlet*

"Seven, eight, nine, and ten. Ready or not, here I come!" Jaryd jumped up and playfully searched for his hiking group after hiding in the forest. Scanning the area, the little boy ran up and down through the trees, feet covered in pine needles and fallen leaves. Sounds of life surrounded him but none offering the familiar comfort of humanity. Trying to find his way to a familiar path, he thought, *This is going to be hard. There are a lot of great places to hide on this mountain.*

He climbed onto a large cold rock to get a better view of the playing field and thought, *I'll never find them up here.* While Jaryd searched the aroma-filled mountain, the thought occurred to him, *I wonder if they played a trick on me, and if they did, my daddy is going to be mad when he finds out these people took my sister.*

Jaryd was on a short hiking expedition with a group of people, some he knew and trusted, one being his older sister.

Unbeknownst to her, she was the one he was primarily playing hide and seek with, although right now, finding anyone from the group would be a welcome treasure.

Everything about Jaryd's existence was a game, as it should be when you are three, and that was why he never realized his life was in any danger when he first ran into the forest to play. After scouring the mountainside as best as he could for anyone who was hiding, he decided he needed to find something to eat in an attempt to calm the noise echoing in his stomach. The need for food slowed down his little engine, and eventually, fright concealed the noise of hunger coming from his body. For all his courage, his youth was not to be ignored, and once he realized he was alone, panic overcame him.

The sun had dropped below the horizon, taking the warmer temperatures with it. As the heat escaped from the mountain, panic flowed through Jaryd's little veins as he finally realized he was all alone, cold, and hungry. A small tear pushed itself from his eye as he whispered, "Daddy, where are you? Daddy, please tell me you didn't forget about me."

When darkness finally engulfed the mountain, Jaryd's frantic panic quickened. He knew his daddy could not sleep without holding onto his hand. He thought, *I only kissed Daddy once today. He probably needs another one about now.*

He wanted to continue searching for those who had betrayed him, but he could not find the will to move on. The sights and sounds of the dark mountainside brought to life nightmares he never before imagined. The innocence of his youth disappeared as swiftly as the evening's hours. Eventually, his body grew weak from fatigue. Jaryd knew he was tired, and the soft noise of the river flowing nearby beckoned him to its edge as if it were saying, "Jaryd, come here. I will help you fall asleep."

With the moon glowing softly in the evening sky, showering its silk rays through the trees from high above, Jaryd decided it was time to snuggle up tightly next to a large rock. As his eyes closed, and with a familiar thumb nestled securely in his mouth, he reached out as if the rock were his daddy and searched for a hand to hold on to.

Before long, the cold Colorado autumn air dropped its temperature below the freezing mark, and Jaryd began to shiver. He forced his little body to pull itself closer together in a fetal position, to generate and conserve what precious heat he could.

Eventually, the fear of being alone was lost to the fatigue brought on by the midnight hours, and Jaryd fell into a deep sleep. He dreamed his daddy was standing just above him, reaching down to hold onto his hand. Jaryd then released his warm soul into what he thought was his daddy's outstretched hand.

The headlines never made the paper. Nobody would ever know the story about how little Jaryd continues to hold on to his daddy's hand every day. In retrospect, the truth of the evening would be far worse than this scenario echoed, for what Jaryd thought was his daddy's hand was actually hypothermia. He died that night, never to be seen by his father again.

Jaryd would always be known as the little boy who won the very last game of hide and seek he ever played.

Scenario Two

At the edge, at the depths...I am here.

—Wm. Hamilton, *Whisper of the Water*

Jaryd casually walked up the meandering trail, admiring all the beauty the vast wilderness had to offer. The light brown, dried-out leaves crackled beneath the soles of his sneakers as he darted and danced along the way. For a moment, his eye was distracted by an energetic squirrel chasing another into the bushes, and that was when his own thoughts began to churn. His little mind thought about all the different games he could play. Finally, he decided to hide behind a tree in order to frighten his sister when she walked by.

Josallyn, a couple of years older than Jaryd in both age and spitfire, was marching up the trail with arms bouncing, singing one of the songs she had recently learned in her kindergarten class. "Criss Cross and go under the bridge then you got to pull it tight. Make a loop but keep a long tail, that's how to do it right. Then you take the other string and you wrap it 'round the loop, pull it through the hole, now you got the scoo—"

"Boo!" Jaryd jumped out from behind the tree and yelled, scaring his sister more into dismay than fear.

Josallyn yelped in response then turned away from her little brother and continued her way along the trail. "Don't, Jaryd, you messed up my song!"

Jaryd laughed and scampered up the path to hide again. As he did, a small smooth rock caught his attention, black and brilliant against the fall, earthy colors. Picking it up, he noticed its size, weight, and texture would be perfect for skipping in the nearby river that he could see just a few yards to his right. He had just recently learned the fine art of rock skipping and wanted to give his new treasure a try. He hesitated and then assured himself it was okay and quickly made his way to the water's edge for the purpose of flinging the rock.

Jaryd ran to the river, pulled his arm back, and as he was getting ready to make the throw of his life, a trout jumped from the water and made a large splash right in front of him. Mouth open, Jaryd dropped the rock into his pocket and watched the huge fish swim back and forth as if it were saying, "Catch me if you can!" That was a challenge, and Jaryd had never lost a challenge in his young life.

Slowly, he put his right foot into the river, standing very still. The water was colder than he anticipated, but the thrill of the "hunt" far outweighed his discomfort. Still and silent, he waited to see what the fish would do next.

The trout taunted Jaryd, swimming from side to side, waiting to see how daring the little boy could be. As time passed, the fish became more comfortable and swam a little closer to the frozen statue that still had one foot in the water and one foot on dry land. Here was Jaryd's chance to make his daddy proud by catching a fish with his bare hands. Quickly, he made his move into the water and reached out.

With barely any effort, the fish swam away from the lunging boy, but Jaryd wasn't ready to lose the challenge yet. Water spewed high into the air with every step he took, echoing both sound and stream all around him. He ran into the chilling water with abandon, not realizing the danger. His fourth step proved to be too tempting for fate, as he was suddenly pulled into a deep hole in the riverbed that was waiting to steal his last breath.

Jaryd panicked as the thick, cold mud gave way beneath his weight, pulling him down beneath the river's current. He kicked his legs, fighting to free them as his arms thrashed violently in the water. He tried without success to grab hold of the water's surface, reaching for anything that might help anchor him above the water. As he tried to yell out for help, a large gulp of water filled his mouth and washed down into his throat. Jaryd thrashed about more and more, his actions only forcing him deeper beneath the water line. He took a deep breath, and his lungs filled with water as his last thought raced through his mind. *Daddy...I can't breathe!* His eyes were wide open, and as his salty tears mixed with the fresh water of the river, his last thought was a final plea to his father. As Jaryd sank to the bottom, he tried to yell one more time, *Daddy...* Within seconds, his desperate movements were transformed into a motionless body.

The river had simply claimed another victim.

Scenario Three

Lying broken I surrender to the arms of unseen angels.

—Ericka Jordan, *Angels Among Us*

Jaryd stood tall on the mountain trail, looking around. He could not believe he was getting the opportunity to run around in an unfamiliar environment without holding onto some nagging adult's hand. He scanned the area—nothing but secure freedom all around him. No strangers to worry about, no cars or other familiar dangers, and he could hear the familiar voices of his troop off in the distance. He was safe and free to do what he wanted. A smile formed on his face as he thought of his daddy, who Jaryd knew would never give him the type of freedom he was enjoying that very moment. "Boy, would Dad be mad," Jaryd said out loud as he pranced his way along the trail.

Jaryd, acting older than he actually was, soon took off, running up the trail as if he were another one of the adults on a short hike into a forest filled with adventure.

After a long while, the trail climbed high into the foreboding mountain, becoming narrower with each step. The familiar voices had long dissipated into nothingness, overcome by the natural sounds of the surrounding forest. At the base of the mountain, the trail had been about four feet wide, but now Jaryd saw the trail squeeze itself onto a ledge that was barely ten inches wide.

Jaryd looked to his right and down over the edge. The drop was long and treacherous, especially to the innocent eyes of a three-year-old boy. *If I fall off this cliff, I'll never stop falling,* he thought to himself as his heart jumped within his chest. Despite his young age, he knew he needed to focus all of his attention on the task of getting past this hazardous section of trail. With his little heart racing, he continued to climb, hand over hand against the mountain wall, foot over foot along the dirt path, clinging to the steeply rising trail with all his might.

A squirrel ran down a tree on the mountainside next to Jaryd and came to a sudden stop when it made eye contact with Jaryd's big, brown eyes. They looked at each other with equal wonder and awe, as if they had never seen another creature like this before. The squirrel stood up on its hind legs, pushed its head forward, then jerked it to the right as it tried to get a better look at the giant animal standing before him. Seconds passed before the squirrel dropped to all fours and scampered down the mountain, running right past Jaryd. Jaryd turned to his left, following the cute and entertaining animal, stepped back, lost his balance, and tumbled down the steep embankment. His head struck a sharp rock, which knocked him unconscious.

Up along the mountainside on a different path, Josallyn continued walking along the trail with her accompanying group, never realizing her little brother's body lay motionless just beyond sight. She was about fifteen minutes up the trail when Jaryd regained consciousness, only to observe he was wedged between two large rocks. He looked at his leg and saw something white protruding through his torn pants. The compound fracture continued to bleed as Jaryd's life gradually flowed from his now-quivering body. He fought and struggled to free himself, but the pain was too much to endure and eventually sent him into an unconscious shock. At last, his young body gave way, releasing his fragile spirit into the waiting hands of God.

Scenario Four

No sacrifice is sweet when it is your own life.

—Matthew Mooring

Standing alone, kicking at the dirt, Jaryd was tired of waiting for the adults who had brought him onto the trail. He thought it would be much more fun than this, perhaps running and playing with his sister while everyone else had a nice walk. He had no idea he was going to be left alone to entertain himself. He would much rather have stayed with his dad, who at least would be playing with him right now.

Not wanting to be alone any longer, he decided he could find his own way home. He wasn't sure what direction to go, but he knew leaving was better than standing around, waiting for someone to come to his aid. Looking all around, he walked in the direction he believed he had come. He took his time, stopping, playing, looking around, and having the time of his life, as he headed in what he hoped was the right direction.

As he walked up the trail, he saw a giant rock hill just to the east of him. He thought, *Wait a minute. I think I live on the other side of that big rock.* Not understanding the importance of staying on the trail, he took off to conquer the rock.

One step at a time, Jaryd tediously climbed over the boulders, walked around the trees, and jumped over the fallen logs that once lived in the area he was climbing. The higher he climbed, the more often he needed to stop and take a deep breath of fresh air to rejuvenate his small but strong muscles.

After making it nearly three-quarters of the way up, he sat down on a rock and yelled, "Josallyn!" not realizing he was being watched the entire time. He took a short rest and was about to continue his goal of getting home when he heard a scampering noise in the grass off in the distance. He stopped, looked in the direction of the noise, and cheerfully yelled, "Josallyn, I'm over here!" Excitement ran through his veins as an elated comfort swelled within him at the thought of his older sister.

He stood there waiting for a response but heard nothing. His eyes searched the area, looking for the person who was playing a trick on him. He waited—but again, nothing. Frustrated at his sister for teasing him when all he wanted to do was go home, he decided to move on.

Unbeknownst to Jaryd, the noise in the grass was not Josallyn but rather a cougar. As Jaryd slowly moved up the mountain, the cougar planned her attack on the prey that would be her food for the night. The cougar raced ahead, watching and waiting for the perfect moment to pounce on the little boy who had unexpectedly wandered into her territory.

This game of cat and mouse went on for fifteen minutes as Jaryd moved ever closer to the trap that was waiting up ahead. Jaryd heard a noise, but before he could turn around to see what it was, the cougar attacked with a hungry ferocity. Blood painted the rock like an ancient hieroglyphic, as Jaryd succumbed to the beast in mere seconds. The cat dragged her victim to a den of waiting cubs, leaving a trail of blood, shoes, and small pieces of clothing in the wake of her destruction.

Jaryd's life was sacrificed so her cubs could thrive.

Scenario Five

Certain dangers come to children for whom care is undone.

—Parenting Proverb

Jaryd was hiking with the slower group of people when his patience began to wear thin. He thought there would be much more adventure and excitement along the mountain trail, as he had seen so many times before in his morning cartoons. But no, this hike was downright boring. To make matters worse, it seemed as if his sister was getting all of the attention anyway. Frustrated, he decided to entertain himself and took off down the path. His pace quickened, and before he knew it, he could no longer see the group he had left behind.

A few minutes passed when Jaryd's eyes made contact with a faster-walking and more animated group ahead, and he became excited to see the people he was so desperately trying to catch. His walking turned into a sprint as he feverishly tried to capture the rest of his group. He huffed and puffed as the gap between him and the group shortened. He was almost there!

A minute later, he playfully tapped a stick, his pretend rifle, on the back of one of the ladies walking at the back of the faster group. She jumped and turned, saying, "Jaryd, where did you come from!" Then she thought, *Somebody needs to be watching this child a littler closer.*

Her reflection was short-lived though, as her attention quickly turned back to her own friends. She gave no more thought to Jaryd as he continued to wander right past the group of people who may have been the last hope to save his life.

Both groups continued their pace as they took in the beauty of the mountain, wanting to see more. Someone said, "Let's sit down and rest and wait for the rest of the group." A very agreeable "okay" came from several of the hikers.

As the small groups joined together to form a larger one, they discussed the wonders they had seen and heard on their way into the beautiful forest.

The relaxed atmosphere was broken when an anxious voice yelled, "Where's Jaryd?"

By then, though, their delayed care was too late; they would never see him again.

Just after Jaryd had passed the second group, he ran into a man walking down the trail from Peterson Lake. The man approached the little boy with interest. As he looked down the trail Jaryd had just hiked up, he asked, "Hey, little guy, are you lost?"

Jaryd responded as he pointed with an outstretched hand, "No, mister, my friends are way, way back down the trail."

A wry smile formed on the man's face as he thought to himself, *This is too easy. How come they all can't be like this?* He warily approached Jaryd, but being a firm judge of character, the little boy could sense an overwhelming evil emanating from the pedophile. As Jaryd turned to run back down the trail, the larger and stronger man grabbed him and placed his hand over Jaryd's mouth. Jaryd let out a quick scream that later was said to be heard by a few others from the group but was never investigated. The man carried him quickly back up the trail toward Peterson Lake and was gone before the sheriff's office was even contacted.

......

I am sure it has pained you as much to read through these scenarios as it did for me to recollect them while writing this text. The truth is, I was so numbed by the sorrow and pain of losing Jaryd that eventually the how and what behind his disappearance mattered little to me. All my mind could focus on was the similar result each scenario ended with—Jaryd no longer being with me. The more I sat back and focused on his final moments—the pain, fear, anxiety, hopelessness, solitude, and worry—the thicker and darker the solemn cloud overshadowed me.

As I talked to every friend, family member, search official, rescuer, tracker, medic, journalist, and seemingly everyone else in the world, the number of possibilities analyzing his final moments increased exponentially. Everyone seemed to have his or her own viewpoint. These five, or a variation of them, were the most frequent and the most likely.

Trying to Face My Reality

There were a lot of strange things happening in the following days, weeks, and months after Jaryd disappeared.

Kelly and I tried our hardest to get the FBI involved with the search for Jaryd, but for some reason, it didn't happen.

The law enforcement community accepted the results of Jaryd's search because of the sheriff's reputation as a competent and thorough investigator. It's not a common practice in any profession for others to rush to judgment and second-guess those responsible for executing operations of this size and nature, and I'm not suggesting he should be second guessed. Although I appreciated the efforts of the sheriff and search and rescue, it is not the nature of a parent in my position to give up. Considering this, it was only natural for me to press forward and ask difficult questions that were sure to intrude into the comfort zones of others. My efforts to recruit assistance from outside agencies were often met by resistance, and I was fully aware that I would confront intense desires to not become involved.

It was a couple of weeks later when I received a copy of a letter that was sent to Congressman Tancredo. The letter was sent from the Department of Justice and then forwarded to me.

The letter stated, "The investigation...has revealed absolutely no evidence of foul play, which would allow the FBI to initiate an investigation of its own." Basically, the FBI would not get involved because there was no evidence of a crime or abduction. If they were presented with evidence Jaryd was taken, then they would get involved.

The sheriff and his team suggested that a majority of the evidence pointed in a specific direction when, in reality, there was no evidence on the mountain to support any theory.

The letter confused me, and I took it upon myself to call the local FBI office. I read the agent the part of the letter that upset me, and the agent was very nice and understanding. I tried to explain to him all the things we had come across that were not investigated, especially Mesa Verde National Park.

I told him my son had passed all of the hikers in his group, and it would have been possible for someone to come down the trail from Peterson Lake. They could have taken my son back up the trail with them.

I then asked the agent what type of physical evidence a person would leave if they picked up a child. We both agreed, not much. He was very sympathetic and said the FBI would look into some of the allegations that had been presented.

Don't get me wrong, I understand my son could be dead on the mountain, but I wanted those in authority to look into every scenario presented. I did not want them to ignore one just because they think it didn't happen. I promise you, I have thought at length about every possible scenario regarding my son.

One day while I was teaching, I visualized my son being attacked by a mountain lion. It gave me an instant headache that I suffered through for the rest of the day. I have seen my son in the river, dead under a tree, lost and crying, being attacked by a predator, and abducted by a person. Because there is no evidence that supports any theory, I consider each scenario every day, looking for the answer. I don't discount any possibility, and I wish the authorities would give Jaryd the same consideration.

I received several phone calls from people who had called the sheriff's office, and they were told abduction was completely ruled out. When I called the sheriff's office, they reassured me they were not saying that, and they realized abduction was a viable theory.

After speaking with the authorities from the sheriff's department, I continued getting calls from people in the media telling me the sheriff had ruled out abduction. Each time I called the sheriff's department, I was told, "No, we didn't say that."

A reporter from the *North Forty News Paper* called me to ask a few questions about Jaryd. I vented and told her my frustrations. I informed her I was very disappointed because people kept telling me the sheriff's office had ruled out abduction, but when I called, they told me they hadn't.

Her response turned my stomach. "I just got off the phone with them, and that's what they told me about five minutes ago. Abduction had been ruled out." I was furious and asked her if she remembered whom she had talked to. She said, "Sure, let me check my notes." I finally had a name!

I called several people at the sheriff's office and asked them to stop telling people that abduction had been ruled out. They once again assured me it wasn't happening. I told them it was, and I gave them the name of the lady who was doing it. A couple of people from the sheriff's office called me back and told me they would check into it.

Fifteen minutes later, I received my first response to my complaint. The first caller told me the lady making the comments said she made them off the record. This first caller from the sheriff's department was very upset and said, "That witch, I wish she would keep her mouth shut. If she says something off the record, she needs to back herself up."

About ten minutes later, another person from the sheriff's office called me to tell me what had happened. This person said they just talked to her, and she said she was misquoted.

I replied, "Really, someone else just told me she said it off the record. I think she's changing her story to protect herself."

I have a very good friend named Cindy who lived close to the area where Jaryd disappeared. She couldn't believe he was missing, so she went to the vicinity to check out the area for herself. I don't remember what exact day it was, but it was within a few days of the end of the official search. While she was snooping around the area where she thought Jaryd might be, she saw a Volkswagen van. The people occupying the van were staying in a cabin back in the sticks, and they were acting somewhat suspicious.

Cindy watched this family closely because she was hoping to find Jaryd there. While she watched, she noticed the adults were painting the van a different color. When they realized she was there, one of the people jumped into a truck and raced toward her. This person approached her and wanted to know what she was doing, and then they demanded she leave the area right away.

Cindy was terrified, but she didn't have to be told to leave again. She raced down the mountain and told her friend Jane about the strange behavior she had encountered.

Jane called the sheriff's office and gave them the information that was conveyed to her by Cindy. A couple of days later, Jane called me and told me what had happened. She told me she called the sheriff's department, but no one had contacted Cindy to question her about the incident.

I took Jane's information and called the sheriff's department myself. I told them what had happened to Cindy, and I asked them why she hadn't been called. They said they would get right on it. I don't know if they ever looked into this situation, because Cindy never provided me with any information concerning an interview about the incident. I never followed up because I always hit a brick wall.

About two weeks after Jaryd vanished, a woman in Colorado Springs called me. She wanted to know if I was the father of the little boy who was missing in Northern Colorado. After telling her I was, she proceeded to tell me she thought Jaryd was living in a mobile home next door to her. A lot of her story sounded as if it had some merit, but I was skeptical.

She told me there was a guy in a green truck who visited her next door neighbors every once in a while. The truck had a decal on the door that said forestry department. I had learned to keep my hopes in check, but the decal got my attention. My mind raced, and it made sense that if Jaryd had been abducted, someone from the forestry department would have had the knowledge and ability to get him out of the area.

I continued listening to her story, but some of the information she gave me didn't sound like the boy was Jaryd. She wanted to know what type of haircut Jaryd had, because this little boy's haircut was different. I told her it was short, but it wasn't like a military cut.

She said, "Yes, that sounds like the little boy living next door."

There was one problem with this little boy's hair that convinced me it wasn't Jaryd. She said the little boy had a small tail about six inches long running down his back.

I told her Jaryd didn't have long enough hair to make a tail, and then I asked her if it was okay if I passed this information on to the sheriff's department.

She said, "Yes, but if you'd like, you can spend the night at my house and take a look at the little boy for yourself."

I politely declined her offer, and then I thanked her for her concern. I called the sheriff's department and passed on the potential sighting.

A couple of weeks passed, I struggled getting back into the flow of what had been my life. There was nothing smooth about my transition, and the road was not only bumpy, but the traffic was stop and go. Concerned about my well being, my friend Cindy decided to bring her son and pay Josallyn and me a visit. She arrived just in time for dinner. We went to a restaurant close to home and talked about everything except Jaryd. I believe she was trying to help me focus on what I had to live for and not what I was missing in my life. After dinner, we went back to my place, put our bathing suits on, and tried to enjoy the comfort of the hot tub.

While our kids played in the pool, we tried to solve the great mysteries of life, and our conversation slowly drifted toward Jaryd. We asked each other how this could have happened. As Cindy and I talked back and forth, she told me she was still bothered by the people she had seen painting the van.

We couldn't get Jaryd out of our minds, and little did we know, he was about to become the focus of the evening. Although he was not present, he always had a way of making himself known.

It was around 7:00 p.m. when my cell phone rang. I got out of the hot tub, asking, "I wonder who that could be?"

I answered the phone, and it was Susan from the sheriff's department. My heart raced as I considered all the possible reasons for her call. None of them were appealing.

"Allyn, this is Susan. I'm sorry to be calling, but I wanted you to hear this information from me first. We got a call that someone had found a shredded blue tank top up on the trail. Mark is on his way up the mountain right now to check it out. I'm sorry I have to call you to give you this information, but I was worried one of the reporters may have overheard our conversations by monitoring our radios. I want you to be prepared just in case someone tries to call you."

I thanked Susan, and then she told me she would call back as soon as she got an answer concerning the clothing.

Mark is awesome. He is the lead investigator in Jaryd's case, and I knew he'd do everything humanly possible to get to the bottom of the newly found clothing. I calmly hung up the phone, but I had this deep desire to grab it and throw it down onto the pavement as hard as I could. Cindy had been quiet during the entire conversation, and for a second, I forgot about her because all I could think about was the blue shredded tank top.

Cindy broke my spell when she asked, "Is everything all right?"

I turned with tears in my eyes and said, "They think they found Jaryd's blue tank top. It's torn up, and they have an investigator on his way up the mountain to check it out."

All kinds of thoughts swam through my mind as the vision of the tank top continued to dangle in front of my eyes. My mind wrestled back and forth as it attempted to form a conclusion about the blue shirt.

I thought, *Allyn, you know it doesn't belong to Jaryd. Have faith. If Jaryd was abducted, it couldn't be his top.* The other side of my mind responded quickly. *Allyn, they finally have proof of what happened to your son. He was attacked by a wild animal.*

Both scenarios collided in my mind. They were polar opposites of what could have happened, and I had already been tossed back and forth by the rough seas of Jaryd's disappearance. There was no smooth sailing, and I had been seasick once before. This was beginning to feel a lot like that. Each wave of possibility slammed into me, causing my mind to wobble between the two possible truths. It was a strange struggle because I knew there wasn't any evidence that supported either side of the argument. I tried to steady myself as the chatter in my head became faster and louder. *Stop it! Don't torture yourself! Quit trying to draw a conclusion without any accurate information.*

I looked at Cindy and said, "I'll call Butch up at the resort. He probably knows what's going on, and he can fill me in on the facts."

I picked up the phone and called the resort. The operator came onto the line and said, "All circuits are busy. Please try your call later."

The phone system on the mountain wasn't working. Anyone trying to make a call to or from the mountain was out of luck. The wind had knocked out the service, and it wouldn't be up and running until the following day.

It was about one in the afternoon when a hiker walked into the store at the Poudre River Resort. He was looking for someone to help him identify a blue tank top he had found on the trail where the little boy had disappeared.

He walked up to the counter where Butch was working and asked, "Can you guys look at this shirt and tell me if it was the one Jaryd was wearing when he disappeared?"

The shirt was bundled up with a lot of twigs and dirt. Butch remembered being told that if we found anything, we were to put it into a plastic bag and hold it until the proper authorities had a chance to pick it up. Butch took the shirt and put it into a plastic bag and called Deputy Jose Romero. Jose advised Butch that he was on his way to inspect the potential evidence. Jose is great guy, and he wants to find an answer to Jaryd's mystery as badly as I do.

Butch had kept his emotions to himself since Jaryd had vanished. I'm not sure how he was doing it, because Jaryd was like his own son. I wasn't there, but I heard the blue tank top was like the straw that broke the camel's back. When the hiker left the store, Butch walked out from behind the counter and went into the apartment for a short moment to release the frustration that had been building within him. He looked around, doubled up his fist and then beat a hole in the unsuspecting wall. Somewhat relieved of his aggression, he walked back into the store and waited for Jose.

Jose arrived about an hour later. He delicately removed the blue tank top from the plastic bag and inspected it. After the two came to the same conclusion, there was one thing left for Jose to do. He needed to drive the shirt down the mountain to the sheriff's office so he could enter it into evidence.

Jose left the resort around two thirty that afternoon.

....

I got back into the hot tub and thought about Jaryd. I tried to enjoy my company, but when I looked at the water, I kept seeing a blue tank top floating on the surface.

Cindy looked at me and asked, "Are you okay?"

I said, "Yeah, I think so."

We lingered in the hot tub for another half hour, waiting for the phone to ring. It never did. I couldn't handle it anymore, so we went back to my apartment and waited.

Any new information about Jaryd required patience, and this was no exception. It was one of my virtues that had been stretched to the breaking point, but what choice did I have? I was frustrated and extremely restless. I knew Butch could provide some answers, and believing I would get through, I continued calling the resort every five minutes. My soul was on fire, and the hole left there by Jaryd's disappearance was expanding. My calls became an exercise in frustration, and I had to accept the fact that contacting Butch was a craving I had to release. Accepting the situation for what it was, I waited for Susan to call back.

It was around 9:00 p.m. when I got the phone call I had waited for. Susan told me the shirt was an adult size, and it didn't belong to Jaryd.

I thanked her, and I asked myself, *Why were you stressing? You knew all along the shirt didn't belong to your son.*

That evening, I assumed the shirt episode was unwinding as I waited, but it wasn't. It was two in the afternoon when Butch and Jose realized it wasn't my son's shirt. Being called at 7:00 p.m. with the news that Jaryd's shirt had possibly been discovered only worked to mock my sanity. It was another two hours of hell that I should not have had to experience, but each of these walks through the valley of the shadow of Jaryd's possible death sucked part of my life right out of me. It is said that the things that don't kill us make us stronger. Was it possible I was being turned into a superhero?

A couple of weeks later, someone on the trail found some bones, and they took them to the sheriff's department to be analyzed. Susan called me about the incident after the bones were confirmed to be those of a deer. She said she didn't want to put me through the pain of waiting again. I thanked Susan from the bottom of my heart for her consideration.

There were eleven adults on the trail with my son when he somehow pulled his vanishing act. It is hard to believe, even ten weeks after Jaryd's disappearance, that I have only heard from two people who were there with him. Nine of them have avoided all contact with me. As difficult as it may have been for each of them, I would have appreciated a call. I can't find a place in my heart bitter enough to hold a grudge. I don't blame them for this ordeal, and the agony that each of us has had to endure should have never been cast upon us. I fear they feel their lives will forever be tainted by the events that now bind us together. I hope guilt has not constructed a wall between us, and although my journey has been grueling, I can't imagine the judgment they place upon themselves. To be forgiven is to forgive. I hope all is well with each of them. With this said, I must share a story I later learned.

When Jaryd disappeared, I heard about what had possibly transpired. I was under the impression that a single group started up the trail. With a quicker pace, several of the hikers went forward, creating two smaller groups, one in front of the other. I was told Jaryd was with the slower group, and they let him walk up ahead, thinking he was trying to catch up with the faster group.

When the two groups came together farther up the trail, neither one of them knew Jaryd was missing. The lower group thought Jaryd had made it up to the leading group, and the leading group had no idea Jaryd was trying to work his way toward them. This is when they first realized Jaryd was missing.

This is the same story I told *Good Morning America* and the *Today Show.* I thought my son became a victim of the mountain because he wandered off, searching for the upper group. I believed this story up until a month after his loss.

I was on the phone with a friend named Karen, and we were talking about what had happened with Jaryd. She wanted to know if they had come up with any new information. She told me she had just gotten off the phone with one of the girls on the hike, and they had discussed the entire situation in detail.

Karen told me she heard how Jaryd had passed the upper group, and they did nothing to stop him. I couldn't believe my ears. This was the first time I was hearing this. I questioned, "I don't understand. Are you telling me the first group let my son walk right through them, and they let him continue up the mountain by himself?" I was mortified!

What I heard next made my heart stand still. Karen continued telling me about the conversation she had with her friend. She said the person she had spoken with said, "Jaryd walked right by me, and I said to myself, *Someone should be watching him a little closer.*" Then she let him continue up the trail.

I responded in a deranged voice. "You mean my son was lost because no one accepted the responsibility for his safety?"

"That's not all. They heard a scream, and they didn't do a thing to check it out."

"What do you mean 'they heard a scream?'"

At this time, my daughter was playing in the same room I was sitting in, and I didn't know she was listening to my conversation. She jumped in, saying, "Yes, Daddy, we heard a scream."

I put the phone down and looked at my daughter with disbelief and said, "You heard the scream too, honey?"

"Yes!"

I looked into her eyes and asked her, "What kind of a scream was it? Did it sound like he was being attacked by an animal, or did it sound like someone was trying to grab him and take him away?"

Josallyn's response was chilling. "No, Daddy, it didn't sound like anything was attacking Jaryd. It sounded more like someone was trying to put their hand over his mouth so they could take him."

I picked up the phone and told Karen what Josallyn had just told me. I told Karen I had to get off the phone with her because I needed to make a couple of phone calls.

I called my friend Brenda and told her what Karen had just shared with me. Brenda confirmed the full story. "That's what I've heard all along, and that's why I'm so upset about the entire situation."

So my son was ahead of both groups, and the sheriff's department keeps telling everyone there is only one way off the mountain, and that's back down the trail the same way you come up. That's not true! If you keep going up the trail the way Jaryd was headed, you can leave the trail at Peterson Lake. If that's the case, someone could have come down the trail and taken Jaryd back up with him.

It's frustrating because more questions surface every day, but answers never follow. It seems as if we have been searching for answers as much as we've been searching for Jaryd.

The Truth and the Strange

Remember Craig, the ranger who believed he saw Jaryd the day after he went missing? I originally spoke with him the week after Jared's official search. A couple of days following our conversation, I called Chris Shauble of KCNC-TV and informed him of the conversation I had with Craig. Mr. Shauble wanted to know if Craig was willing to talk to the media, and if he was, could he interview him. I told Mr. Shauble I'd give Craig a call and find out.

Craig had no problem talking to the media. He was frustrated because everyone was reporting someone from the sheriff's department had already interviewed him, and they hadn't. He wanted to set the record straight.

Mr. Shauble called Craig and recorded the entire conversation. Craig believed the boy he saw could have been Jaryd, and he wanted someone to investigate his sighting. Mr. Shauble knew he had to get both sides of the story, so he drove to the sheriff's house and interviewed him about Craig's claims. I could not believe what happened when the official interview was concluded.

The Learning Channel was filming a documentary about news reporters, and they had a crew shadowing Chris Shauble. A typical day in the life of a reporter seemed to be the primary goal, but the crew inadvertently recorded a gaffe made by the sheriff. When the interview about Craig and Mesa Verde was over, Shauble's news team began packing up. The objective of *The Learning Channel* was not the interview, so unbeknownst to the sheriff, they continued to film from the shadows. The sheriff was looking in the direction of the Channel 4 cameraman, so he must have thought it was safe to drop his guard.

The sheriff stood and looked at Chris and asked, "Are you as tired of this story as we are?"

Mr. Shauble, being the professional he is, attempted to deflect the question. The comment didn't make the evening news that night, and it was probably a question that was supposed to just fade away. The question wasn't intended for me, and the sheriff probably believed I would never hear it. I don't believe he would ever attempt to intentionally hurt me, and Jaryd had a way of compromising our intentions. Although I was later offended by this comment, I had no desire to see the sheriff in this position.

Innocently, I looked forward to watching *The Learning Channel* documentary. I know many people around the country who also watched the program when it aired. When Chris Shauble's interview ended, I heard the sheriff's disturbing question. Obviously, many others heard the question, because my phone took on a life of its own. Sadly, I wondered if the sheriff would ever do another thing to help with Jaryd's search. I couldn't help but think his true feelings had just been exposed. Was Jaryd just another case, and would the little thorn that he became ever go away?

As I reflected on what the sheriff had said, I wondered who he was talking about when he used the word "we." I didn't have to think long, because a few sergeants quickly came to my mind.

The sheriff didn't know it, but I received a couple of calls from deputies because they wanted to apologize to me. They wanted me to understand that they did not have the same feelings as the sheriff. One deputy informed me that he approached the sheriff the next day and said, "You really blew it this time, didn't you!"

For almost a year, I would hear how Craig was interviewed, and they didn't find anything credible to his story. Craig was so upset that he sent me a letter addressing the fact that nobody had spoken with him. The following letter was dated September 11, 2000:

Sept. 11, 2000

To whom it may concern,

This letter has been drafted to make a statement as a matter of fact, and for the record, that I, Craig W. had not and never had any contact with the police or sheriff's department concerning the disappearance of Gerad Atadero, who went missing as of Oct. 2nd, 1999.

While working as a park ranger at Mesa Verde Nat. Park, I witnessed what I believed to be young Gerad and another man, traveling in a 1998/1999 Suzuki SUV. I completed a report with the National Park on the 3rd or 4th of October 1999, but have since received no contact with any of the sheriff's department.

The ranger's letter was written almost a year after Jaryd had disappeared, and it gave me comfort because I was tired of explaining myself to the media. I was never taken serious about Craig's claims because the media would always counter that the sheriff told them they investigated him. I never understood why they chose to believe him over me. It was nice the day I had the chance to pull out the letter and show it to someone who had doubted my claims.

....

Nine months had passed since Jaryd had disappeared, and there was no sign of him. The Arapahoe Rescue Patrol volunteered to go up the mountain and conduct a search with my family. We had the date picked, and we planned to be on the Big South Trail that entire Saturday.

Stan Bush, the president and founder of the Arapahoe Rescue Patrol, contacted the sheriff's office in order to get the sheriff's permission and blessings. Everything was approved, and the search team prepared for that weekend.

As the weekend got closer, Stan was contacted by the sheriff. He was told the Arapahoe Rescue Patrol was not welcome in the area, and they would be arrested for trespassing if they showed up. Again, why was someone trying to stop my family from trying to locate my son? This story was never made public because too many things are controlled by politics.

Stan called me and asked, "Allyn, what's the sheriff's problem up there? He wants to stop this weekend's search, and we don't know why." I discussed the options with Stan, and we decided to conduct the search anyway. The plan was to have the group arrive on the mountain without their search and rescue uniforms. The search and rescue team would then conduct the search as a bird-watching club. And that's exactly what happened.

On the day of the search, everyone met in the parking lot of the Big South Trail to organize the search. It was hard to tell the difference between the Arapahoe Rescue Patrol and my family because everyone blended in as if we were a group of tourists. There was a little anxiety floating through the air because everyone was waiting for someone from the sheriff's office to arrive and cause a scene. I was thankful it never happened.

When the search started, everyone walked up the trail in a single-file line until we got to the area where Jaryd was last seen. The search group broke up into small teams and thoroughly searched the area in question. My family was hoping the search team would find something that would indicate what may have happened to my son.

While I was walking back down the trail, a United States congressman approached me and introduced himself. During our conversation, he asked me, "Hey, what's the problem with the sheriff up here? Someone from his office called my office three times and said, 'Tell the congressman, if he knows what's right for his career, he better not show up on the mountain during the search.' What's he hiding?" This was not Congressman Tancredo.

I didn't know what to say. I couldn't believe what I was hearing, but the stories kept coming. I laughed and said, "It doesn't surprise me!"

I know this story is hard to believe, but it really happened. I tried to contact one of the members of the search and rescue team to confirm this story for my book, but they told me, "I can't! You don't understand how political this thing is."

I received an e-mail from one of the searchers on the mountain that day that confirms my information. The following is from that e-mail:

> Our county sheriff contacted the county sheriff in charge of the search area and he received an OKAY to do a one day search around the last seen point.
>
> We were scheduled for a Saturday but two days before the activity we received word that we were not to do the search.
>
> Much discussion. The area is not private land, but along a forest trail. Numerous times over the years we have gone ahead and done searching at the request of citizens although we prefer to have law enforcement authority.
>
> We heard unofficially that other teams from around the state had volunteered and been turned down.
>
> We were not involved in the after action reports or critiques. We concluded that—for some reason—the Sheriff believed it to be a crime scene and so wanted all non official groups and individuals kept out of the area but this was just a presumption.

When I spoke with Stan on the phone, he informed me there were a lot of questions surrounding Jaryd's search. When things take place at this level, it's best that assessments remain behind closed doors. Politics are a way of life in our daily activities, and I had no desire to get mixed up with those where I had no business. My focus was Jaryd. However, I felt the strong pull of local politics on my drive to find answers concerning my son.

Another thought comes to mind. If Jaryd had drowned or had been attacked by a lion, a crime scene did not exist. If a crime had taken place, the event would continue to be worked regardless of whether the authorities were tired of it or not. I was pretty tired not knowing the answers myself. If the trail is a crime scene, why won't the FBI get involved?

I often try to understand why certain areas were searched and others somewhat ignored. I remembered how frustrated I was when we first asked the sheriff to send a search team to the area where Seaux, the tracker, thought Jaryd may have wandered off. The more I put the pieces together, the more I realized everything was predicated upon a belief or a hunch. This had to be the case, because certain areas were ignored, and other areas were searched and then re-searched again.

I remember seeing footage of the dive team searching every nook and cranny of the river, hoping to find my son. They did this for days because the sheriff's gut feeling was Jaryd had fallen into the river and drowned. I didn't realize this until six months later when I called the sheriff to ask him a few questions. I remember when I asked, "Sheriff, man-to-man, what do you think happened to my son?"

He replied, "I think Jaryd drowned in the river, and his body won't resurface for five years because the water is too cold."

Okay, everyone is entitled to their own opinion, especially if there isn't any evidence to refute their belief. I thought about it and asked, "Do you really believe that?"

The sheriff said, "Yes, that's exactly what happened."

Almost six months had passed since Jaryd had disappeared, so I figured the sheriff had taken a close look at the lack of evidence and drawn his own conclusion. I had a conversation with Don Bendell six years later, and he relayed a conversation to me about what the sheriff had said to him on the second day of the search. I asked Don if he'd write down what the sheriff had said and e-mail it to me so that I could include it in Jaryd's story. The following is part of the e-mail Don sent to me on December 28, 2005:

> It was late in the day when I arrived in the rugged mountainous setting. I had been pulling a loaded trailer over 1,000 miles, and my head felt like it was filled with Elmer's Glue-All. I spoke with a deputy who stood guard at the National Forest trailhead parking lot, which was taped off with police tape. National news media trucks were clustered everywhere, and I first spotted Allyn Atadero with news cameras and microphones shoved in his face.
>
> On the other side of the bridge was a National Guard encampment and no news media. That is where I wanted to be. I am a publicity-hound in that I write paperback books and own karate schools. In both businesses, you have to provide your own publicity and promote yourself and your business. When it comes to tracking missing people though, I shun all publicity as much as possible and do not want any. It is one of the things I do privately between God and me. Most of the searches I have been on, most people do not even know about.
>
> I saddled my horse, put a search vest on my dog, loaded my saddle bags, and put on my tactical vest, 9mm, and around my neck I wore my universal law enforcement badge, which reads Don Bendell, Tracker Special Investigator. I learned to carry one around my neck when I am on searches while I was working with the FBI and Navajo Tribal Police looking for some cop-killers on the big Navajo Reservation in the Four Corners area.

I rode over to the search headquarters, and a deputy at the police line tape put his hand up, but a Larimer County sheriff's sergeant walked up and said, "Let him in. Look at the badge. He's one of us."

I winked at the sergeant, and he said, "Who are you with?"

I grinned, saying, "God."

He chuckled and pointed out the Larimer County sheriff to me. The man was tall, distinguished-looking, and wore a gray suit with a maroon power tie, and at that time, was facing half a dozen TV cameras with twice as many microphones shoved in his face. I caught his eye, and he excused himself. He walked over, and we shook hands, and I pulled out a letter from the then-Fremont County Sheriff Sean Green basically saying I was okay as a tracker and played well with others. I also showed him a similar letter from the then-head of Fremont County Search and Rescue.

The sheriff read the letter, handed it back, and dismissed me with, "That's nice, but we don't need your help. You can go back home."

After driving over 1,000 miles non-stop pulling that horse trailer, and several days of adrenalin-pumping interacting with fans and many people, that was not what I was in the mood to hear.

I handed my reins to one of the deputies and said, "Sheriff, can you and I speak privately for a minute?"

He said, "Sure," and I grabbed his upper arm in a friendly manner and guided him away from his deputies, news people, handlers, or whoever was surrounding him.

Taking him between two parked cars, I stopped and faced him, speaking softly, "Sheriff, do you remember the two missing boys in the southern Colorado Mountains last year who died of hypothermia, and they could not find the stepdad for weeks?"

He said, "Yes, it was in all the news."

I said, "You know, many people kept saying the stepdad had molested them and got them lost in the mountains while he took off."

The sheriff said he heard all those rumors.

Then I said, "You know I was down on my hands and knees up on that mountain, holding my horse's reins in my teeth, wearing reading glasses, and finding his tracks that were several weeks old by turning over leaves and pine needles. I worked out his whole trail, Sheriff, and found him face down dead in a stream, after over 400 searchers from four states, including search dogs, and Army Blackhawk helicopters with IFR could not find him. I even got pneumonia the day I found him, and it was well past midnight when we came down off that mountain with his body. My horse and I were dead tired, sore, and sick, kind of like I am now, and I found not a half dozen, like here, but over fifty microphones and TV cameras shoved in my face. At that point, I had to make a decision. I could make the Fremont County Sheriff look like a good guy, which he is, or a fool. I might end up having to make that kind of decision here. What is your opinion on that, Sheriff?"

He looked at me for a second and grabbed my upper arm now in a friendly way, saying, "Mr. Bendell, you make a good point. Let me take you to our command post, and I'll introduce you to my head of search and rescue, and they will give you a sheriff's radio to carry. I don't think you'll find anything though. You'll see how rough the river is. His body is wedged under some rocks or roots in the Cache la Poudre. I guarantee it. It will come loose sometime in the future and somebody will find it."

I smiled, saying, "Sheriff, I'm just going to look for signs and try not to narrow myself down to any conclusions right now."

I didn't realize the sheriff was so adamant about Jaryd's body being wedged under some rocks or roots in the river. One night it came to me, I finally understood why the sheriff wouldn't search the area on Seaux's map and why he wouldn't call in the National Guard: he'd already solved the case.

Jaryd wasn't missing, he was dead in the river, and the sheriff was going to prove it by having the dive team search the river over and over. Wait a minute, I thought the media reported the sheriff believed Jaryd was attacked by a mountain lion. Which was it? Was he in the river, or was he attacked by a mountain lion? In either case, how was it a crime scene?

....

I know some people might think I'm an upset father, and if I am, I believe I have plenty of reasons to feel that way. I had a lot of things to say, but no one would listen to me; and if they did, they didn't believe me. I'd tell people part of the story, and they'd respond, "Really, your family was actually told they would be arrested if they tried to help with the search?"

I'd look them in the eye and say, "Yes. Can you believe that?"

Their response was usually, "Wow, that's hard to believe."

For instance, there was a letter written by Wendy Johnson, and it was published in *The Poudre River Reporter* in November of 1999. The following is a copy of the letter:

> An opinion, by Wendy Johnson
>
> This letter is written as a mother, grandmother, friend, and locals of the Poudre Canyon. In Concern to Jaryd, who was lost.
>
> The sheriff and search and rescue did a great job.
>
> Dogs were sent in along with search teams, the area was closed to the public. We agreed, but Jaryd was not found! Spending his first freezing night, the next day, still Jaryd was not found! We decided to search or help somehow. Living here all or most of our lives we know every aspect of this country. We couldn't understand after this amount of time why they wouldn't be thrilled to see local volunteers.

When Mom asked if we could search she was treated like nothing mattered except reporters and interviews, being shrugged from one person to another. What really was important here? Chances became slim sooner than four nights and five days. What could be wrong with another set of eyes looking? I know there are procedures and ways of doing things "by the book," but as procedures are checked, Jaryd is out there alone.

A man from Steamboat Springs also chose to search. When he saw search teams, he asked if he could continue to the trailhead. He was told they were investigating the helicopter, it was being guarded, to leave or he would be thrown in jail! What exactly is important here?

We feel for the searchers of the crash but…thank God they are alive and fine. All that is left is the helicopter, metal, plastic, nuts, and bolts! Shouldn't we find Jaryd instead of making the cause of the crash more important?

Society is becoming too dependent on everyone with a title or badge instead of relying on each other. Let people help people. Granted there is a time and place, but in this situation, after a few nights and days it's time to let people who want to help, Help! Thank you for your time!

—Wendy Johnson

I realize when one is questioned, one feels the need to respond and set the record straight. While I was researching information to include in my book, I came across a response to Wendy's letter that was written by one of the search and rescue members. I believe the search and rescue team did an awesome job, but I didn't feel Wendy's feelings needed a rebuttal.

The rebuttal gave Wendy credit for wanting to help, but it also went on to say Wendy wouldn't help the fire department or paramedics even if children were in danger because she wasn't trained to respond to these emergencies.

I understand this response, but I don't agree with it. If this were the case, Don Bendell would have never been treated the way he was because he is a highly trained person and was there on the mountain for Jaryd's best interest. I also know a lady with search and rescue dogs, and she was treated the same way. Being trained had nothing to do with the way the sheriff treated those who wanted to help.

The competition and lack of communication isn't something new when it comes to searches in the state of Colorado. Back in the sixties, a couple of different agencies fought over control of a search that was being conducted up on Rollins Pass. The argument lasted two hours while fifty searchers waited to begin their search for a missing boy. This is just one example of how people forget the real reason for conducting a search. It has nothing to do with notoriety; it's all about the extreme jubilation one gets when reuniting a family (Bush, Stan. http://www.coloradosarboard. org/CSRBHistory.shtml).

One of the things that comes to mind when I think about Jaryd's search is the amount of people who where actually involved. There were approximately sixty searchers on the mountain at any given time, and it was reported that authorities asked those not assigned to the official search to stay away from the mountainous scene. All those involved in Jaryd's search should be considered heroes, and they should be treated with the greatest respect. But on the other hand, those who wanted to help should not have been hastily turned away.

In September of 2005, Michelle Vanek went missing in Eagle County, Colorado. I found this story interesting because searchers were calling this situation the largest search effort in Colorado history, and the organizers of the search said anyone wanting to volunteer should come on up to the search area. They didn't threaten to arrest anyone, and they didn't say people had to be properly trained. All they wanted was help.

In June of 2005, Brennan Hawkins became lost in the Utah Wilderness on a Friday afternoon. The next day, civilians began showing up to search for him; and by Sunday, there were three thousand volunteers involved. Four days later, when all hope was gone, Brennan was found alive and was reunited with his family. I'm absolutely positive not all those who showed up were officially trained search and rescue members.

I'm excited for Brennan's family, and at the same time I think about Jaryd's search. I wonder if the outcome would have been different if they would have allowed volunteers to participate. That's a thought that will never be answered.

Now for the Strange

I wrote a poem about two weeks after my son's disappearance called "What Did Jesus Say?" The words were very comforting, and they helped me with my daily struggles. I knew the rest of my family was having a hard time with Jaryd's plight, so I decided to share my words with them. This story, about the poem, is somewhat strange, but it makes me feel as if my son continues reaching out for my hand.

It was about 7:30 p.m., and I was in my apartment, all alone, talking to my mom on the phone. She tried extremely hard to find the words that would comfort my aching heart. Our conversation about Jaryd stirred several emotions, including tears and a little laughter. Toward the end of our discussion, I told her I wanted to e-mail a poem to her because I thought she would enjoy reading it. As we said our good-byes, I hit the send button on my computer and hung up the phone. I couldn't wait for my mom's feedback.

I walked into my living room and immediately called my dad because I was in desperate need of emotional support. About two minutes after sending the e-mail, and while I was on the phone with my dad, I heard a loud noise coming from my bedroom. It sounded as if something was being blown against my bedroom wall. After hearing the crashing sound a couple of more times, I told my dad something was going on in my bedroom. I continued talking to him while I walked into my bedroom to investigate.

I looked at my computer, which sits right below the window, and I could see the cord that opens my curtains swinging back and forth. The loud clacking sound was coming from a small weight that was attached to the bottom of the cord. A wind gust must have blown through my open window, causing the weight to fly up and crash back down onto my computer monitor. I didn't think anything of it, and I told my dad I needed to put the phone down in order to use both hands to close my window. When I pulled back the curtains, I noticed my window was closed and locked. My mind raced in different directions because I couldn't understand what had caused the cord to swing. At that moment, fear raced through my body, and I freaked out.

I hastily picked up the phone and told my dad what had happened, and then I informed him I had to go because I was terrified. I hung up the phone and ran into every room and turned on the lights. About a minute after I ended my call with my dad, the phone rang. When I answered it, it was my mom. She told me she really enjoyed the poem, but she wanted to know what 8217 meant. Her question pushed me over the edge. I had no idea what she was talking about because I never wrote 8217. She told me 8217 was written throughout the poem, and she didn't understand why I would put that number in it.

Okay, this wasn't funny anymore. I was all alone, yet it seemed as if someone or something was right there with me. By this time, the events of the night were scaring me. I could tell my mom was confused because her voice cracked and she asked, "What's going on, honey?" I had no idea what to say to her or how to explain anything that was happening. Maybe there was a good explanation for 8217, but what caused the weight on the curtain to swing back and forth?

I asked my mom to send the e-mail back to me, and when she did, the number 8217 was nowhere to be seen. We both became somewhat hysterical because the situation had a strange effect on us. My mom's voice continued to crack as she said, "I'll print the page and fax it to you at work tomorrow morning."

I was blown away. I remembered that I had e-mailed the poem to my brother, Arlyn, at the same time I had sent it to my mom. I thought my brother's e-mail would show the same phenomenon since they had the same Internet service provider and received their e-mail from the same company. I called my brother, but he didn't know what I was talking about. The number 8217 never showed up on his copy of the e-mail.

That night, I went to bed with all the lights on in my apartment. If I could have gone somewhere else for the night, I would have. I had a hard time falling asleep because I was afraid things would start moving around in the night.

The next day, I called my mom, and she faxed my poem to me. It had 8217 written throughout the poem. That day, I showed the fax to everyone at school, and no one could explain this strange event. For the next week, all of my friends tried to figure out what 8217 meant. Was it part of a phone number, or was it part of a license plate? We didn't know. About a week later, my mom called me and told me Jaryd had sent us a hug. If one takes the eighth, twenty-first, and seventh letter of the alphabet and puts them together, it spells *hug*. To this day, I'm convinced my little man caused the weight to swing back and forth because he wanted me to know that he loves me, and he wanted to show this by sending a little *hug*.

....

About a month after Jaryd was gone, I was taking attendance in the gym for one of my classes. While my students sat quietly in their spots, the radio in the equipment room came on and blared loudly.

My students were curious, and they wanted to know who was in the equipment room. I told them the room was empty, but they thought I was kidding, and they wouldn't believe me. They were positive someone was in the room playing a trick on them and wouldn't calm down until a search party was dispatched to investigate the abrupt noise the radio was causing. I laughed, and I told them I knew what was going on, but I didn't try to explain it to them.

A couple of my students asked if they could go into the room to surprise the person who was messing with our class. I knew they wouldn't find anyone, but I let them check out the room in order to satisfy their own curiosity. After I gave them my permission, the two students ran to the room hoping to prove me wrong. To their surprise, the room was empty. Each of the students looked at me and asked, "How did that happen? There's no one in the room."

I laughed and replied, "You don't want to know."

I always attributed the strange and weird happenings in my life to Jaryd. It was a way of keeping my son close to my heart, and I knew if Jaryd were around, he would have probably turned the radio on to give me a hard time.

I knew it wasn't him, but the thought that it could have been was comforting.

....

About four weeks after Jaryd disappeared, I was walking through the locker room on a teacher in-service day. What happened was strange because there were no students at school.

I walked past the lockers toward the gym. As I got to the doorway, I heard two cries as if they were yelling for help. The words were chilling because I heard, "Daddy! Daddy!"

I ran back into the locker room and said loudly, "Jaryd, Jaryd, where are you?" I sat down and cried because the time on my watch was exactly the same time of the day Jaryd was lost.

I don't know where the calls came from, but I was frustrated because I knew at one time, my son was calling for Daddy, and I never responded.

It was a chilling experience I'll never forget.

One-Year Anniversary

Eleven months had passed, and the one-year anniversary of Jaryd's disappearance was quickly approaching. Time was passing faster than a blink of an eye, and no matter how hard I tried, I couldn't slow it down.

The last month before the anniversary, I found myself trying to relive each day as if it were the one the year before. I'd get up in the morning and ask myself, *What were Jaryd and I doing on this day a year ago?* The closer I got to October 2, the harder it was to look in the mirror and face the tragic reality of what was quickly approaching. I felt as if I were reliving every minute from the year before, except there was one difference: I knew the horror that was lurking just beyond the horizon.

I got that sick feeling all over again because I knew the media was preparing to contact me on October 2. I hated answering all of their questions, but I also understood it was an avenue to get Jaryd's picture in the public's eye once again. It was a price I had to pay, and as long as Jaryd was listed as officially missing, I would do anything to have his face shown all over the world.

About three weeks before the anniversary date, Susan called me with a proposal. She had quit her job as the victim's advocate for the sheriff's department and was now working for Allison Funeral Service as their director of business development. Susan told me she had talked with Mark and Ben, and they wanted to have a service for Jaryd on October 2, 2000.

I was surprised that Susan had come up with the idea to honor my son and bring attention to the fact that he was still missing. I thought it was great, but I wasn't sure how I would emotionally hold up having the services in a funeral home. Susan asked me to bring pictures and toys that belonged to Jaryd because she wanted to reintroduce the community to him. She wanted everyone to meet the real little boy who had vanished on that horrible day a year earlier. I agreed and went to meet Susan that Friday.

I arrived at the Allison Funeral Home and slowly walked in. I had an eerie feeling when I entered the front door because I was facing the fact that I was in a place where family and friends gathered to pay their last respects to someone who had died. I did not want to be there because I did not want to deal with the emotions and feelings that accompanied the thoughts of my son being dead.

I had an uneasy feeling as I searched the foyer looking for Susan's friendly smile. After a few minutes of searching and trying to get used to the idea that I was in a funeral home, I walked into the office and told the receptionist I was looking for Susan. The receptionist called Susan and informed her that I was there. A minute later, I saw Susan walking down the stairway from the second floor. She approached me and gave me a welcoming hug and then escorted me to a nicely decorated room that had freshly baked cookies and hot coffee sitting on a conference table.

I sat down and poured myself a cup of coffee. I closed my eyes, put my head back, and daydreamed about the special times and fun I had with my little man. These pleasant thoughts calmed my nerves and allowed me to release the anxiety that had built up all morning. As I drifted off into my past life, Susan went to get Mark and Ben for the meeting.

When they walked in, they introduced themselves and expressed their condolences for the pain I had been experiencing during the past year. I could feel myself slowly falling apart as we talked about Jaryd and the plan they had developed for his services.

When it was my turn to respond, the dialog stopped because I couldn't handle the situation. Every time I opened my mouth, I cried. It was strange, but it seemed as if I was being forced to deal with the pain and reality of what I had experienced the year before. It was like a time warp, and I was back on the mountain, crying for my son's safety.

Mark was in tune with my pain as he talked softly and told me not to worry. He wanted this to be a positive experience, not a painful one. Susan interjected that she didn't consider the service to be a funeral, and she didn't want me to think of it as one. She said, "We want to call the commemoration Services of Hope and Healing."

That thought made me cry. I sat there, looked intently at the ground, and rubbed the tears from my eyes. I took a deep breath and slowly let it out as I tried to grasp any composure I could find. I gradually raised my head, looked at Susan, smiled, and said, "Jaryd, I can't believe all of the things people want to do for you. I love you, man."

My breathing became somewhat normal, and the words that Susan said echoed through my mind. I thought, *Hope and healing. I really like that.*

Susan went on to explain to me that the entire community of Fort Collins was searching for answers, and there were a lot of people out there looking for some type of closure. We discussed some protocol and things we might want to include in the services. Susan told me about helium-filled black and silver balloons that they wanted to pass out to everyone in attendance. When the service was over, everyone would go out to the parking lot and release the balloons in Jaryd's honor. I thought the balloon idea sounded awesome, and I knew my little guy would like it. The thought that he might see one was welcoming.

We talked about music that could be played, and Susan told me she had a song she wanted me to hear. I told her I had a couple songs too, so we went into the chapel and sat down to listen to "He's My Son," performed by Mark Schultz.

As I listened to the words, I closed my eyes and lowered my head into the palms of my waiting hands. Mark's lyrics stirred my emotions, and within seconds, I turned into a bowl of melting Jell-O. I cried uncontrollably until the song was over. I was embarrassed, and I was afraid to raise my head because I could feel fluids oozing from every opening on my face. I grabbed Kleenex after Kleenex and wiped the tears from my eyes, the snot running from my nose, and the slobber that was flowing from out of both sides of my mouth. I didn't have to look in a mirror to know I was a complete mess.

I waited for a couple of minutes, and as soon as it was safe, I raised my head, looked up, and said, "Thanks, Jaryd."

I was numb, and I couldn't believe I was sitting in the chapel of a funeral home. Little by little, I looked around. *No parent should ever have to experience what I'm going through right now. It isn't fair.*

As I was getting ready to drive back to Littleton, Mark asked me if I would be willing to return the following Friday to meet with Pastor Kevin Jones. Pastor Jones was one of Mark's friends, and Mark recommended that he perform Jaryd's services.

At that moment, I knew I would be spending a lot of time with my newly found friends at the Allison Funeral Home.

....

The following week, my friend Chris Schauble from KCNC-TV called me and asked if I would go up the canyon with him on

Sunday, October 1, to film a one-year anniversary story. I said yes because I wanted to go back up the mountain to visit the site where Jaryd was last seen anyway.

The day Chris and I went back to the Big South Trail, his cameraman accompanied us as we retraced the steps that Jaryd could have taken. Chris was easy to speak with, and he made me feel comfortable. As we were filming, two ladies approached us and inquired as to what we were doing. After all, how often does one encounter a news crew on a quiet and secluded mountain trail?

The two ladies were a mother and daughter. The daughter, who was originally from Italy, had relocated to Fort Collins. She said her mother had watched the story about a missing boy a year ago from Italy. When she came to visit her daughter, she asked her to take her to the place where the boy had vanished because she felt compelled to have a look for herself. Chris introduced me as Jaryd's father, and this revelation was communicated to the mother in Italian. The mother took my hand and spoke in a language that I didn't understand. Condolences have a way of bridging language barriers, and for a moment, I truly felt our hearts were one.

Friday quickly approached, and I prepared myself for the trip back to Fort Collins to meet with Pastor Jones. I wasn't sure what he would say or how he would act since he had never met Jaryd, but the more I thought about the meeting, the more frustrated I became. I had a hard time comprehending I was involved in planning what could be construed as a funeral for my son. I thought, *No, Lord, this can't be happening.* I had to remind myself there was no evidence that indicated my son was dead. On the other hand, there was no evidence my son was alive. I was at a point in my life where I would give anything in the world to know Jaryd's fate. Maybe God was protecting me because something terrible had actually happened to him.

At times, in the back of my mind, I see my son struggling in the river as he fights for his survival. At other times, I see him turning around just in time to see a mountain lion ripping at his body. Either way, the thought of my little guy experiencing any pain or fear destroys me. And believe me, those thoughts have destroyed me a million times in the past year.

I walked through my apartment and searched for anything I may have forgotten the week before. I grabbed the poems I wrote about Jaryd because I wanted Pastor Jones to incorporate them into his service. When I was sure there was nothing else to take, I hiked down to my car and headed for Fort Collins.

About a mile into my trip, I pulled out a CD that I wanted to listen to and inserted it into the CD player. I skipped to the song that reminded me of Jaryd and pushed play. I waited for a few seconds and then Pink Floyd's "Wish You Were Here" began playing. I turned up the volume and sang along and thought about how much I wished Jaryd was sitting right here with me. When the song was over, I played it again and again. That was the only song I listened to for the entire hour-and-a-half trip.

The words "so you think you can tell heaven from hell" echoed through my mind. It was ironic. The thought of my son being dead and in heaven gave me some comfort, but not having him with me was putting me through my own living hell. I was in heaven every minute of the day while I had both of my children by my side. Since the day Jaryd vanished, I've been living in hell. My surroundings haven't changed, but my emotional status has. So you think you can tell heaven from hell? I'm not sure I can. What I once thought was heaven is now hell.

When I arrived at the Allison Funeral Home, Susan took me upstairs to a private room where Mark, Ben, Susan, Pastor Jones, and I could talk. Pastor Jones wanted me to tell him as much about Jaryd as I could so that he could somehow get to know the little guy himself. There were a couple of times Pastor Jones referred to Jaryd as passing on, and I would stop him and say, "There's nothing that points to Jaryd being dead."

Pastor Jones asked me if I would like to get up during the service and say a few words about Jaryd, but the thought freaked me out. How could I stand up and say anything if I couldn't stop crying?

I decided to put the entire service into Pastor Jones's hands because Pastor Jones had already worked with Mark on several occasions. As I listened to the entire group, I knew the service was one Jaryd would be proud of, but it was something I was not looking forward to.

I remember attending a party once and being asked a simple question, "What would you do if God revealed to you that you only have two more months to live?"

I quietly sat back and listened to the basic answers that one would expect to hear, but when it was my time to answer the question, I think I kind of surprised everyone with my response. I said, "I'd be very excited, and I would throw a party every day."

People looked at me as if I were crazy or if I were some sort of an idiot, but all my friends knew from where I was coming. One lady came up and asked me why I had such a bizarre response. I told her about my son, and I said, "If by chance he's dead, I'd celebrate because I'd be seeing him soon."

During the first year without Jaryd, I experienced many situations where special people reached out to help me. This story would be incomplete if I failed to mention the efforts of Congressman Tom Tancredo, Colorado's sixth district representative. In the Afterword section of this book, I write in detail about what this man did for me. In short, he was able to get the Jaryd Atadero Bill through Congress. Its focus was on child safety while visiting wilderness areas, and it was eventually signed into public law by President Clinton.

The Kelly Factor

When Jaryd first disappeared, several people called the resort to offer me their support. Most of them were normal people, but one lady took the cake since she was crazy and lived in a land of deceit. I told you about her in the beginning of my book. Her name was Kelly, and I thought she was there to help.

I remember, quite well, the first time Kelly called. Her words were calming, and she spoke with a confident demeanor as she lured me into submission. It wasn't hard for her to do because I was helpless and was at the mercy of anyone who claimed they could bring order and peace back into my life. Kelly went on to explain that she understood the feeling one experiences while searching for missing loved ones because she was abducted as a child and had been searching for her parents for most of her life. My desperation clouded my decision, and the only words I could get out of my mouth were, "Yes, please help me. I'll do anything for you if you find my son."

Let's face it. I didn't have the time to investigate her background, and I thought I was working with a true professional because she had identified herself as a criminal profiler. Kelly told me she'd reunited other families with their missing children, and she could possibly do the same for me. At first, she was a lot of help, but as each day passed, she began acting a little weird. Her help turned into a game of lies, and she slowly turned my life upside down with strange stories and fantasies about Jaryd's whereabouts.

One day, she called to inform me she had some important information about my son, but she couldn't tell me what it was because it was confidential, and she needed to keep it that way for my own safety. That irritated me because there was no way she was going to keep information away from me, especially when it was related to my son. I was mad, and I yelled at her, "Who do you think you are? You have secret information you can't share! That's ridiculous! Don't call me again unless you're willing to talk to me."

I went to hang up the phone when she replied, "Wait, I'll tell you, but you can't share this information with anyone."

I was silent and somewhat skeptical, but I wanted to know about her little secret concerning Jaryd. I waited a few seconds and replied, "Okay, I won't tell anyone."

Kelly told me she had evidence proving Jaryd had been abducted and was living in a child labor camp somewhere in Mexico. She wanted me to set her up with one of my friends in the media in order to get her story out to the public. Her plan was to fly to Mexico with a camera team and document the children while they worked in the labor camps. When they came across Jaryd, they would grab him and fly back to the United States and return him to me.

Have you started laughing yet? I laughed to myself as she continued with her ridiculous daydream about kidnapped American children working in the remote jungles of Mexico. I told her she was crazy, and I would never go to the media with such a strange and unfounded story. Besides that, how many three-year-olds can one find doing any type of work throughout the world?

I didn't hear from Kelly for several days, but her next phone call was more bizarre than the one I had received a few days earlier. She knew I didn't believe a word she had said, so she changed her story to include secret photos of Jaryd.

She claimed she was working with a company that utilized satellite imagery to photograph different coordinates, and they had faxed her several pictures of Jaryd working at a labor camp. She said this because she knew I would not believe her story without any tangible evidence. As I listened, I realized her lip service was hollow because she tried to dodge every question I had about the pictures. I thought the situation was pretty simple—either produce the pictures or shut up. I asked over and over to see her evidence, but her response was always, "The pictures are top secret, and they can't be shown to anyone." I thought, *Right, it's hard to see the photos because they're invisible.*

Her immature antics drove me crazy, and they caused a heated argument about the authenticity of the pictures. I told her our conversation was over unless she could produce something that could validate her amusing fairy tale. Since she couldn't, I abruptly hung up the phone.

I knew something didn't add up because Kelly told me she got all her information from a reliable source, yet she couldn't reveal him to me. Each time I asked who it was, she would snap, "I can't tell you because you won't believe me anyway." This went on for several months, and for some reason, she was beginning to buy into her own little escapade. Was she crazy? I don't know, but she was beginning to make me feel that way myself. Every time she called, I wanted to hang up the phone and pull out my hair.

I was done with her games, and I told her I wouldn't talk to her unless I received the pictures in the mail. I waited a couple of weeks to get a response, but Jaryd's labor camp pictures were as mysterious as his own disappearing act. No matter where I looked, there was no sign of either one of them. Since Kelly couldn't produce any evidence concerning Jaryd's pictures, she changed her approach and tried to get my attention in one more hurtful way.

One night, I was sitting down eating dinner with my daughter, and the phone rang. When I answered it, Kelly was on the other end, crying and acting as if someone had just shot her. She sobbed uncontrollably and mumbled, "They have Jaryd, and they want to return him."

I thought, *Oh my goodness, what is she talking about now?*

I have to admit, she startled me with her story because I didn't think she'd call and fake an uncontrollable cry. My heart wanted to believe her, but my mind wouldn't let me. I listened as Kelly told me the story of what had happened to her earlier in the day.

Kelly told me a lady had called her at work and confessed to the kidnapping of Jaryd on October 2. Kelly cried a little more and then said, "They didn't want to hurt you. They were hoping to extort money from you and your family because they wanted your resort up in the mountains." The lady also told Kelly they wanted to give Jaryd back to me, and they would contact her in a few days with the details.

Kelly's story floored me because I wasn't sure why she would go out of her way to make up something so ludicrous. I came to one simple conclusion: her story was either true, or she was the daughter of the devil.

I knew one thing: there was no way a couple of ladies could have kidnapped Jaryd when we already had pictures of him working in a child labor camp in Mexico. I thought, *What a freak!*

The next night was filled with more desperation. Kelly called me again because there was more to her story. This time, she informed me the lady not only called her at work but she had left a couple of messages on her answering machine at home. I know, I should have asked to hear them, but I didn't because there were several things going through my mind. I wanted to know how this lady got Kelly's work and home phone numbers, and why wasn't she calling me? Kelly was an out-of-control menace.

Just when I thought it couldn't get any worse, it did. Kelly called me the next day at work and informed me the lady who had Jaryd wanted to set up a time to return him to me. That freaked me out, and yet for some reason, it kind of got my hopes up. I started shaking, and I ran to the office at my school and told them about the phone call. I was extremely nervous and was falling apart because I really wanted to see my son. My mind was no longer dealing with her information in a rational way, and I had a euphoric feeling that I was actually going to be reunited with Jaryd. I knew it was crazy, but it is hard to convince a desperate father of the difference between reality and fantasy.

I drove home and called the authorities and reported Kelly to them. There was one person I trusted at the sheriff's office, and I was hoping he could help me by giving Kelly a polygraph test. I figured the results would discredit her story and she would leave me alone. When I talked to Captain Newhard, he was all for the test and willing to set the trap that would expose one of the strangest people I'd ever met. He wanted me to ask her if she was willing to be tested because he had a hunch she'd run and hide when she was confronted with the truth.

The next day, Kelly called me again and told me she needed me to pick a time and place where the kidnappers could hand Jaryd over to me. I told her I no longer believed her story and asked her if she was willing to take a polygraph test. I thought, *This is it, you lying little witch. I've got you now.* I was wrong. She got all excited and said she wanted to take the test to prove she was telling the truth. Her response was strange because I thought she'd say no and recant her story.

What was it that made her believe she was telling the truth? Maybe I was wrong about her and she had stumbled into something that was hard to comprehend. I wasn't sure what to think, but I couldn't wait for the results of the test.

I called the captain, and he informed me he'd talked with her, and she had agreed to meet at 5:00 p.m. to be tested at the sheriff's office the following night. This was it. The fairy tale was about to crash and burn, and it would force her to run home with her tail between her legs.

I thought the test would take about half an hour to complete, and I'd have the information I was waiting for by five thirty or six that night. That was wishful thinking. Several hours had rolled by, and I hadn't received a phone call from anyone. Did Kelly get cold feet and run before she had the chance to take the test, or was her story true and they were looking into the phone calls? I had all kinds of things going through my mind, and I was starting to lose patience with everyone.

It was about 8:30 p.m. when the captain called me with the results of the test. I listened anxiously as he said, "Allyn, she made the entire thing up. What would you like us to do with her?"

Fury ran its course through my entire body, and I responded with a rage, "Lock her up! I want her arrested for making up these stories!"

The captain replied, "That's what I was hoping you'd say."

The next day, Kelly was charged with a felony because she attempted to influence a public servant with false information. The captain reported her story to the media as a hoax, and he said she preyed on a family's vulnerability and her actions violated the law.

It's kind of funny, but when a reporter interviewed Kelly, she said the only thing she lied about was who gave her the information. Kelly went on to say, "I was trying to protect the source, and so I couldn't say who he really was. Now I'm in hot water because of it. I guess I'm not a very good liar." To this day, her source is a mystery to everyone, *but I know who it is because she told me.*

When Kelly was asked about the child labor camps, she replied, "I can't discuss the labor camp tip because I don't want to interfere with an ongoing investigation. All I'm trying to do is the right thing."

I found her response strange because she was willing to comment on each story as if they both had credence. Either Jaryd was in a child labor camp, or he was with the two ladies who abducted him. He couldn't be in both places.

Kelly eventually plea-bargained to a lesser crime. I believe she received three years probation and was instructed to never contact any of Jaryd's family again. I am not sure what happened to her, but maybe she's in Mexico continuing her incredible investigation into the daily lives of those who kidnap little children for the sake of cheap labor. And to think she actually accompanied my family and friends on our bird-watching search.

The Amber Alert

The next few years came and went without any new information concerning Jaryd's disappearance. I wasn't afraid to stand up for what I believed in, and I wished the effort to find my son was more of a priority to some. About once a month, I would hear in the back of my mind, *Are you as tired of this story as we are?* I was upset, and I didn't want anyone to experience the frustrations I had gone through. I wanted to become an advocate for missing children because I knew what a parent in that situation experiences. It was hell, and it wasn't fair at all.

One day, out of the blue, a reporter called and asked if I would help support a new law that was introduced by Representative Joyce Lawrence of Pueblo and Senator Ken Gordon of Denver. The new law would establish the Emergency Alert System in Colorado, and it would be called the Amber Alert. The Amber Alert would notify broadcast media statewide when an abduction of a child was confirmed.

I thought, *You bet! This is something I'd love to support.*

A few days went by, and before I knew it, I found myself at the State Capitol testifying in front of several lawmakers in support of the Amber Alert. The first time I spoke in front of the committee was an educational experience in itself. The committee had a list of people who would be called to testify. When each person was called to the front of the room, they had to state their name and then give the name of the organization for which they were speaking. After this, the chairperson informed each speaker they had three minutes to talk. The time was measured with a three-minute sand timer that was turned over as soon as one started speaking. When the three minutes were up, the person was informed time had expired.

I had been going through my mind trying to figure out how I was going to consolidate my speech into three minutes when I heard, "Next up is Allyn Atadero."

I got up and grabbed my folder that was filled with the articles I wanted to use while I was talking. When I got to the front of the room, the chairperson said, "Please state your name and tell us who you represent."

I stood up tall, tried not to cry, and responded, "My name is Allyn Atadero, and I'm representing my son, Jaryd Atadero."

The room got quiet, and then I heard some of the representatives whispering back and forth, and one quietly said, "This is that high-profile case about the little boy missing in the Poudre Canyon."

I tried to keep my composure as the chairperson and I made eye contact. She continued to gaze at me and said, "Mr. Atadero, the three-minute rule is being waved on your behalf. Please take all the time you need."

I talked for about ten minutes and explained how a ranger thought he saw Jaryd the day after he'd vanished. I informed them that if the Amber Alert were in existence at that time, the ranger would have known there was a missing child, and he could have taken appropriate action. I was totally in favor of the Amber Alert because I believed it would provide the help that keeps the hope burning in the hearts of any family member who, tragically, is faced with the pain and anxiety one feels when learning their child is missing. Not all nightmares associated with missing and abducted children are preventable, but this could be a step in the right direction.

When all testimonies were complete, the committee voted unanimously in favor of the Amber Law and sent the bill to the next committee. On my way out of the committee room, several of the lawmakers hugged me and gave me their condolences.

On April 1, 2002, Governor Owens had my daughter, Josallyn, sit next to him as he signed the Amber Alert into law. They conversed back and forth during the signing, and when the ceremony was over, Governor Owens gave Josallyn one of the pens he used while signing the bill.

After the signing, I had the opportunity to address the media about the significance of the Amber Alert. I spoke about Jaryd and Amber Hagerman and thanked the lawmakers for passing a bill that would help bring comfort to families when they learn one of their children is missing.

When I got home that night, I had a chance to reflect on what had happened earlier in the day. The day was long and difficult, but it was one of the best birthdays I'd ever had.

Divine Interventions

Unwillingly, we are part of the mysteries of the universe. A speck on the earth's surface with a lifespan that expires in a flash, our purpose, or meaning of life, leaves us asking more questions as we age. Are we swept away in a sea of chance only to react to situations as they materialize? Is it possible that chance or coincidences actually have order, or do we credit the strange to the supernatural? Is there a higher being or spirit world influencing the randomness we accept as part of being human?

It was March 15, 1950, in Beatrice, Nebraska. The West Side Baptist Church choir practice was held on Wednesdays at seven twenty. It was Wednesday, and the time was seven twenty, but not one of the fifteen choir members had arrived. There were random reasons for the tardiness. Car problems, ironing a dress, homework, etc., and every one of them was over five minutes late. A coincidence or intervention? At seven twenty-five, the church exploded.

We have all heard of or experienced similar stories. I went to San Diego one weekend and checked into a room in a hotel I had never stayed in before. I'm sure there are thousands of hotels in the area. The next day when I left my room, I ran into my twin brother leaving his room a few doors down. It was his first time there, and neither of us realized the other had gone to San Diego, over one hundred miles from where we lived.

After returning from a business trip to Sacramento, my sister-in-law, Robyn, began to discuss the challenges of her trip with her sister who was living in Palm Desert. As they spoke, the two discovered they were in Sacramento at the same time and had both stayed in the same hotel.

There are times when things appear hopeless, and this book is full of examples. I will never know why I was chosen for this journey and wondered if Jaryd had left me with a new purpose. Was I on the verge of fulfilling my destiny, whatever that might be? I had been struggling with the Colorado legislature to help raise funds for search and rescue organizations. I thought I had a plan that nobody could deny, but everywhere I turned, I ran into obstacles. After meeting with Governor Owens and being instrumental in getting the Amber Alert passed in Colorado, I was sure I could use our relationship to move my plans forward, but he left office. The door to my purpose driven opportunity was slammed, and I had no idea of how to pry it back open.

Some things may be bigger than we can imagine and their complexity so extreme that a way out can't be fathomed. An example of this would be the Gordian Knot. According to Greek legend, a poor man named Gordius had entered the public square of Phrygia in an oxcart. An oracle had told the locals their future king would arrive riding a wagon. When the people saw Gordius, they made him king. Gordius later dedicated his ox cart to Zeus. The cart was secured by a knot that was so difficult to undo that an oracle predicted that the person who untied it would be the next ruler of Asia.

Many years passed, and countless people tried their luck with the knot, but nobody succeeded in its undoing. Enter Alexander the Great. Only twenty-three at the time, he had a lot to prove. The cart had been placed by the Temple of Zeus over a hundred years earlier by the king of Phrygia. Alexander saw himself as the future ruler, but when a crowd gathered as he worked on the knot, he was left with the same result as those before him—failure. It is said that he shouted, "What does it matter how I lose it?" He pulled out his sword and with a mighty blow, severed the knot. That night, a huge electrical storm hit the area, causing many to believe Alexander was the son of Zeus. Alexander did go on to rule Asia. The governor being gone had become my Gordian Knot. Would I have to take my sword to it, or would it fall on its own accord?

The local magazine, *Imperial Valley Magazine*, where I'm from, contacted my brother shortly after we initially published our book. They were interested in writing a story about the details of Missing and were looking for additional background on its publication. Betty Miller, from the magazine, made contact with Arlyn and the interview was started. They discussed many things about Jaryd and spoke about the local connection surrounding the story. My brother talked about the things I was trying to accomplish in Colorado and spoke of my frustration concerning efforts to raise money for search and rescue teams. Toward the end of the interview, Arlyn talked about the Amber Alert in Colorado and the role I played in helping it become law. He also discussed my disappointment in losing my contact in the governor's office and spoke about potential ideas in establishing a connection with Governor Ritter.

There are small towns and cities all across this country, places like Haven, Kansas, and Paradise Park, Florida. Or Madras, Washington, and El Centro, California. The odds are that the majority of their populations have never been to Colorado. There's a great chance that most of these people don't know anybody in Colorado either.

Unseen, something was stirring in the room as the two conversations began to converge on a common point. Had a quantum fiber stretched from the front range of the Rocky Mountains to settle in our small town, its destination deliberate?

Was it possible that a mysterious energy could be generated from a simple act of randomness? Could it have been a planned manifestation surging forward with a purpose and distinct target, or was it an extraordinary act of coincidence contributed to luck? Arlyn wasn't sure, but something was there, and it was about to snap. He spoke, and she spoke, and they shared thoughts and stories about my tragedy.

Silence.

"I think I might be able to help you," Betty replied.

Oblivious to what Betty had said, Arlyn sat in deep thought and considered impossible options. The odds of getting into any governor's office were slim, at best. Betty's words rattled through Arlyn's mind without making sense then began to fall in line. Did she say what he thought she said? Arlyn stared inquisitively, then asked, "Did you say you might be able to help?"

When she replied yes, Arlyn was sure there was no possible way a stranger from a small neighboring town would be able to do anything that hadn't already been attempted. Was she going to send a copy of the magazine to the governor and hope for a response? Arlyn admired her ambition, but even a stunt of this nature had a slim chance at life.

Betty was confident and repeated that she might be able to help us return to the Colorado governor's office. She didn't say she could make a meeting happen; she said she *might* be able to help. A search *might* find a missing person, the purchase of a lottery ticket *might* make one a millionaire, and the Colorado Rockies baseball team *might* win the World Series someday. Arlyn asked how she might provide this help.

There was no attempt to boast or brag. Betty was humble in her statement. "You're probably not going to believe this, but my sister, Barbara, is the lieutenant governor of Colorado."

Snap! We were meant to meet!

She was an angel.

My Gordian Knot instantly fell at my feet as the governor's door swung back open. Jaryd's purpose would not be denied. I was on my way back in, and we had a lot of work to do. Arlyn would end up going to Governor Ritter's office with me, thanks to Betty's sister.

The Beginning of the End

Since Jaryd vanished, I have reached into several directions hoping to find something that would help me with my sanity. There have been several situations where I felt tremendous guilt because I was laughing or smiling, and I wasn't sure it was okay to experience any positive emotions. I had this strange feeling that Jaryd was in heaven watching me, and he would cry every time I laughed. I was convinced he perceived my joy as moving on, and he believed that I had forgotten him. I struggled with this, and each time I experienced any joy in my life, I apologized to him.

I held on to those feelings for three and a half years because I knew the only thing that could bring me true joy would be the discovery of something that would point toward what may have happened to Jaryd. I had no idea that one of the most unforgettable days of my life was just around the corner. Would I finally have the answers to all of my questions, or was I getting ready to take another ride on the rollercoaster of mystery?

On Friday, June 6, 2003, my friend Chuck and I were shopping at an American Furniture Warehouse store in Littleton. As we looked around, a salesperson approached us and asked if we needed any help. While showing us around, our conversation slowly turned to laughter, and we carried on like a bunch of comedians who were trying to outdo each other. The laughter was so loud it was hard to hear anything going on around us. As the roar continued, Chuck reached over and shoved me, yelling, "Hey, Allyn, I think your phone's ringing." I reached down and pulled my phone out of its holder and looked at the number to see if I recognized it. The number didn't look familiar, but I answered the call anyway.

"Hello."

"Hi, is this Allyn?"

"Yes, it is!"

"Allyn, this is the sheriff. I'm sorry to call you right now, but we think we found Jaryd's clothes."

My mouth fell open, my body quivered, and tears welled from my eyes. What was I hearing? What was the sheriff trying to tell me? I replied in a shaky voice, "What do you mean you think you found Jaryd's clothes?"

The sheriff answered, "A couple of men were hiking on the Big South Trail a few days ago, and they found what appear to be Jaryd's shoes, pants, and his jacket. Is there any way you can come down and identify the clothing?"

I thought, *I can't wait that long. That's a two-hour drive!* Then I responded, "Do you have any pictures of the clothing, because if you do, I'll be able to tell if they're Jaryd's by looking at them."

The sheriff said, "Yes, we do. If you give me your e-mail address, I'll send them to you right away."

When I got off the phone, I turned away from Chuck and our newfound friend and broke down crying. I searched for a place to sit because I was trying to digest what I had just heard, and I wasn't sure my legs would hold me up any longer.

Chuck yelled, "Hey, bro, what's wrong?"

I kept walking because I didn't know what to say, and I wasn't sure I could stop crying.

Chuck raced up to me, grabbed my shoulder, and said, "Are you all right, man?"

I gradually looked up, wiped the tears off my face, and said, "That was the sheriff, and they think they found Jaryd's clothes."

Chuck immediately screamed, "What! What do you mean they found Jaryd's clothes?"

I told him about the conversation I had with the sheriff, and I informed him we needed to leave immediately because I wanted to see the pictures of the clothing.

As Chuck questioned me, I turned and walked away because my crying intensified, and I desperately wanted to sit down. After I sat down, I mumbled to myself, *How could they find Jaryd's clothes and not find him? Where's his shirt, and why isn't there a sign of his body? Where exactly did they find his clothes? Why didn't they come across them during the search?*

My mind was experiencing a meltdown as I relived the entire episode again. I told myself to calm down because this wasn't the first time I had been called concerning the possible discovery of Jaryd's clothes. As I inhaled, I felt my lungs expand. The sensation that this was somehow different covered me like a warm blanket, and the significance of this call was beginning to work its way into every cell of my body. This was not like the other calls...my skin tingled with anticipation.

I slowly got up off the couch and looked over at our salesman. Even though I was going through an intense heartache, I felt sorry for him because I could see his pain and frustration as he tried to comprehend what was going on. Chuck turned to him and gave him a quick overview about Jaryd and informed him that I was Jaryd's father. The salesman made eye contact with me and quietly replied to Chuck, "I remember the story, and I prayed that he would find his little boy."

I got up enough courage to look at Chuck and said, "We've gotta get outta here, bro. I need to see those pictures right *now!*"

As we hurried from the store, I threw my car keys to Chuck. There was no way I could drive in the shape I was in. When we got into the car, I sat back in my seat and closed my eyes, knowing I would see my son that very moment. This was a technique that helped me deal with the anxiety that was trying to destroy my life. All I had to do was close my eyes, open my mind, and Jaryd was there with me. With my eyes closed, I reached over and grabbed Jaryd's little hand and thought, *It's okay, little brother. Daddy's right here with you.*

I kept my eyes closed for most of the way home because I knew the twelve-mile trip would seem like a lifetime. I prayed, questioned how Jaryd's clothes were found, prayed some more, and then prepared myself for the moment when I'd open my e-mail. Was I about to observe the clothes I hadn't seen in over three and a half years? If this was the truth I was about to face, I wasn't sure how I would handle it. My driveway came into view as the rest of my life strangely loomed before me. As we parked, the burden of the past thirteen hundred days crumbled at my feet as my spirit fought to free itself from Jaryd's secrets.

I jumped out of the car and ran to my computer to check my e-mail. I nervously fumbled with my keyboard while I tried to type in my ID and password. There it was, the message read, *Forward photos.* I quickly moved my curser over to the e-mail the sheriff had sent and clicked on it. The sheriff wrote the following message to me:

> Allyn,
>
> Attached are five photos, front and back of the top, one of the pants, and two of the shoe. Over the years, we have had several discoveries of bones, clothing, etc.—none of which panned out. However, this seems to match in all aspects.
>
> In some ways, if this is Jaryd's clothing, this is a blessing in that it finally can bring you some closure. On the other,

I can only imagine it would be devastating in that it denies you any hope. My heart goes out to you, and I'm having trouble even writing this little bit through misty eyes.
God bless!

I appreciated the kind words offered by the sheriff as I scrolled through his e-mail. A picture of a pair of blue pants appeared on the screen, then a picture of a jacket, then a shoe, and another shoe, then a second picture of a jacket. I gazed at my monitor in disbelief. My heart struggled to beat as a kaleidoscope of memories flashed in my mind, each alive for a brief nanosecond. *This can't be true! They're his! They're all Jaryd's clothes!* I had visualized this day on so many occasions, and in an instant, it fell into my lap. I cried and reached out to place my fingers on the computer screen as static electricity welcomed my trembling touch. Jaryd's energy gently surged into my body as our hands finally met again, and I couldn't let go. It became difficult to breathe because my chest felt paralyzed. My gasps for air tuned to broken sobs while I apologized to Jaryd for not being there on that dreadful day. I whispered, "Jaryd, Jaryd, Jaryd, what happened, little bro?" The only answer I heard was the steady hum of my computer.

Chuck didn't say a thing for a few moments because he knew by my reaction the pictures were of Jaryd's clothing. Chuck was very close to Jaryd, and the sight of the pictures caused him to break down and weep right along with me. I stood, put my arms around him, and tried to understand what was happening. I had many questions, but I knew I had to call the sheriff to inform him he had Jaryd's clothing in his possession.

I got up from my desk and stumbled slowly to the phone. I wasn't sure how this next conversation would go, and I dreaded having to be part of it. Reluctantly, I picked up the phone and punched in the sheriff's number and waited for someone to answer my call.

"Hello, sheriff's office, can I help you?"

"Yes, can I speak with the sheriff, please?"

"May I ask who's calling?

"Allyn Atadero."

"Thank you, one moment please."

My hands got cold and sweaty as I waited for the sheriff to come on the line. I thought, *Please hurry. I want to get this conversation over with.*

"Hello, this is the sheriff."

"Sheriff, it's Allyn."

"Hi, Allyn, did you get the chance to look at the pictures?"

"Yes, I did, and the clothing belongs to Jaryd."

"Are you sure?"

"Yes, Jaryd was wearing Josallyn's jacket, and I have Jaryd's jacket right here next to me. They're identical jackets, so I'd recognize it anywhere."

The sheriff proceeded to explain more of the information to me. "The clothes were found a couple of days ago, and we have since sent the search and rescue team up to cover the entire area where everything was found. The team has not been able to find any signs or remains of Jaryd. If you look at the picture of his pants, you can see that one of the legs is missing, but that can be explained. The area where the clothing was found is scattered with tiny pieces of blue material because the birds and rodents in the area were tearing apart the pants and using the material as nesting. The search team is planning to go back up the mountain a week from tomorrow, and you can join them if you'd like."

That was a lot of information to swallow, but I responded, "Yes, I want to see the area where the clothes were found."

The sheriff continued, "Allyn, you know we have to put out a press release because the media is going to want to hear about this. I know you're probably having a hard time dealing with this right now, so if you'd like, we can put off the release until Monday."

His consideration of my condition was much appreciated, and my answer was obvious. There was no way I wanted or needed the imminent onslaught of media in my house that day. I replied, "Yes, please give me the weekend to comprehend the magnitude of this. I don't want to be bothered, and I need to contact my family."

The sheriff responded, "No problem. We'll put out the press release on Monday, and you try to get some peace this weekend. I'll talk to you later."

"Thank you, Sheriff. I'll talk to you later."

After I hung up, I knew there were a lot of things I wanted to accomplish in the next hour. I needed to call my family and forward the pictures of Jaryd's clothing to them.

I picked up the phone and went through the painful process of calling my mom, dad, and brother, Arlyn. About a minute before I called each of them, I e-mailed them the pictures so they could examine them as we talked. Each of my family members was in complete shock by the news, and each responded to the pictures in a different way. The one person who caught me off guard was my father.

As my dad evaluated the pictures, he said, "There's something about the picture of Jaryd's pants that bothers me."

Being intrigued by his comment, I responded, "Really, what's that?"

My dad said, "Look closely at Jaryd's pants. Are they inside out?"

Wow! He was right. I examined the pants and tried to come to a conclusion of how and why his pants ended up that way.

Somewhat dismayed, I said, "Dad, I think you're right. Jaryd's pants *are* inside out."

The apprehension in my dad's voice became more apparent as it got louder and louder. "How do you think his pants got that way?" his troubled voice asked. "An animal isn't going to take the time to undress Jaryd. If someone tried to take his clothes off, they would grab a hold of his waistband and pull them down quickly. That type of action would turn Jaryd's pants inside out, wouldn't it?"

Oh my goodness, he was right. The discovery of Jaryd's pants had now created more questions, and the scene on the mountain provided so little information about what had happened to him. I talked a little longer with my dad, but I still needed to make the hardest call yet.

I had sent my daughter, Josallyn, to San Diego to visit her mother the previous Saturday, and I needed to call her and attempt to explain what was happening. I was regretting the call because I didn't want Josallyn hurting anymore. She had always hoped Jaryd was alive, and I didn't want to say or do anything to take that hope away. Yet I knew Josallyn would want to know this new information about her little brother. This part of my day was going to take some courage, so I whispered, "God, please be with me." I then dialed her number.

I put the phone to my ear and could hear it ringing. On the other side of the line, I heard a sweet, soft, "Hello, Daddy." Because of the caller ID, she always knew it was me calling, and her voice made me feel as though I was talking to a little angel.

I said, "Hello, honey, how are you doing?"

She joyfully responded, "I'm doing pretty good, Daddy. What about you?"

"I'm not sure, but I think I'm all right."

The other end of the phone was quiet for a few seconds and then she asked, "What's wrong, Daddy?"

Josallyn had the innate ability to know something was bothering me, especially when it came to Jaryd. We had been through so much, and at times, it seemed as if she was the caregiver and I was the child. I can remember the many times she walked up behind me, put her arms around me, and ask, "Is missing Jaryd bothering you right now?" I never understood how she did it, but she was always right.

I continued my conversation with my daughter and said, "Jos, I need to talk to you about Jaryd."

"Okay, Daddy."

"The sheriff just called me, and they found Jaryd's clothes."

"Are you sure they're Jaryd's clothes?"

"Yes, I saw pictures of them."

"Was Jaryd with them?"

"No, honey, there was no sign of Jaryd."

"I guess that's okay then, Daddy?"

"What do you mean?"

"Well, if Jaryd wasn't there, then maybe somebody has him. But if Jaryd is dead, then God has him. Either way, Daddy, Jaryd is either alive or he's with God."

Hearing those words come out of my daughter's mouth made my heart melt, and the tears flowed down my face. The innocence of my daughter allowed her to comprehend the situation with such clarity. Wow, what a thought! Either he's alive or he's with God. Why wasn't it that easy for me?

During my conversation with Josallyn, I told her that Uncle Arlyn and Aunt Robyn were driving up from El Centro, and she informed me that she wanted to come home with them. Her plans were to spend at least one month with her mother, but her heart wanted to be at home with Daddy and Jaryd.

I thought about Jaryd's clothes all weekend, and the situation about his pants kept me up each night. Why were his pants inside out, and where is he? I was baffled because his shoes looked as if someone had thrown them onto the mountain a couple of months ago, and his jacket looked fairly decent. Heck, if a mountain lion had taken him, one would think his jacket would be torn to pieces, and there would be visible bloodstains. At least that's what I believed.

I was so frustrated that I later called the senior wildlife biologist from the state of California and asked him about some of the mountain lion attacks he's investigated. He assured me there would be bones somewhere, and he'd never seen or heard of a mountain lion pulling off someone's pants until they were inside out. Considering the situation, his comments were comforting.

I wasn't sure what to believe anymore, and now, for the first time, I couldn't help visualizing a vicious mountain lion attacking my son and carrying him off into the wilderness for his own private meal. I think about Jaryd standing there, having the time of his life, then suddenly he's faced with a fear he's never experienced. Did he yell for me, or did God take his precious spirit before he knew what was happening?

Each time the mountain lion vision surfaces, I try to suppress it because the image is extremely graphic. This mental picture has a life of its own, and it reminds me of a thief in the night trying to destroy and steal the remaining joy in my life. When the vision attacks, I shake my head in an attempt to obliterate its grip, and then I try to think about the happy times I had with my son. My struggle with this vision is a mental conflict, because the past few years taught me there is a fine line between reality and fantasy, and I was starting to have problems deciphering the difference between the two.

I am not sure how God deals with painful situations that happen on this earth, but if Jaryd was taken by a mountain lion, I'm sure Jaryd's remains were something God didn't want me to see. I wanted to find my son badly, but God wouldn't allow me to be exposed to images that would have a destructive effect on my emotional stability. This would have been a life-long affliction that would have been difficult to overcome.

I didn't know what to think, but I knew the weekend was almost over. The discovery of Jaryd's clothes and the feast the press was about to experience were about to collide in my living room. Once again, I imagined I had everything under control. It appeared that way until I received a phone call from a reporter named Bob that Sunday afternoon.

Bob worked at one of the local television stations, and he claimed he'd heard a rumor that Jaryd's clothes were found, and he wanted to confirm it. I was baffled because this information hadn't been released, and I was curious to find out how he had obtained it. During Bob's questioning, I realized I needed to put a stop to his probing, so I cut him off in the middle of his sentence and emphatically responded, "I have no idea what you're talking about. Who did you hear this from?"

There was no way I was going to let the cat out of the bag because I didn't want to deal with this until the next day. It's hard to explain, but I needed to get into the proper mindset, and I knew I wasn't mentally prepared or emotionally capable of answering his list of questions.

I continued my conversation with Bob, trying to convince him he didn't know what he was talking about when he said, "I got my information from our sister station in Las Vegas."

I thought, *Great, I know who the source is.*

I needed to get off the phone because I wanted to do some damage control before the entire episode came apart. As soon as I hung up, I called one of my reporter friends from the station where Bob worked and gave her a heads-up about the upcoming press release. I told her about my conversation with Bob, and I wanted her to know there was more to the story. I knew Bob's source was reliable, and it was possible he would continue digging until the truth was revealed. I didn't want him to call me again, and I thought I could shut Bob down, so I made her a simple offer; if she could wait, I'd talk to her first. If she couldn't, I wouldn't talk to her at all. She agreed, and I told her I would see her the next day.

I got off the phone and waited a couple of minutes before making my next call. I wasn't sure what to say, but I wanted to talk to my dad because I knew he had to be the source in Las Vegas.

When Jaryd first disappeared, a Las Vegas news station accepted the responsibility of arranging a flight to Denver for my dad. Because they were able to meet his travel needs, my dad promised himself he would respond to their generosity by contacting Deborah Clayton concerning any news about Jaryd. The Vegas station received their information through my dad's innocent attempt to fulfill his obligation.

After speaking with my dad, I confirmed my hunch. If he would have anticipated the domino affect produced by his actions, the call would have never been made until after my authorization was given.

It was late, and time was on the move. Sunday evening was fast approaching. I wanted to hold on to the day because the perils of a long and sleepless night would eventually give way to another torturous flood of microphones, cameras, and curiosity. I looked forward to greeting the morning sun of a normal day.

....

Monday

My past experiences with the media were somewhat tumultuous, but Sunday night's anxiety and dreams produced an intense anguish that weighed heavily on my heart. In the morning, my eyes lazily opened, expecting to meet the surroundings of an ordinary day, but the nausea that jumped me made it difficult to get out of bed. The air in my room was stale and my mouth tasted bitter. My tongue licked at my dry lips as I rubbed my right hand through my disheveled hair. I sat up and kicked my legs over the side of the bed, immediately aware of the dull throbbing in my temples. *Good morning, Monday mourning!* I needed to get to the kitchen and make a date with some coffee.

I walked through the quiet living room and thought about the mass of reporters who would soon overrun it. My expectations were mixed, and I questioned the direction Jaryd's clothes would take us. Would today bring about the end to a tragic story, or would the clothes and their condition interject new theories worth investigating? Either way, the hills surrounding my valley of peace were beginning to swarm with a multitude of questions poised for their attack. The thought of it all caused my chest to tighten. Where was the coffee?

I finally relieved the aching of my body with the hot water of my shower. I got dressed and attempted to make myself presentable for the media, who had no idea they would visit me again today. I wasn't sure when the news of Jaryd's clothes would be released, but I was sure my neighborhood would later experience a parade like few had witnessed. Waiting for the media axe to fall was tedious. Needing some company, I went to find my roommate, Chuck.

I found Chuck downstairs sitting on the couch. I smiled at myself because Chuck looked like how I felt. His appearance was a wreck, and my gut and head were a scrambled mess. As I spoke to him, his demeanor revealed he had no idea about the pending storm. This was probably a good thing because there was no need to have both of us running around the house like the sky was falling. His experiences with the media paled when compared to mine. It was possible he would be faced with a few frivolous questions, but I was facing center stage and the crippling heat of the lights. I had been there before, but today's hurdle was snuggly lodged somewhere between me and my future, and I wasn't sure I could clear it. I needed Chuck to be here for me today, and he would do anything to ensure I made a safe landing. He kept saying, "I'm here for you, bro. Just let me know if you need anything." He really meant it too.

The morning passed without the phone ringing. My anxiety increased as each hour faded away. I was positive every minute would yield itself to the ring of my phone, but the minutes trickled by uneventfully. I paced through the house and prayed for someone to call. I wanted the day to be over because I was consumed by unexplained fear.

I didn't wait long. It was shortly after noon when the silence of the house was disturbed by my first call. I took a deep breath and walked over to look at the caller ID. When I saw the ID, I thought, *This is it.* I slowly picked up the phone and said, "Hello?"

"Hello, can I speak to Allyn, please?"

"This is Allyn."

"Hi, Allyn, my name is Gail, and I work for one of the local TV stations. We just received a press release stating Jaryd's clothes were found and I was hoping we could come by and talk to you?"

"No problem, what time do you want to come by?"

"We'll be there in about an hour."

I wasn't sure how many more calls I'd receive, but knowing the press release was out brought me a little relief. I put the phone down, and before I could walk away, it rang again. It was Mary, the friend I had talked with the day before. She said she was around the corner and wanted to know if she could come over right away. I told her yes because Gail was coming over in about an hour.

That was the wrong thing to say because Gail was from another network. Mary was frustrated when she said, "Allyn, you can't talk to Gail until after five. Her station airs their news an hour before us, and we want to break the story. Please get out of the house and go to a movie or get some dinner. I'll pay for it."

I didn't know what to say. These reporters were my friends, but I didn't want to get caught up in the "We broke the story first" race, and I couldn't leave because I knew there would be several more phone calls the next hour. I told Mary I'd think about it, and then I hung up.

When Mary arrived, she pleaded her case again and asked me to put Gail off until after five. I told her there was no way because I wanted to get the day over with and didn't want to put anything off any longer. She tried to ask again, but the phone started a perpetual ringing that lasted for several hours. It got so bad that Chuck had to grab a notebook and write down everyone's name, phone number, and the time they were coming. As the afternoon passed, the knocking at the door sounded like an out-of-control woodpecker. Chuck took the phone outside and set up a makeshift command center as he made everyone line up to wait for his or her turn to speak with me.

The questions were like a broken record. "How did you feel when you first heard about Jaryd's clothes?"

"Have you had the chance to go up the trail to the area where Jaryd's clothes were found?"

"What do you think really happened to him?"

"Does this bring your family any closure?"

Closure. What the heck is closure? Closure is a word someone made up because they will never understand the feeling one experiences in a situation like this. Do people really believe I could experience *closure*? I should have answered that question by responding, "Sure, I have closure now because Jaryd's clothes were found and they're safe. I feel a lot better, and I can sleep at night because…wait a minute! Where's my son? What do you mean 'closure?' There's no such thing as closure here! I may never see my son again, and that should make me feel better? Come on! Have a clue! Nothing will make it feel better!" That's what I should have said, what I wanted to say, but I didn't.

There were several situations where I wanted to say one thing, but I didn't want anyone to think I was an out-of-control maniac. At times, there were media personnel who approached this story as if this was their big break at investigative reporting. Their questions were not directed at my feelings or reactions to recent events, but they believed their cleverness would expose the truth the rest of us diligently worked to conceal. I have learned this approach can make one look rather ridiculous, especially when one has no idea what he is doing.

When Jaryd first disappeared, several TV stations dispatched reporters to the trail's head so reporting could be conducted from ground zero. These reporters were the top of their class, as professionalism and responsibility ruled the air of the Big South Trail. For the majority, I felt great admiration and respect, but there were exceptions. One guy irritated the life out of me because of his amateur antics and insulting questions. The first time this fellow called on me, I couldn't believe a reporter could be so animated. He asked questions as though he had written the media guide for reporting, and he placed himself in a caring and compassionate light. He would go into the local mountains and stage an area as though it were the trail where Jaryd had vanished, but none of us were allowed on the trail. His stories were extremely sensationalized, but his efforts to deceive the viewing public were exemplary. He may have fooled a lot of people about his ability to report from the scene, but I knew he was miles away from the Big South Trail. I learned to avoid this guy, and his tactics caused me to lose respect for him and his network. Contrary to his belief, my son's tragedy was not a big show; and if he calls, I won't talk to him.

As the afternoon faded away, I realized I didn't have the time to comprehend who I was or wasn't speaking with. The media spectacle was incredible, and the street outside my house looked like a parking lot for all of the news employees in the Denver area. During the chaos, one of my neighbors came up to me and said, "Allyn, why don't you tell them to leave you alone?"

That was a good question, but there was no sign of my son, and I knew the media would be responsible for splashing Jaryd's face on millions of televisions. Although my neighbor believed he was watching out for my welfare, and I appreciated this, he didn't realize some of the reporters had been by my side since Jaryd had vanished. I owed a dept of gratitude to them, and time with me was payment in kind.

....

The day slowly came to an end, and one would think the worst of the week was over. The cat was out of the bag, and for the most part, I was sure we were approaching the bottom of the hill with the clothing issue. I had no idea the theme song for the next few days would be "We've Only Just Begun," by the Carpenters. Heck, I was tired and wanted to go to bed, close my eyes, and finish the day off with a wonderful dream about my son. I had no idea the greatest calamity loomed beyond the horizon.

I went to bed early because I knew I had to get up at the crack of dawn and drive an hour and a half to the sheriff's office for a formal news conference concerning Jaryd's clothing. I hadn't had the opportunity to see the clothes firsthand, but I was looking forward to touching them. To me, the clothes were my son himself. The last time I had seen his clothing was the day I put them on him, but seeing them up close would bring reality back to the nightmare I had been trapped in for the past few years. It was a bittersweet thought, *Would Jaryd's clothes reveal answers to my questions, or would they bring death to the hope I'd been holding onto?*

The arrival of Tuesday morning was a welcomed occasion. I had the feeling things were about to change because as the sun climbed into the western sky, it looked a little brighter. To me, events were taking place with a purpose. I could distinguish a pattern that was beginning to emerge, a form with a confidential message of hope that was being ushered into my inner heart. The day Jaryd walked into the unknown, he was three years and nine months old. Only a parent would know this modest fact. Jaryd's clothes were found almost three years and eight months later. The days with my son were almost equal to those of my search, and I wanted to believe this was Jaryd's way of communicating with me. His plan to demonstrate all was fine.

It didn't take long to ready myself for the day. Anticipation stimulated my nerves as I allowed my newly found enthusiasm to wash over me. Chuck understood what I was going through because he also had a special relationship with little Jaryd. Being one of the links that held the Poudre River Resort family together, Chuck shared the strenuous journey for answers with me. This adventure had mocked my sanity as we attempted to untangle the clues that had been left behind. Thankfully, Chuck was familiar with the man I was and the one I had become. Because of our ties, he insisted on accompanying me to Fort Collins so he could ensure I would be all right. He was correct; I didn't want to be alone.

Shortly after leaving the house, I slipped one of Pink Floyd's CDs into my stereo. The familiar strumming of the guitar began as I listened to "Wish You Were Here." The music and the lyrics were a comfortable reminder of the trip I had taken a few years earlier, and it became the official theme song for Josallyn and me. The melody brought back memories of Jaryd, and it gave us hope we would see him again.

I was in the middle of singing, "So you think you can tell heaven from hell," when I was interrupted by the ringing of my cell phone. It was a friend of mine who worked as a cameraman for one of the local television stations.

"Hey, Allyn, this is John!"

I replied, "Good morning, John."

"Allyn, are you on the way to the sheriff's office yet?"

"Yes, I'll be there in about forty-five minutes."

"Do you think I can meet you there, because my station manager wants me to ask you if you'll allow us to get footage of the moment you first see Jaryd's clothes? I know it will be emotional for you, so if you don't want me there, I'll understand. Honestly, it's not my request. I'm only asking you because I was told to."

Wow, I needed personal time with my son, and this wasn't the time for me to share my emotions. I waited for about ten seconds and responded, "I'll let you know how I feel when I get there."

John replied, "Thanks. I'll see you in about half an hour."

I shared the conversation with Chuck, and with a gaze, he questioned, "You're not going to let him do it, are you?"

I shouted back, "No, no way. I want to be by myself when I see Jaryd's clothes." At that moment, we sang the song as if we hadn't missed a beat. I played the song over and over until we pulled into the parking lot at the sheriff's office.

I parked my car and took several deep breaths. I had a lot to think about, but even for me, it was difficult to control the emotions I was experiencing. The thought that I was about to touch the clothing that belonged to my beloved son made my skin crawl. I cried, wiped the tears away, tried to smile, and hoped it was actually my son himself. I wasn't sure if I was ready, but I knew it was time.

I opened my car door, slowly stepped out, adjusted my clothes, and walked toward the front door of the sheriff's office. About ten steps into my trip, John approached me and waited for the answer to his question. I looked John in the eyes and said, "Not this time, John. I need to do this one alone."

John understood exactly what I was saying and responded, "I know. I'd do it the same way." We shook hands, and then I continued my trip toward the front door.

When I entered the front door, an employee of the sheriff's department approached and asked if I was Mr. Atadero. After informing her that I was, she led me to a room that was about the size of an average bedroom. As I waited, I became somewhat nauseated because this was a place I had never felt comfortable. The sheriff's office was giving me the chills, and if it wasn't for the fact I had official business here, I would have run away as fast as I possibly could. My past experiences with the sheriff's department were cordial at best, and although I had grown close to several members of the department, I never experienced a true sense of being treated with courtesy, respect, dignity, and compassion by others.

I sat down and impatiently waited for the arrival of Jaryd's clothing. The few minutes that passed seemed more like hours. I grew restless and wondered what was taking so long as the yearning to hold Jaryd's clothes intensified. *Come on, I want to see Jaryd's clothes. God, please have somebody bring my son's clothing to me!*

A few seconds later, the door opened, and a deputy entered the room carrying a poster board that had Jaryd's clothing displayed on it. The clothes were covered with some sort of plastic wrap that was designed to prevent the evidence from being touched.

The deputy introduced himself and asked me a few questions, but I didn't hear much because I was transfixed on the clothes. I wanted to reach out and touch them, but the plastic wouldn't allow my curious hands to explore what was rightfully mine. As my eyes searched each item for clues, I thought, *Jaryd's jacket and shoes look pretty good considering they have been lying out in the wilderness and exposed to the elements for almost four years.*

My eyes wandered toward my son's tattered pants, and I wondered what everyone would think when they saw them. I guess it's not what they would see that bothered me; it's what they wouldn't see that would conjure up many questions. One of the pant legs was missing, and it looked as if something had torn the leg right off the pants. I knew this wasn't true because the sheriff had already informed me that rodents and birds in the area had been busy for the past few years, slowly dismantling Jaryd's pants to build their nests. This was evident because the area where the clothes were found had small particles of blue material scattered all over the ground.

I sat down because something else about Jaryd's pants bothered me. I thought about the original picture the sheriff had sent me, and I knew for a fact, Jaryd's pants were inside out. I focused on Jaryd's pants again and realized they were displayed with the right side out, as if someone had just turned them right-side-out and laid them onto the display board. I didn't understand why they hadn't displayed the clothes the way they were found.

My thoughts were interrupted when two more deputies and the sheriff entered the room. We chatted a little, and then the sheriff told me about potential evidence discovered on Jaryd's jacket.

"Allyn, we found two different types of hair on the jacket, and we're not sure what that means."

I laughed to myself and said, "I do. One set of hair belongs to Jaryd, and the other belongs to Josallyn. The jacket was originally Josallyn's, but she outgrew it and gave it to Jaryd."

The sheriff replied, "I guess that could be it."

We talked a little more, and then I asked the sheriff the question that was really bothering me. "Sheriff, Jaryd's pants were discovered inside out. Why aren't they displayed that way?"

The sheriff was quiet, and with a perplexed look on his face, he tried to digest the question of the moment. He looked at his subordinates and said, "I'm not sure what you're talking about. I didn't know his pants were inside out. Did any of you know notice this?"

The deputies looked at each other and replied in unison, "No, we didn't know that."

I quickly jumped in and said, "All you have to do is look at the original pictures you e-mailed me, and it's obvious the pants were inside out. Why aren't they displayed that way?"

Again, no answer was provided.

The conversation quickly changed because it was almost time for the press conference to begin, and we needed to migrate to the room where the media had gathered. As I prepared to leave, the sheriff stopped me and said, "We're not going to have any problems out there, are we?"

I looked at him and snapped, "No, I don't think so."

He gave me a satisfied look and then led me to a room that was filled from wall to wall with media personnel and cameras. For most people, this would have been somewhat intimidating; but by this point, it was routine for me. I stepped to the front of the room where there was a podium and chairs and sat and looked out into the audience. Everyone watched each move I made.

Being a teacher, it reminded me of the times I had to review a science unit with my students. They would look at me as though I was the king of knowledge, and I held the answers to all of science's great questions. Through me, they could fill their empty cups.

Today was different. These people weren't my students, and I was the king of nothing. My lack of knowledge about what may have happened to Jaryd was obvious because I sat there shaking my head in disbelief.

The sheriff walked up to the podium, and before he got into his speech, he introduced me, several deputies who were there, and the two gentlemen who found the clothing. As he rambled on, he talked about the two different types of hairs found on Jaryd's jacket and acted as if these hairs were critical to the case. He then said, "Officials will test the two hairs in order to determine their origin."

My mouth fell open and I thought, *Wait a minute, didn't we just have this discussion about ten minutes ago, and didn't I tell you the hairs probably belonged to Josallyn and Jaryd?*

He had no plans of diverting from what appeared to be his preplanned speech. He failed to mention the fact that the jacket originally belonged to my daughter, Josallyn. I guess he didn't think the information I had provided was pertinent enough to relay to everyone else. I sat there and bit my tongue because I'd given my word we wouldn't have any disagreements in front of the gathered media, and I had no desire to challenge him on his presentation. However, my state of aggravation increased because I thought the facts were once again being misrepresented. I thought, *Should I say something when it's my turn to speak, or should I keep my mouth shut again?* It's interesting to watch a master spin a story. I wanted to speak out, but I knew this wasn't the time.

When it was my turn to speak, I tried to make eye contact with everyone, and I calmly said, "I'm not certain Jaryd is dead because the clothes don't tell me what may have happened. Let's not say, 'This is it.' We need to understand that all that was found was his clothing, and it proves nothing. Regardless of how I feel, I'd give anything to hold my son right now."

When I was done, I got the generic, "How do you feel, what do you think, and does this bring closure?" The canned questions got the typical canned answers, but there was one question I was willing to answer. "Allyn, have you been to the spot where Jaryd's clothing was found, and if not, will you be visiting the area soon?"

I gladly responded, "Not yet, but the search and rescue team is going back up this Saturday, and I'm going to join them."

When the press conference was over, I retreated into one of the back rooms to discuss the details about Saturday's planned search. I was somewhat sideswiped when I was cornered and asked if I'd be willing to sign a death certificate. I thought, *A death certificate? Why would I sign a death certificate?*

I replied, "I didn't know they issued death certificates for clothing."

I was immediately told the given circumstances would allow the county to issue a death certificate, especially if I agreed to it. I was then informed that this action would allow the sheriff's department to close Jaryd's case, and we could all put this episode behind us. They also reassured me that if any new evidence was discovered, they could reopen the case.

I thought about it for a long time. I think an entire second went by before I retorted, "I don't think so! I'm not willing to sign anything just because Jaryd's clothes were found."

I was frustrated because I believed they thought they could get me into a room and strong-arm me into waving a white flag and surrendering. No way, not this boy! My son was still missing, and his clothing didn't prove a thing.

I got up and left the room and relayed the information to anyone who would listen. I couldn't believe they wanted me to sign a death certificate.

How Were Jaryd's Clothes Found?

The following information was taken from the official sheriff's report. The two statements below were provided by the two hikers who found Jaryd's clothing.

Statement from Hiker One

On June 4th 03 my hiking partner and I discovered clothing we believed to be Jaryd Tarakero. We had known of his disappearance Oct 2nd 1999 and had hiked Big South on 3 other occasions prior to, and often commented on this childs disappearance. While we were hiking past camp 2 we deviated off the main trail and wound up to the east of it. At this time, we thought the main trail was further to the east of us so we started bush wacking in that direction. As we hiked we climbed the side of the gorge, and early on we realized the trail lay to the west of us—we were having fun bush wacking, so we continued up the side of the Mtn. heading east. Within about 20 minutes of our climb up, my hiking partner called out to me that he had found something and could not believe it. When I saw a shoe—I immediately assumed it was the 3 year old boy who had been reported missing 3 years earlier. We came across another shoe, sweat pants and shirt within about 30 feet of the shoe. These items were photographed where they were located having not been touched. The shirt and one shoe were placed in a bag and brought to the sheriffs department June 5th along with the photographs at 1:00 p.m.

Statement from Hiker Two

Day hike up Big South Trail stayed on main trail up to camp I went to camp 1 then bushwacked up and to the rt of camp I hit a skee rock field and went mostly straight up. Spotted kids sneaker. Then 2nd sneaker was spotted then blue sweat pants? And then beige fleece vest. All within 20' of each other. Looked above for any signs of any thing—nothing. Looked below the 4 items nothing. Started to sleet and rain went back to trail head and we drove home went to sleep then work and then sheriffs office.

I was a little confused by the two statements because there were a couple of things that didn't make a lot of sense. First of all, the second hiker stated they found both shoes, but the first hiker said they only bagged one shoe and a shirt to take to the sheriff's office. Why didn't they take all of the clothing, and where is the shirt? Maybe he is calling the jacket a shirt, but I don't know.

The part of the statement that really frustrates me is, "We drove home went to sleep then work then the sheriff's office." If I were hiking and found what I thought was something important about a missing child's case, I'm going straight to the authorities, not to sleep and then to work. I don't understand that behavior at all.

The Fight for the Truth

I had no idea the rest of the week would generate a battle for the truth. Philosophies, beliefs, and reputations would be challenged in order to persuade the general public into believing one story over the other. I was a bystander watching as the two forces came together to produce their side of what they believed happened. What a story it was turning out to be. What was going to be found, and what would never be found? Our expert is more of an expert than your expert. Yes, the mountain was now willing to speak, but would it be more of a whisper than a shout? The clash took place on national TV, and within the next four days, a winner would be declared. As I observed the confrontation, I believed this entire situation had nothing to do with what really happened to my son. Jaryd's plight was being lost in the hysteria of the situation.

I was under the impression that a few deputies at the sheriff's department were trying to convince everyone there was enough evidence to issue a death certificate. I was under this belief because I watched one of the national networks interview the sheriff about the latest developments in the case. He tried to reiterate the fact that he believed there was a good chance the remains of Jaryd would never be found.

After the network anchor finished interviewing the sheriff, they brought on a well-known forensic pathologist named Dr. Michael Baden and asked him what he thought about the situation. I wanted to hear what he had to say because I recognized him from different news clips. I knew Dr. Baden was the Chief Medical Examiner for the City of New York from 1978 to 1979. He also worked on the O. J. Simpson and Claus Von Bulow trials, the death of John Belushi, and investigated the remains of Czar Nicholas II and his family members. His credentials are incredible, but the statement at the bottom of his web page gave me the most comfort because it says, "Remember, we answer to God." This statement is great because I don't believe God would have said on national television, "Leave me alone. I'm already tired of this story."

During the interview, Dr. Baden's words gave me comfort and hope. He said, "Finding someone's clothes doesn't prove they're dead. If the boy were killed by a mountain lion, there would still be human remains, even four years later."

I thought, *Wow, finally someone is looking at the situation the same way I am.*

I sat there listening to every word that came from his mouth because I knew this man had the knowledge and experience to know what he was talking about, so I moved closer to the TV. I didn't want to miss a thing.

Dr. Baden continued, "If you're attacked by an animal of any kind, they won't leave sneakers behind in good condition, and they won't consume your entire body. As a forensic pathologist, I would expect to see some type of human remains, even four years later."

What he said next sent chills racing down my spine. Dr. Baden said animals don't remove clothing, and he believed the way the clothes were found left open the possibility of abduction. He thought an abductor could have removed Jaryd's clothes and kept them during the search and then put the clothing back at a later date.

The new gauntlet was set, and the challenge to find the truth was back upon us. I don't believe the sheriff knew Dr. Baden was going to be interviewed after him, but I'm sure he was watching, and I bet he was completely frustrated and upset with everything Dr. Baden said.

The next night, I discovered my hunch was correct. The sheriff was back on TV, and he was trying to disclaim everything that was said by Dr. Baden the night before. He made a comment about being a backwoods sheriff not knowing what he was doing, and then he went on to explain his belief. The sheriff told a story denying a test that was performed by the Colorado Bureau of Investigation where they buried a pig in the wilderness, and four months later, no evidence of the pig was found. I knew differently though. If the pig had been wearing clothes, I'm sure they would have found his shoes, jacket, and pants.

Dr. Baden was interviewed after the sheriff again, and he restated the fact that something would be found. His exact words were, "You would at least find a tooth." This would become a profound statement, and it would conjure up more questions about the whereabouts of Jaryd. Could it be the stage was now set for me to find a tooth? Now wouldn't that be a strange coincidence, and would this type of discovery be a signal from my son?

Dr. Baden was my latest hero. His thoughts and beliefs were intriguing, and I wanted to talk to him. I searched everywhere until I found a way to contact him. It took about thirty minutes of digging before I found what I thought was his phone number, but I didn't think I'd be lucky enough to talk directly to him. I knew it was a shot in the dark, but I grabbed my phone and dialed his number. I listened as the phone rang, and then I heard a quiet yet secure voice say, "Hello?"

I shook with anticipation when I asked, "May I speak to Dr. Baden please?"

"This is he."

"Hi, Dr. Baden, my name is Allyn Atadero, and I'm the father of the little boy who was lost in the Colorado Mountains."

"I'm glad you called. How can I help you?"

"I want to thank you for the information you've provided, and I want you to know it gives me comfort."

"Thank you, but I want you to keep one thing in mind. Finding someone's clothes isn't a reason to issue a death certificate. Don't let them talk you into it because there's no evidence the little boy is dead. Make them find something."

I reassured him I wouldn't sign a thing unless they could accurately determine the status of my son. He then told me he was there for me, and he wanted me to call him if I needed anything. When I hung up, I had a hard time believing I had talked to Dr. Baden. I was overwhelmed knowing there was a person out there who wouldn't jump to conclusions and try to convince me that wrong was right, especially if its purpose was to close this case.

It was Thursday, June 12, and the struggle to determine if remains would be found on the mountain continued to heat up. The philosophical tug-of-war didn't influence my beliefs because I thought the facts were clear, and there was no real sign of Jaryd. I wanted to believe my son was still out there, so I focused my thoughts on the area where the two hikers had found his clothes. I had a lot of questions going through my mind, but I wanted to know how far apart his clothes were, and I needed to see the blue fibers that were strewn all over the mountainside.

I didn't want to tackle this adventure by myself, but I didn't know whom to turn to. I sat down and read the notes Chuck had written and noticed I had received a phone call from Andy Lovato, the president of the Child Recovery Network in the Denver area. I'd never met the man, but Chuck had scribbled next to his number, "Wants to know if he can be of any help." I thought about it for an hour and then decided to give Andy a call.

Andy told me he had heard I was going up the mountain on Saturday and wanted to know if he and his son-in-law, Manuel Herrera, could accompany me. Andy informed me they were experts in child recovery, and he assured me they would do whatever it took to help me locate any remains of my son, if they were there.

I was intrigued and needed someone on the mountain who wasn't afraid to be upfront with me, so I invited Andy and Manuel along contingent on receiving permission for their inclusion from the under sheriff.

After our conversation, I immediately called Eddie Newhard, the under sheriff, to ask if he would allow a couple of experts to join me on Saturday. Eddie was a captain when I originally met him, but he was moving up the ladder in his department. I had no trouble talking to him because I knew he wanted what was best for my family and me. After listening to my question, he happily replied, "I don't have a problem with that, Allyn. You go right ahead and bring those two guys up with you. Just let the person in charge know that we talked, and I gave my approval."

I knew he would agree to my request because our prior relationship demonstrated he was a reliable man. I was excited and couldn't wait to call Andy and give him a formal invitation to join me on the trail.

After talking to Andy, I was pumped and ready to attack the mountain on Saturday. I closed my eyes, thought about climbing the trail, and tried to visualize a positive outcome to the search. As my spirits rose, anticipation swelled within me because I knew something good was going to happen that day. Saturday was still a day and a half away, but I was ready to leave right then.

....

Saturday morning quickly arrived, and I hoped the day would bring answers to a lot of the questions I've had for the past three and a half years. I was extremely anxious and looking forward to sitting in the exact spot where Jaryd's clothes were found. I know it sounds strange, but something inside kept telling me Jaryd and I would have some sort of connection the moment I arrived at the spot where he may have perished. But on the other hand, if he was still alive, I knew I wouldn't feel a thing. As Jaryd's father, this was something I was looking forward to.

I knew I wasn't going to be alone because I had about ten friends, including my father, who were going up the Poudre Canyon with me. We were all looking for answers, and we thought we could deal with any new information that was presented. Regardless of the outcome, I was hoping today would be the final chapter to an incident that had consumed me with pain ever since my son's disappearance. Today was going to be rough, but it had to be done.

It was 7:00 a.m., and five of my friends had already arrived at my house. We were aware we needed an early start in order to meet the search team at nine thirty on the mountain. The rest of the group was driving from different areas, so they decided to meet us at the entrance of the Poudre Canyon.

The group at my house joked around because the anxiety level kept rising as each minute passed. They were trying to lighten the mood and help me relax. After all, if we had the choice, none of us would be taking this trip. We were doing it because it was something we had to do, and there was a creepy kind of therapy going on since we were all related in one way or another due to Jaryd's life. Today wouldn't bring healing; it was more like taking a drug that was created to relieve intense pain generated from our sorrow.

We piled into a couple of vehicles and started our long journey toward the Poudre Canyon. We had two different destinations that were significant to our voyage. One was Ted's Place, a gas station at the bottom of the mountain, and the other was the Big South Trail. Even though Ted's place was only forty-nine miles from the trailhead, the time it would take to get there would be over an hour due to the winding roads in the canyon.

When we left my house, the group in my car started off with a lot of small talk, but the closer we got to Ted's Place, the more focused we became. Our game plan was simple: we wanted the truth, regardless of what it might be. It was something that had eluded us for a long time, and we didn't want to see it go on any longer.

The trip appeared to take a lifetime because I was looking at my odometer every two to three miles, and it seemed as if we'd never get there. My emotions were twisted in knots because I was looking forward to going up the trail, but the canyon brought back bad feelings, and I hated being there. I struggled because there were also a lot of good memories, and it was obvious the good and bad were fighting to dominate my current mental state.

As we got closer to our first destination, I couldn't wait to get into the parking lot to a take a short break. My body was full of nervous energy, and I needed to burn some of it off so I wouldn't go crazy on the second half of the trip.

There it was. I made a left onto Highway 14 and then a quick right into the parking lot of Ted's Place and parked my truck. I turned the vehicle off, got out, and looked around for my other friends who were going to meet us here. While I was scanning the parking lot, I saw an emergency vehicle parked next to a car on the far side of the parking area. The man in the car was talking on a cell phone and waving his hands in an animated fashion. During the conversation, the man in the emergency vehicle got out of his truck and into the car with the man on the phone.

I thought, *I wonder if one of those people can tell me who's in charge of today's search.*

I walked the twenty yards in order to ask them if they could point me in the right direction. When I got closer to the car, the man talking on the phone looked over at me, hung up his phone, and laughed with the man sitting next to him. I didn't think anything of it, and I continued toward the car.

When I got there, the window was rolled up, and the man who was on the phone made no effort to roll it down. I thought that was kind of awkward, but I knocked on his window anyway. He rolled down his window and yelled, "I don't want to talk to you, and I don't want anything to do with you," then drove away from me and parked in a different place.

I thought, *What the heck is his problem?*

My anxiety spiked, and I could feel my blood pressure rising because I was getting angry. Who was this guy, and why did he have to treat me the way he did? I didn't care. I was going to talk to him anyway.

I walked toward his car again, but this time, I was ready for his rude, childish behavior, and I was going to let him know how I felt. I walked up to his window and observed both men laughing like they were a couple of bullies claiming their turf on the playground. I doubled up my fist, banged on his side window, and screamed, "I just want to ask you a question."

The man, who was a member of the sheriff's department, rolled his window down about four inches and shouted, "You don't listen very well, do you? I told you I don't want anything to do with you." Then he rolled up his window and drove away again.

By this time, I was steaming and was ready to hurt someone. Nobody deserves this sort of ridicule from a public servant. I followed him with my eyes and watched to see where he'd park this time. He parked next to the emergency vehicle, where he originally was, and he let the other man out of the car. I didn't want him to leave, so I jogged over to his car, banged on the side window again, then roared, "Hey, man, I just want to ask you a question. Do you have a problem with that?"

The man looked at me and finally responded, "I'll answer your question if you leave me alone."

I thought, *I'd have left you alone a long time ago if you would have answered my question in the first place.*

I looked at him and asked, "Do you know who's in charge of today's search?"

He snapped back, "I am, why?"

I replied, "The under sheriff gave me permission to bring a couple of guys up the trail with me, and he wanted me to inform you that he'd already given his approval."

For the life of me, I never expected his next response. He yelled like a mad man, "You're a liar! I'm in charge of this search, and I make all of the decisions around here. And besides that, the under sheriff would have never told you that."

It took every ounce of my energy to hold me back, and then I yelled, "Who are you calling a liar? Why don't you pick up your phone and call him and verify what I'm telling you?"

He cracked, "My phone doesn't work out here, and I wouldn't call him anyway because you're a liar."

I thought his last statement made him look kind of ridiculous, so I questioned, "If your phone doesn't work, then why were you just talking on it? Are you afraid to call him because you might learn I'm telling you the truth?"

He got mad, rolled up his window, and without saying another word, drove out of the parking lot toward the trail. I stood there and told myself I was tired of the way they were treating me, and I wasn't going to put up with it anymore. At that moment, I realized people needed to know the truth, and I was ready to give it to them.

I walked back to my car, and my dad could tell I was irritated. He looked at me and asked, "What was that all about?"

I explained to him what had just happened, and then I reached into my car and grabbed my cell phone so I could call the under sheriff. I looked at my phone and realized my signal wasn't strong enough to place an outgoing call, so I threw it back into the car and ran into Ted's place. The manager was my friend, and I knew she would let me use her business phone.

When I entered the front door, my friend approached me and said, "I thought I'd see you today, Allyn. Is there anything I can do for you to make your trip a better one?"

After I explained to her what had happened in the parking lot, she led me to her phone and said, "Have at it."

When I picked up the phone, I could see my hands were still shaking due to the anger that was flowing through my body. I took a deep breath, dialed the under sheriff, and then waited for him to answer. After several rings, an answering machine responded. I waited until the end of the message then calmly yelled, "I talked to your man in charge, and he treated me with disrespect, and then he called me a liar. You need to contact him right away because I'm tired of being treated like this, and I'm ready to blow this entire situation out of the water. He needs to know you gave me your approval, and he needs to back down."

After I got off the phone, I walked out to my car and tried to calm myself because I knew I had enough anger in me to cause a heart attack. I took several deep breaths and then told everybody to saddle up because we were going into a hostile environment to search for my son.

I relived the parking lot situation over and over all the way up the mountain. Why was that guy such a jerk, and do people really believe they can act anyway they want just because they're carrying a badge? I can never imagine having the audacity to treat another person the way he treated me. Then I remembered that insensitive comment, "Are you as tired of this story as we are?" He must have been part of the "we" group.

I fumed all the way up the mountain, and for some reason, I expected a brawl when I arrived at the Big South Trail. My negative demeanor was directly attributed to the search commander whom I no longer trusted. I couldn't believe this man had my best interest after he displayed his true colors by yelling at someone he'd never met.

We pulled into the parking area at the base of the trail, and I could see a man and a woman standing next to a sheriff's vehicle. My blood boiled again because they walked toward me, and I could tell it was the same thug who had verbally attacked me at the bottom of the mountain.

The lady approached me, stuck out her hand, and said, "Hi, Mr. Atadero. Is there anything we can do to make today easier for you and your family?"

I replied, "Yes, you can keep that jerk away from me."

She gave me a stern look and said, "We don't want any problems now. We're here to accommodate you, and we want to make this day as easy as possible for you."

I glanced at the man and asked, "Why are you trying to be so nice? Did the under sheriff talk to you?"

The lady jumped in and said, "Yes, the under sheriff informed us about the conversation he had with you concerning your two friends helping with today's search."

It was kind of funny watching the deputy backpedal and squirm while I looked at him. He knew I was right, and I could tell he hated it.

I looked at the man, grasped his arm, and said, "Why don't you take a walk with me."

I didn't want to say a word to him until we were far enough away from the rest of the group. When we were a safe distance away, I looked him in the eyes. "You're a jerk, and you owe me an apology for calling me a liar."

He was caught in a dilemma, and he had a hard time owning up to any of his previous behavior. All he said was, "I was told I was responsible for everything that takes place up here today, and no one would interfere with my search. If there were any decisions that needed to be made, I'd be the one to make them."

I argued, "That doesn't give you the right to call me a liar and treat me like a criminal. I'll tell you what. I'm willing to forget it happened because we need to work together today."

We agreed, and then the deputy gathered his equipment and raced up the mountain ahead of us. I was tired of being treated as if Jaryd's case was somewhat trivial, and I was keeping people from the important stuff.

The female deputy escorted my family and me up the trail to where campsites two and three are located. The trail leading to the campsites goes up and down and meanders along the river, and at times, it gets very narrow and is somewhat tricky to navigate. The beauty of the area can cause accidents because one wants to take in the scenery, and when one does, there's a good chance of tripping over something.

Several hundred yards up the trail, I looked down and saw the words "We miss you, Jaryd" inscribed into the dirt. I stopped and took a knee because it tore my heart out, and I couldn't hold back my tears. I was hammered emotionally, and it took a couple of minutes to get up enough strength to continue my journey. Another hundred yards up the trail, I felt like I was hit with an arrow because I saw another message that was written into the dirt. This time, it said, "We love you, Jaryd." Man, I wasn't sure I could go any farther. This was killing me, and it was slowly extrapolating every ounce of energy from my body. I was depressed, but I was glad to see there were others who cared for Jaryd, and they wanted my family to know their feelings. I saw these messages several more times before I came to the end of my journey.

After the forty-five-minute hike, we approached an area about five hundred feet below the spot where Jaryd's clothes were found. I walked around a few trees, and I saw several media personnel, waiting for me to arrive on the scene. I didn't exchange many words with them because there wasn't a lot that I hadn't already said, and I knew they didn't want to talk to me until I retreated back down from the search area.

A few minutes later, two members of the search and rescue team approached me and informed me that my safety was their responsibility. They handed me a helmet that was hideous-looking and asked me to put it on. I looked over at my dad and laughed because I know I looked ridiculous, and I knew everyone would laugh at me as soon as I started my climb. I guess this was the perfect way to loosen up because we were all stressed.

I was ready. One of the members from the search team led the way up the steep embankment, and the other stayed behind me in case I slipped or fell backward. I was in great hands because these two experts brought water, gloves, and a walking stick for my disposal, and they stopped about every two to three minutes to see if I needed a rest. I was fine; I just wanted to get to where the clothes were discovered.

On the way up, Andy and Manuel from the Child Recovery Network checked every nook and cranny as they searched for clues that would possibly yield information concerning Jaryd. I was excited to have them with me because I knew they were searching as if Jaryd was their own child.

As I climbed, I felt a special kinship with my guides. They were awesome, and they were determined to get me to the search area in one piece. I lost my footing several times and almost fell, but the two people wearing the bright orange shirts saved me from the imminent danger that continuously surrounded us. I was amazed because these strangers loved what they were doing, and they performed their jobs with passion.

We climbed over boulders, under fallen trees, and through different types of plants that had their own way of reaching out and causing pain. On my way up, I thought about the different scenarios that could have taken place, and I became more baffled. I thought about Jaryd, and there was one thing I couldn't get out of my mind. Jaryd hated wearing socks and shoes, and he preferred to play barefoot all the time. The day he disappeared, I had to force him to wear his shoes, but I couldn't get him to tie them. If a mountain lion attacked Jaryd then dragged his body up the side of this mountain, his shoes would never have ended up in the area where his clothes were found. It's impossible, and I'm sure it never happened. Someone or something could have dragged, pulled, or carried me today, and if my shoes were untied, I would have lost them within the first ten feet of my trip.

The higher I climbed, the more I paused and scanned the area, looking for any missing parts to the puzzle. I found it strange because most of my son's clothing was found, but his T-shirt was still missing. I kept shaking my head back and forth because I couldn't understand how and why someone would be on this part of the mountain in the first place. Who, in their right mind, would want to hike up here if they didn't have to? Not me!

We climbed for another five minutes then we heard voices, and we could see people walking about one hundred feet above us. I picked up my pace because I desperately wanted to touch the ground where my son could be resting. My emotions were extremely acute because if Jaryd were here, I wanted to feel him.

Finally, I stepped onto an area that had little flags marking the areas where Jaryd's clothes were found. I looked around and saw small particles of blue material scattered all over the general search area. The actual spots next to the flags looked as if the ground had been moved about and sifted through by someone searching for that elusive tooth Dr. Baden had talked about.

I stood there and tried to comprehend everything because the entire scene wasn't making a lot of sense. About a minute had passed when a deputy, the one who called me a liar, approached me and asked if I'd like to help with the search. I was happy to see that he was being somewhat amenable, but I looked at him and said, "I don't think so. I'm going to sit down on this rock for a couple of minutes and try to figure out what happened up here. After that, I'm getting my butt off the side of this mountain."

The deputy acknowledged my comments with a shake of his head. "I understand."

I sat down, looked back to where we had just come from, and saw the river flowing below us. It looked as if the water was several miles away. My spirit calmed as I took in the majestic scenery that surrounded me. I closed my eyes and thought, *Jaryd, if you're here, you sure picked a beautiful place to rest.*

My emotional silence was broken by the cracking of the deputy's radio. I opened my eyes and tried to listen to the conversation he was having with one of the searchers on the other end.

"Yes, Mr. Atadero is here...You found something...We'll be right there."

I couldn't believe what I was hearing. I arrived here less than two minutes ago, and they find something. I'm no dummy, but one of two things had just happened. Either Jaryd had waited for his daddy to arrive before he revealed himself, or someone waited for me before they discreetly found something worth celebrating.

I knew this was the second day searchers had combed the area, but this must have been one of the greatest coincidences known to man. This was happening too fast, and it was making my head swim. A part of me actually thought I was being set up because I was trying to figure out why the deputy wouldn't let me look into his car. His actions didn't make any sense.

The deputy looked down at me and said, "Come on, they found a tooth. Let's go check it out." Now wasn't that the biggest surprise of my life. My mind couldn't let go of how coincidental this was.

I hastily got up off the rock and followed the deputy about twenty yards until we came upon a group of people. These people were standing around an area that looked like a foot-wide wash with a tiny log stretching from one side to the other. They quietly talked and pointed at something sitting on top of the log. It was strange because the closer I got, the lower the chatter became. They were acting as if Jaryd himself were stretched out across the log.

As I got closer, one of the searchers pointed to the log, glanced at me, and said, "Do you see it? It's a tooth."

I looked down at the tooth, and tears flowed down my face. I wanted to reach down, pick it up, and hold it as close to my heart as possible. I glanced up, looked at everyone, and I noticed the entire group was crying along with me. Like a child, I looked at the group and asked, "Can I touch it?"

One of the ladies said, "Yes, go ahead and pick it up."

I slowly reached out and touched the little tooth as if it were the very first time I had touched my son. I then picked it up, put it into the palm of my hand, placed my hand over my heart, and cried.

While I was in a faraway place with my son, another voice said, "Did you see what else is laying there? If you look closely, you can see the top of a skull lying just below the log, sitting upside down."

She was right; it looked like a small bowl filled with dirt and pine needles. I tried to figure out how it got there, and I came up with my own little theory. I know this is going to sound kind of sad, but when one searches for the truth, all things must be considered.

If an animal had come across Jaryd's body, it must have dragged his skull to a higher location and placed it above the area where it was actually found. If a thunderstorm blew into the area and created a flash flood, then the small river could have carried the skull down the wash. As the skull rolled down the mountain, the top part of the skull (as it rolled upside down) could have hit the log and broken, leaving both the tooth and skull cap where we found it. If this scenario is correct, then the rest of the skull must be in the same wash, but farther down the mountain.

I couldn't stop myself from analyzing everything because I wanted to understand all the evidence as it was presented.

I reached down and picked up what I believed to be the top of Jaryd's cranium and cuddled it as close to my body as possible. Some men would be horrified if they were put into my situation, but I was happy because I had part of my son with me once again.

No, this wasn't the answer I was hoping for; but it was my son, and Daddy didn't want to let go this time.

I spent about five minutes caressing what I thought was my son, and then I reluctantly handed everything back to the search team in order for them to process the body parts as evidence. I thanked everyone who was involved and then said, "It's time for me to go down the mountain and tell my dad what you found."

I located one of my escorts and told him I was ready to go back to where my family and friends were gathered. On the way back, I stayed toward the area where the water had carved a gully because I wanted to find my son's shirt. The area was treacherous, so we moved in a southward route away from the directional flow of the wash. This bothered me, but I knew it wasn't going to be my last time up here.

About thirty minutes after we started back down, my escort and I could hear voices coming from the area where the media had gathered. We knew we were close, so we stopped to reflect upon what we had experienced up in the wash. My escort looked at me and asked, "Are you sure you're ready for this, or do you want to wait here for a few minutes?"

I leaned toward this gentleman and reached out my hand and thanked him for everything he had done for me. As I acknowledged his heroic efforts, our eyes filled with tears of pain, frustration, and camaraderie. I hugged him and said, "Let's do it. I need to get this over with."

We walked side by side the rest of the way down the mountain until we reached the staging area. When we arrived, the commotion got loud, and everyone acted as if I were Moses coming out of the mountain holding onto the Ten Commandments. My family and friends were anxious to hear if anything was found, and the media scrambled to capture the first words out of my mouth.

I stood there, quietly searching for the correct words, waiting for my emotional pain to subside. I knew if I opened my mouth too soon, no one would be able to understand my weeping words.

I took a deep breath and tried to pull myself together, yet I couldn't formulate any comprehendible sounds.

My dad looked at me and asked, "Well, did you find anything?"

I reached out, grabbed my dad's arm, and tearfully said, "We found him."

As soon as those words left my mouth, I could hear everyone sighing and moaning loudly as they tried to come to terms with what I had just said. Some of my friends broke down right where they were standing, and some of them surged toward me, seeking comfort.

My dad lost it. He pulled away and yelled. "No! No! No! Don't tell me you found him!" Strangely, our family had held on to the hopes that Jaryd had been abducted. How often does one find himself in a place where he hoped one of his children was actually the victim of abduction? *It's a crazy world*, I thought.

I cried more and more, and then I howled, "We found a tooth and a part of a skull."

The media rushed over and pushed their microphones toward me and wanted to know every detail about our discovery. Their actions didn't bother me because they were my friends, and I knew they were searching for the same truth that had been eluding my family and me for the past three and a half years.

After answering several questions, I looked for my dad to see how he was doing, but I couldn't find him. I had no idea what had happened to him until Butch informed me that he took off running back down the trail, heading toward the parking lot. He said, "Don't worry, Chuck followed him to make sure he's all right."

Disbelief floated throughout the area because everyone believed we wouldn't find a thing today. They were right; we came to see the area where Jaryd's clothes were found. We could have never imagined Jaryd was there with them.

I thought, *Wow, everything's happening too fast. I need to get off this mountain and go home.* A couple of days ago, I was shopping for furniture.

I gathered all my friends, said a prayer for my son, and then headed back to the bottom of the Big South Trail.

On the way down, I passed several members of the search team, heading up to the search area to continue with their mission. Two men who walked by had a strange affect on me because they wouldn't make eye contact. I could tell they were having a hard time holding back their tears. I didn't know why, but I later learned these two men were on Jaryd's original search, and the past few years had been a real struggle for them.

When I arrived at the bottom of the trail, I saw my dad and Chuck sitting on the back of my tailgate having a conversation. I walked up to my truck and asked my dad, "What happened to you?"

He replied, "I didn't know how to handle the situation, and I wanted to be alone."

Chuck laughed and jumped in, "Yeah, I saw him take off running, so I chased after him. Did you see the deputies riding up the trail on horseback?"

The entire group responded, "Yes."

Chuck pointed to his knee and continued, "I fell down right in front of them and tore a hole in my pants. It was embarrassing. I got up and asked them, 'Which way did grandpa go?' They pointed me in the right direction and told me I wasn't far behind him."

His story caused us all to laugh, and it was kind of nice because we really needed something to lighten the somber feeling that was in the air.

Jaryd had been found in the area where Seaux had said the search needed to be refocused. Almost four years later, I wanted to know why my request had been turned down. I could only wonder how different this story's ending could have been if that area had been searched. Seaux, who had been a member of the Army's Special Forces, was highly trained in tracking enemy militia. Seaux reenlisted shortly after Jaryd's search, and he is currently in the Army as a Green Beret.

The following is part of an e-mail from Seaux that can be read in its entirety in the Afterword section of this book. Also included are the maps he provided me.

> I was lucky to be the primary tracker for the search of a young autistic boy named Evan Thompson last Memorial Day. The search was successful, and I told the boy's uncle about Jaryd and how I had been waiting to heal my own emotional wounds for a long, long time.

Seaux's map and alternative outcome will always be a part of me.

The following Sunday was Father's Day, and several reporters spent time with me because they wanted to know how I was handling the day without my son. I knew there were a lot of fathers receiving phone calls from their children, and others were spending the day with theirs, but I wasn't that lucky. Sure, I was extremely happy knowing I had my beautiful daughter; but I missed my little buddy, and nothing could change that.

Later, I went outside on my deck and prepared my own Father's Day barbeque. It was nice because I looked up into the heavens several times and asked if my son were there, and if he was, I wanted to know if the tooth we found belonged to him. If it did, I was willing to celebrate the fact that my son was having a great day with his Heavenly Father.

I know my heart has the right to be heavy and sad on occasions like Father's Day, but when I put everything into perspective, I'm proud of my son, and I'm thrilled that my grandparents in heaven are taking care of him. He brought me a lot of joy, and I know I'll see him again some day.

I walked over to my barbeque grill and opened it up to check the status of the pork that was cooking. As I turned the meat over, one of the reporters asked me, "What is the true meaning of Father's Day, and what does today mean to you?"

I laughed to myself and then replied, "I'm probably the only father in the world who can say I wanted to find a dead son for Father's Day. Isn't that sad? It's kind of strange, and it's hard to comprehend, but this is what I've been praying for."

I stopped, paused for a few seconds, and then continued, "The true meaning of Father's Day is being able to smile when you think about your children. Today, my children made me smile." I'm not sure that was the response he was looking for, but it was true, and there was a strange kind of joy that came along with today. I wasn't happy, but at least I could look up into heaven and smile.

I thought, *What makes a dad anyway?* There are those who have been called a father because they are biologically related, yet they never experience the joy of fatherhood. There are those who experience fatherhood, yet they are not biologically related. We, as fathers, regardless of how that title was given, need to step up and love our children as the gifts they are. Lord, thank you for allowing me to be the father of my children.

Test Results from Jaryd's Clothing

Jaryd's clothes, tooth, and skullcap were rushed to the Colorado Bureau of Investigation for scientific analysis. The reason the remains were rushed was because they needed to be identified for potential prosecution. His shoes were in good shape, and they led me to believe they could have been placed back on the mountain at a later date. Could this be the reason they were looking to prosecute someone?

I wasn't sure how long the tests would take, but in my heart, I didn't think they would find anything. When I looked at Jaryd's clothes, I couldn't visualize any type of animal attack because I didn't see any signs of it. First of all, I had been told that a mountain lion would attack and feed on its prey by entering the abdominal area. If this were the case, I would expect to see Jaryd's jacket torn apart, and there would be a sign of some type of mutilation or carnage. There are no signs of this, and Dr. Baden said he had never heard of a wild animal undressing a child.

On July 14, 2003, the Colorado Bureau of Investigation issued its lab report concerning the analysis completed on Jaryd's clothing. When I read it, I found it interesting because it did not provide answers to any questions concerning my son's disappearance. Most of the conclusions were consistent with what I believed they would find, and that is nothing at all.

Serological examinations (searching for the existence of blood) were performed on Jaryd's shoes, pants, and fleece jacket, and they didn't find a trace of blood on any of these articles. I was told his clothing was out in the elements too long, and the rain and snow must have washed it all out. I don't believe there ever was any blood present to be washed out. I continued reading the report, and it addressed the fact that hairs, which appear to be of nonhuman origin, were found on everything, including the skullcap. What kind of hairs were these, and from what type of animal were they? I believe if any of the hairs were from a mountain lion, the media and everyone would have been told about it. Since this is not the case, none of the hairs must have been from a mountain lion.

The Evolution of a Theory

The meaning of life is whatever we choose.

—Jonathan Lockwood Huie

Several years have passed since we first released our story about Jaryd. The life of this story always has its way of evolving, and I have discovered there are many people out there who are willing and eager to innocently propel it in different directions. I've watched as it flowed from theory to theory and have decided to make an attempt to shed light on some of the questionable areas that have taken root on the Web or on television. For example, when a child goes missing, I still see stories about Jaryd's disappearance. I'm often the person the media contacts when they are looking for insight on what a family may be going through. I appreciate the media's involvement and their attempt to keep our communities safer, but why they frequently close with Jaryd being the victim of a mountain lion is beyond me. There is no evidence to remotely suggest this happened, yet it seems to not only be a point worth hanging on to, it becomes one some feel needs to be promoted. I know there are people out there who probably disagree with me, so allow me to present my evidence to the mountain lion delegation.

I have revisited this scenario many times myself. I don't do it looking for confirmation of a mountain lion encounter Jaryd may have experienced. Since I'm convinced this did not happen, I continuously search for clues that may yield undiscovered answers. As much as I dislike thinking about this, a mountain lion confrontation would have been violent and I'm positive it would have left evidence to prove the incident actually took place, yet there is none. For those who remain supportive of this conclusion to Jaryd's life, let's go back a step. Jaryd's clothes were found fairly intact. There were small animals in the area that were using Jaryd's clothes for nesting. They were not ripped, torn, or cut in any fashion. The remains of the clothing were tested, and there was no blood found on them. There were no mountain lion hairs discovered either. This is profound enough to put an end to this theory, yet it continues to be repeated.

For those who are not ready to come to my side of this argument, Jaryd's clothes were found inside out. I'll repeat this: they were found inside out. His shoes were in great condition. Mountain lions, or any other predator for that matter, do not remove clothes so that they are left behind in the condition they were found. No physical evidence and being found inside out should be enough to close this argument.

After hearing the drum beat so often for a mountain lion attack, I contacted one of the leading experts in mountain lion research. After sharing Jaryd's story with him, this is the response I received.

> I find it most unlikely that a mountain lion could turn pants completely inside out. I won't say impossible, but I would say 99% unlikely. Inside out with no trace of blood would be about as close to impossible as I can imagine.

Knowing these things, how does one logically support this conclusion? I know there are people who would suggest that one predator is capable of leaving behind this type of scene, and

I agree. This is why I leaned toward it being a man. Or was it something else?

As of this writing, Josallyn is nineteen years old. She recently read Missing for the first time, and she remembers the story and her brother, but the details have since faded. A tattoo of a small hand holding her young lady hand adorns her shoulder. Josallyn is as much of this story as me and Jaryd, and she can often be driven to the Internet for the purpose of initiating her own searches. On May 17, 2013, Josallyn went to my office and turned my computer on. After launching Google, she slowly typed the letters of her brother's name then hit enter. As usual, a collection of pages populated her screen followed by a number of additional pages at the bottom. Meticulously, she began to follow each trail hoping to stumble upon new information concerning her missing brother. Sifting through words with fixed eyes, she followed several trails with nothing new. "Hey, Dad, come here. You're not going to believe what I just found."

Not knowing what she was talking about because I had no idea she was researching Jaryd, I got up and went to my office to look over her shoulder.

"Dad, check this out. I can't believe these people are talking about Jaryd in this forum."

I squinted and tried to read the screen. Before I could follow what was being discussed, Josallyn continued, "They don't believe Jaryd was taken by a mountain lion. They think something else happened to him."

Her voice was all I needed to stir my curiosity, because at this stage of my life, that's usually all that happens when something new is discussed. These are little morsels that bring back the taste of the event enough for me to take another bite, so I began to read the forum myself. What I found and what Josallyn stumbled upon was a friendly debate by two fellows concerning the disappearance of Jaryd. Both people used old articles to present their cases to the other, followed by their takes on the matter.

> So, yea, a squirrel could have put his tooth on the log where his head was. And, his shoes etc., were removed, but no body? Do cougars declothe their victims before they eat them? Do they untie their shoes?

This person was making my argument, but why? I continued to read.

> You mean the same Jared Atadero whose tracks stopped a few feet away from a set of mountain lion tracks, and whose clothes had mountain lion bite marks in them?

Jaryd's tracks stopped a few feet from those of a mountain lion, and they had bite marks on them? I have Jaryd's clothes in my possession, and there are no bite marks on anything. The tracks that had been seen were those of a bear.

> Yep, that certainly sounds like Bigfoot.

I stopped reading and noticed Josallyn smiling at me. "Bigfoot," I said. "They think Bigfoot took him?" That was a new one for both of us, and who am I to question the beliefs of others? One evasive story was being weaved with the other, and I supposed there was no evidence to suggest that Bigfoot didn't take him. It made more sense than the mountain lion theory.

DNA (Do Not Ask)

Jaryd was released from the hospital on January 4, 1996, two days after he was born. I was so excited because I now had a wonderful son to compliment my beautiful daughter. I can remember holding him in my arms as I proudly walked through the lobby of the hospital. I didn't have much on my mind as I made my way out because my entire focus was on Jaryd. Almost to the door, I was suddenly stopped by a nurse who had taken it upon herself to create a human roadblock. Arms stretched out before her and waving her hands in my general direction, it was obvious she was a little irritated with me.

"You can't leave this hospital with that baby until you prove you have a car seat!" she proclaimed.

I chuckled to myself because I realized she was only doing her job, but she wasn't budging. I smiled at her to reassure her that I wasn't a threat and replied, "I don't need a car seat. I live about a half mile from here, and I'm talking my son on his first walk." I could hardly control my enthusiasm. This was the first of many moments we would share.

Jaryd's story was full of mysteries—some that could be solved, some that couldn't, and one that was a secret waiting to be unveiled.

As a parent, I needed to know if the cranium and tooth that were found belonged to my son. It was a simple request. Was Jaryd dead or alive? I've tried for the past fourteen years to solve the mystery of Jaryd's disappearance, but my hope waned as each day passed. Was it that important to know the cause of his fate?

The years have come and gone, and my life has seen several changes, especially when I look in the mirror. I'm not the same person I once was because the pain and frustration I experienced caused me to question reality. In a way, they opened my eyes and allowed me to see things differently. Why did things happen, and was someone trying to protect me throughout this entire event?

I can't answer those questions, but I know the passing of time softened my heart in many ways. I now try to put myself into the position of others who were forced to live this horrific story with me. I want to be empathetic and to understand the total picture, not just my side and how I feel. Sure, mistakes were made, but not with the intent to hurt or mislead my family from the truth. In reality, I hope there is a lesson here for everyone involved.

The truth, whatever it may be, has a way of being elusive. It can be sitting right in front of one's eyes, but if one's eyes are closed or if one is looking in the the wrong direction, it is never seen.

On June 4, 2003, hikers found the tennis shoes, jacket, and pants that belonged to Jaryd. On June 14, the top of a small skull and a molar were found about 150 feet away from where the clothing was found. This discovery set off a new chain of events that would take ten years to unravel.

Was it Jaryd? I didn't know, but a DNA profile would provide the answer to the question everyone was asking. It was my understanding the DNA residing in the cranium would magically identify the body parts as Jaryd's. I'm not sure how it works, but I knew I would have a conclusive answer within weeks.

A month had passed, and I was still waiting for the results of the DNA test. I had no idea how long it would take, but while I was waiting, Kobe Bryant, from the Los Angeles Lakers, was arrested on July 4, 2003, for allegedly sexually assaulting a nineteen-year-old woman in Colorado on June 30, 2003. You might be thinking, why and how does this relate to Jaryd? On July 2, Kobe Bryant voluntarily submitted to a DNA test, and it was reported that it would only take about two weeks to get the results.

The local media jumped on the story, and several people asked why it was taking so long to get the results from the cranium, but Kobe's results would only take a couple of weeks. I had a reporter from channel 4 news call me, and she asked that exact question. She wanted to know why Kobe's DNA took precedence over Jaryd's, and she wanted to know how I felt about the situation. She was right. I thought the same thing, and I wanted to know what was taking so long.

This is where the story becomes more entangled with the greater series of events that were unwinding. Later that night, channel 4 news had a story about Jaryd and Kobe. It was sad, yet it was kind of funny because I thought Jaryd had his hand in making this story happen. The broadcast started with a picture of Jaryd then switched to Kobe. They flashed back to Jaryd's picture and then switched to video of Kobe making a slam dunk with the basketball. Jaryd's pictured flashed back on the screen, and the reporter asked, "Why does Jaryd have to wait so long for his results, yet Kobe gets his right away?"

After the question, they showed another video of Kobe taking a three-point shot attempt, then the story finished with Jaryd's picture on the screen.

The reporter had asked a valid question, and it intrigued me. Why? Because Jaryd knew I was a lifetime Laker's fan, and Kobe was one of my favorite players. It was as if Jaryd was saying, "Hey, Dad, look at me. I'm on TV with Kobe and the Lakers."

I couldn't get my little man out of my mind because I could see him smiling with excitement. I was a proud father seeing my son with the Lakers on that day.

I patiently waited for three more months, and on October 24, 2003, I received the results I'd been waiting for. The test indicated the remains were likely Jaryd's, but it couldn't provide a hundred percent confirmation. The test did indicate the DNA was consistent with a child conceived by Jaryd's mom and me, but I was told the test was inconclusive because the DNA was "significantly degraded." The degradation was due to the four-year exposure of the remains to the elements.

The test was inconclusive? That was baffling because I was hoping for something different. I didn't want someone telling me it could be Jaryd. I wanted to know, beyond a reasonable doubt, it was him!

In hindsight, I should have stopped there and moved on. I should have been happy with the results and thanked all those involved for their hard work. But I didn't! I continued my pursuit for the truth, not knowing I was walking toward something that was beyond my comprehension.

I waited for a few years, and I questioned the results of the original DNA test. What if the results were wrong, and Jaryd was alive, waiting for me to rescue him? That thought drove me crazy because there were too many scenarios that needed to be resolved.

On April 12, 2006, I contacted a DNA specialist out of Ohio, and I sent him the following e-mail:

> Dr. Bruno:
>
> I found your name on the internet and I was hoping you could answer a question for me.
>
> My son was missing for almost four years before a tooth and a skull fragment were found. The sheriff's

department completed a DNA test and sent me the following information:

DNA was analyzed by PCR technology at fourteen loci. The DNA profile developed from the tooth revealed a mixture of DNA at a level below criteria necessary for interpretation. After numerous attempts and using several DNA methodologies, there was an insufficient quantity of quality DNA obtained from the skull fragment to generate a complete DNA profile. However, the DNA profile is from a male individual and is consistent with the DNA profile expected from the offspring of the parents at a single loci. Based on the profile developed at the single loci, 88.6% of the population of biologically capable reproducing parents are excluded as the potential parents. The other loci gave no results.

Can one make a true analysis of DNA by examining only one loci?

Can you please help me?

—Allyn Atadero

I waited for about an hour, and below is part of an e-mail I received from Dr. Bruno:

Hi Allyn,

You have my sympathies regarding the search for your son.

There are two things about the information you provided to me that strike me as being not quite right. First, a sample from a tooth should not be a mixture (which means that it contains the DNA of two or more individuals) if the tests and extractions were performed correctly. At the very least, a mixture for such a sample would mean that some contamination occurred and DNA testing labs are usually very careful to avoid any possibility of contamination/ mishandling of samples. Second, the genetic markers that are used for the purpose of human identification are called "loci" in the plural but an individual marker is referred to as a "locus" (singular). While attorneys and lay people are not sensitive to the difference between the singular and plural form of that word, professionals who work in DNA testing labs are almost always hyper-sensitive to it and rarely use them incorrectly.

It is not that unusual for no DNA profile to be obtained from a sample that has been exposed to the environment for extended periods of time or for the DNA profile that is obtained to be a partial profile. It is possible for a single locus to be used for the purposes of parentage testing but that usually comes at the cost of diminished discriminating power for the test (and that is consistent with the 88.6% number you were told). The more loci that were examined, the greater the power of the test and larger and larger fractions of the general population could be excluded as being possible parents.

The information Dr. Bruno provided was interesting because I had no idea the mixture of DNA from the tooth contained the DNA of two or more individuals. What does that mean, and was the tooth related to the cranium that was found?

Dr. Bruno was an expert at reading the "electropherograms" that were generated during the testing, but he could not perform a new DNA test for me.

My wife, Debbie, and I were involved with several Missing Children's organizations, and we were called upon several times to help other families locate missing loved ones. In June of 2005, we were at the Colorado Capitol building, participating in Colorado's annual Missing Children's Week. After speaking at the event, my wife and I were introduced to a nice gentleman from the Center for Missing and Exploited Children. As we casually spoke, we told him about the original DNA test that was performed on the cranium, and he said he could arrange for another test through the University of Northern Texas.

I could hardly sleep that night because I was excited, and I couldn't wait to get up in the morning and send the cranium to him. Could this be the answer I'd been praying for?

I waited for a couple of months before making my first phone call to see if there were any DNA results. I was told we were in line, waiting, due to the large number of cases that were in front of us, and I would receive a call when the results came in. I waited another month and called again, but Katrina destroyed our hopes.

I had no idea Mother Nature would intervene and create problems for Jaryd's case. Hurricane Katrina hit the Gulf Cost on August 29, 2005, at 8:00 a.m., killing 1,836 people and created one of the largest forensic identification efforts our country has ever seen. The identification process was somewhat arduous, and several bodies needed DNA testing for proper identification. It was really bad. Three years after Katrina, there were over forty bodies that had not been identified.

My frustration continued to grow, but it didn't stop me from making my monthly phone call to inquire about my son. I called for several months, but in late May, I was told to quit calling. The person on the other end of the phone said, "You need to quit calling. Move on and realize you will never get the information you are looking for. We're sorry, but this is all we can do, and we've exhausted all of our efforts."

I was dumbfounded because I now believed I would never know if the cranium belonged to my son, Jaryd. I went home and surrendered. I was finished, and I needed to give up.

I got up the next morning and struggled as I recalled the conversation I had the day before. I thought, *I will never know the truth, and I need to find something else to focus on.*

I sluggishly got ready for work, not realizing I would receive more information about Jaryd later that afternoon.

When I got to work, the day lingered, and my depression grew as each minute passed. I wanted for the bell to ring so I could go home, find a quiet place to sit, and contemplate the conversation I had the day before.

When the bell finally rang, I quickly walked to my car and started a drive that would be interrupted by a phone call from the Center for Missing and Exploited Children.

About five minutes had passed when my phone rang. I answered the phone, and it was Jim, the gentleman who had talked with me the day before. He asked, "Allyn, what are you doing?"

I replied, "I'm in my car driving home."

He calmly said, "Why don't you pull over? I have some information for you."

I pulled to the side of the road, and I asked him what type of information he had.

His answer surprised me when he said, "It's him!"

I was baffled, and I barked, "What do you mean it's him? What happened overnight? You told me yesterday I'd never know, and now you're telling me it's him. I don't get it...it doesn't make sense. You told me to quit calling and move on. Please tell me what happened overnight."

He was as confused as I was and replied, "I don't know what to tell you, and I don't know how they came to this conclusion, but I was told it's Jaryd. I hope this provides closure for you and your family, and you can get some peace knowing it's him."

I thought, *Sure, you tell me to leave you alone, and now you are telling me it's him. I don't believe you, and I feel like you are telling me this to get me off your back.*

I'm sorry, but I didn't believe him, and this information created more consternation for me to process. Why was I called a day later? Was it because my wife, Debbie, contacted Governor Owens and asked for his help? She requested his help because she witnessed the pain I was suffering while waiting almost a year for the results.

I lived with this information for many days. In fact, thousands of days passed before I had the courage to reach out again. I knew science was changing every moment, and the ability to identify DNA had come a long way since the last test. Eight years had passed, and my desire to know the truth was slowly eating away at me.

On August 7, 2013, I contacted a gentleman named Marc Scott Taylor, from Technical Associates, out of California, and I asked him if he could perform another DNA test on the cranium.

I received the following e-mail from Marc:

> I think we can help you with this case. I will need you to send me any remains you have. Teeth, bones, hairs can often be used to establish a profile. I will also need to get any reports of testing that was previously performed. This may assist in the approach we follow.
>
> Sincerely,
> Marc

I sent the cranium to Marc, and I patiently waited five months to get the results. I knew he was a busy man, and I was thankful for any help I could get. As time passed, I received more information from Marc:

> October 25, 2013
>
> Allyn,
>
> I have gotten tied up with some court appearances that required substantial preparation. We have examined the skull cap you forwarded to us and are preparing to isolate DNA from portions of the bone that look promising. Due to scheduling I don't believe we will have results for several more weeks. I will call you with information as we proceed.
>
> Sincerely,
> Marc

January 7, 2104

Allyn,

We seem to have a fairly large amount of DNA, but with inhibitory substances. We are evaluating it to proceed with cleaning it up before amplifying and typing it.

—Marc

Marc called me on January 22, 2014, to inform me of the DNA results. He said, beyond a reasonable doubt, it was Jaryd. This information took the breath out of me, but it was also somewhat calming because I no longer questioned Jaryd's whereabouts.

Life has a strange way of connecting the dots, but this was a coincidence that pulled me back to the earlier DNA test. I had no idea, but I later learned this was the same company that performed Kobe Bryant's DNA test years before. I'm very thankful to Marc and the employees of Technical Associates.

In the following paragraphs, my daughter, Josallyn, shares her thoughts on her brother's disappearance.

A Sister's Perspective

By Josallyn Atadero

I never truly believed Jaryd died on that mountain when he disappeared on October 2, 1999, at least not at the hands of an animal or natural occurring circumstance. Growing up without my younger brother, I always had faith he was still out in the world somewhere. The little evidence we had didn't seem to support the fact he lost his life on the trail. I never considered the possibility Jaryd was attacked by a mountain lion, or that he fell and hit his head; maybe he drowned in the river or died of hypothermia. These situations didn't seem probable, and because of that, I never entertained the idea one of these circumstances truly could have stolen my brother's short-lived life. Awaiting the results of the final DNA test didn't steer my opinions in any different direction. I was almost positive the results would come back, and we would hear that the remains found on the mountain were not Jaryd's at all; that these results would cause some celebration in me; a new search for brighter answers; Jaryd was alive in the world somewhere and I would find out where he was and bring him home to all he had missed in the fifteen years he had been gone.

That January day when the results finally came was no different. As I heard my dad's side of the conversation, I suddenly understood the look on his face and the shakiness in his voice. As he hung up the phone, I had that falling sensation people often have in dreams and I felt my insides rush into my chest. Spinning and twisting through a dark void that seemed to be infinite, I physically felt the blow of the news impact me. I didn't want to cry. I had so strongly believed this would not be the answer we would hear, I failed to remember the other possibility: Jaryd was indeed gone. He wasn't out there waiting to be found anymore; it was like the ending of a search that had lasted my entire life, although it had already finished years ago. I had lost all chances Jaryd was still somewhere out in the world. Was this actually the end? Jaryd may not physically be here anymore, but I know he left clues for our family to find, in hopes we will eventually understand the last day of his life. While the search for answers is not as optimistic as the search for Jaryd himself, it is one that will bring Jaryd home in ways that no one else would understand. Closure doesn't come from knowing Jaryd is gone. In fact, I don't believe closure will ever be a part of my life.

While Jaryd is absent from the world now, my belief remains strong Jaryd was not stolen from us by mere chance: by the animals or terrain on the rugged mountain where he disappeared. The assurance of his death only sparks a new fire; a longing to find the remains of Jaryd left behind in his final moments.

Through the years I have witnessed the revealing of many secrets by Jaryd. The puzzle is complex and I am confident my brother has more to share and the telling of his story is far from complete.

Josallyn lost her brother on October 2, 1999, and because of the results of the last DNA test, I officially lost my son on January 16, 2014. The past fourteen years have been filled with too many questions that created lifelong pain. I'm not sure why I was chosen to take this walk, but it was a journey no man should be confronted with. How can one survive the turbulence and storms that are generated upon this earth? I'm not sure, but I did. My story did not shake my faith; it only made it stronger. I realize no man can survive hell on earth without God, and I'm looking forward to what he has planned for the rest of my life. I forgive all who have caused my family pain, and I hope they forgive me if I have caused any consternation in their lives.

Jaryd, thanks for sharing your little secret. I love you.

Walking Through the Open Door

What does it actually mean when a case is closed? It means the investigation stops and the effort to find out the truth slowly wanes. In Jaryd's situation, his case was closed the day they found his clothing on the mountain top. His clothing gave no clues to what might have happened, but to most involved, his clothing provided proof he was there. Or was he?

In Jaryd's situation, investigators made every effort to close the case—for good! One problem, there was no evidence that indicated, with a hundred percent accuracy, what had happened. The lack of evidence generated many creative theories. Some investigators search for evidence that supports their theory, and others search for evidence to create a theory. Either way, these theories are eye-opening, intriguing, and sometimes hard to understand or believe.

I find it interesting because each theory had a few things in common. For instance, they all believe the tooth found on the log was planted, and his clothing was put up there at a later date. They believe the tooth didn't belong to Jaryd, and that's why the DNA generated from the tooth was contaminated. I've had many questions about the tooth myself, and its size looks to be too large to come from a three-year-old. I could be wrong, but then again, stranger things have happened.

Without any answers, the door remains open, and the search for the truth continues.

....

On April 6, 2014, I was searching the Internet for any new information concerning Jaryd. About ten minutes into my search, I found an article about a book titled *Missing 411*. The article was a book review that talked about missing people, and it mentioned my son. I did a quick search on the book, and I found a website called the CanAm Missing Project. I clicked on the link and read the following:

The CanAm Missing Project

The first website dedicated to understanding the complexity and issues of searching, rescuing and investigating people missing in the wilds of north America.

About Us

CanAm Missing is a group of retired police officers, search and rescue experts (SAR) and other professionals that are dedicated to researching, on scene investigating and generally understanding the issues associated with people who go missing in the wilds of North America. This has typically been a project that is intensely worked by search and rescue teams starting when the victim is reported lost and usually continuing for the following 7-14 days, the case then flounders in a file cabinet. After years of reading thousands of SAR reports, speaking with dozens of victims, we believe the paradigm of this effort needs change.

The project initially started as a meeting with a park ranger and slowly evolved evolved into a study on missing people who vanished in the wild, many under highly unusual circumstances. We found that MANY of the cases we've researched, parents and relatives of the victims believe a kidnapping had occurred. Law enforcement and the media usually do not publicize concerns of kidnapping or abduction when the missing can be explained through traditional means. There are too many of these cases to ignore and there is a consistency to the stories.

Federal agencies are harboring statistics and reports on the missing that need to be intensely studied and applied to the topic for future application. We have applied much of what we've learned and documented this in "Missing 411" and would encourage every SAR coordinator and manager to read it.

I was extremely intrigued about the information presented on the CanAm Missing Project website, and I wanted to contact them. I wasn't sure if they would respond, but I decided to send them an e-mail because I wanted to know if they could provide any information about Jaryd. I let them know I was Jaryd's father, and I would appreciate it if they could contact me.

I was surprised when I received the following e-mail on April 7, 2014:

Allyn

We did receive your e-mail through our website.

I first must say that writing about Jaryd, obtaining his case from the sheriff, having our team travel to the site 4X and later writing about it was a life changing event. Each of our investigators are seasoned law enforcement professionals and we were each bothered by many aspects and facts surrounding the case and loss of Jaryd. We cannot ever understand the the pain and suffering you have gone through. Our prayers are forever with you and your family.

Thank you for reaching out to us.

I am always interested in what others have to say.

—Dave

I quickly read the e-mail and I replied right away:

Dave,

Thank you for responding to my e-mail. I'm not sure what happened to my son, Jaryd, but there are a lot of things that don't make sense. For instance, Jaryd's pants were found inside out, and I've been told by a couple of mountain lion experts that mountain lions don't pull clothing off of someone and leave it there.

My brother and I wrote a book about Jaryd's disappearance .... The book details everything my family and I experienced during and after the original search. I would love to send it to you because I hope there is someone out there who can help me find the truth.

What is the best way to get your book? I look forward to reading it!

Thanks again for doing what you do.

—Allyn Atadero

Our conversation continued:

Allyn

I have your book and have read it numerous times.

There are more unusual aspects to your son's disappearance besides what you've noted. We obtained the crime scene photos from the sheriff and many of the physical attributes to what was found at the scene don't make sense.

I live in Morrison. Perhaps we can meet and I'll give you my book.

—Dave

Morrison is less than fifteen minutes from where I teach, so we decided to meet the next day at a local restaurant. I wasn't sure what to expect or who I was looking for, but I couldn't wait to meet Dave.

I walked into the restaurant and slowly glanced around, searching for this mysterious person with information about my son. I saw a gentleman sitting toward the back, and he stood up and said, "Allyn, it's a pleasure to meet you."

I walked toward him and stuck out my hand to introduce myself. I was surprised when Dave said, "I don't want to shake your hand. After all you've been through, I need to give you a hug."

I didn't realize I was meeting a man who would become a great friend and someone who would become very close to my family.

Dave first told me he knew more about Jaryd's case than I did, and I thought that was a pretty bold assertion. What did I say to him after he made this statement? Nothing. I just shut up and listened. He said he had been on the Big South Trail several times and had read my book. Nothing new there. I've been on the same trail several times, and I wrote my book.

What could David produce that would support his assertion about Jaryd? We talked for several minutes, then David pulled out a large three ring binder that contained everything he knew about Jaryd's case. The binder included several pictures of the clothing, shoes, tooth, and cranium that I'd never seen. I thought, *Who gave you those pictures? I've never seen them before.*

Dave questioned, "You've never seen these?"

I replied, "No. I was told Jaryd's clothing was found in one small location. I had no idea his shoe was up in the rocks and his pants were next to a log. I wonder why they didn't give the pictures to me?"

Dave kind of smirked. "I told you I probably know more about your son's disappearance than you do. I can't believe you haven't seen them before...someone should have given them to you." David showed me a picture of Jaryd's tooth. "Do you see anything strange about the tooth?"

I sat there quietly as I tried to digest what I was looking at. My momentary silence was broken when Dave followed with his next line of questioning. "If the tooth was sitting there for over three years, why was it sitting on top of the pine needles and not covered by them? Doesn't it look like someone staged the tooth in that position? Why is it so clean?"

He was right. The cranium was full of pine needles, yet the tooth was on top of the log as if someone had just set it there. I've always questioned the tooth because it was destroyed during the DNA process, and it contained a mixture of more than one person's DNA. How could this happen, and why was the entire tooth demolished?"

We continued our conversation, then David asked if he could see Jaryd's shoes. He picked up one shoe and turned it 360 degrees to see as much as possible. He slowly handed it back to me and said, "I don't see any drag marks on his shoes. If a mountain lion dragged Jaryd up the mountain with his legs and feet dangling, there would be several drag marks or scuffs on the toe or heel of the shoe."

I believe this evidence proves Jaryd was never dragged up the cliff, and if he wasn't, then he had to make the climb on his own. Maybe he was never there; maybe his clothes were put there at a later date. I wasn't the only person thinking this. The quote below is from one of the people who was on the mountain the day Jaryd's clothes were found.

"Sure, I think a lot of people would like to think we planted the clothes, but we certainly didn't plant them...Jaryd could not have possibly climbed the 435 feet up the steep slope to where the items were found."

This thought was reflected by Dr. Baden, the chief medical examiner for the City of New York from 1978 to 1979. He told me to hang in there because he believed the clothing and shoes were put on the trail at a later date. He did not believe Jaryd's clothing had been sitting in the elements for almost four years.

Did Jaryd climb the cliff, or was he dragged? Was he there, or were things planted? Again, these are questions that can only be answered with more questions. Will I ever know the truth? I don't think so. I've learned that one should never fear searching for the truth because the truth is out there.

I went back to the CanAm Missing Project website a couple of days later, and Dave had posted the following about our conversation:

> Jaryd Atadero
>
> Our primary rendition of what happened to Jaryd is told in "Missing 411-Western United States."
>
> What you are reading here are new details supplied by Allyn Atadero, Jaryd's dad.
>
> In 2010 I was living in California and just starting to research missing people. One of the first cases that caught our eye was the disappearance of Jaryd Atadero from the Big South Trail adjacent to the Poudre River in northern Colorado. The incident has a lengthy section in "Missing 411-Western United States."
>
> Jaryd was three years old when he vanished while hiking with a group of single people who were staying at his father's resort 20 miles away. This is one of those cases that shook me to the core. There is a photo in my book where Jaryd looks at the reader with those innocent, piercing brown eyes, is stuck in my thoughts. There were many nights where my mind traveled to that trail and tried to imagine what happened on October 2, 1999.
>
> Readers know that we have a policy of not contacting victims or their families. If they reach out to us, we will always meet with them.
>
> On April 7 the Can Am Missing Project website got an e-mail from Allyn Atadero, Jaryd's dad. What sometimes seems like destiny may really be something we don't understand. In 2010 I lived in California, I now live in Colorado and Allyn teaches at a school less than 5 miles from my house. We agreed to meet at a restaurant I frequent regularly.
>
> I'm not embarrassed to say that I sat in the restaurant booth with tears in my eyes. I know this story intimately. I've probably been on the trail where Jaryd vanished at

least four times. I felt the same way when I met Dennis Martin's father. The pain that these parents have gone through is unimaginable, but a pain that any dad can only pray they never experience.

Allyn entered the room and I instantly recognized him from press photos. I walked toward him and we hugged. There are a few times in life when you feel an instant bond, I felt it. Allyn and I casually talked about various unimportant issues, how he found us, what he knew, etc. It wasn't long before we were onto talking directly about Jaryd and the specifics of his disappearance.

At the time of the disappearance, the Atadero's owned the Poudre River Resort, and he was a teacher in Littleton. He had a strong Christian background and thought it was important if he put a cross on his resorts sign as a notification to travelers that this was a safe place to ask for assistance. This is a fact I never knew. I did know that Jaryd was walking the trail with the Christian Singles Association group that was staying at the Atadero Resort. As we were talking, I asked Allyn if Jaryd had been baptized. He thought for a few seconds and stated: "I don't think formally. I do remember sitting at the back of the resort with Jaryd in my arms asking for God to protect him."

I won't repeat what I've already written about Jaryd's incident, but I will tell you a series of troubling facts that Allyn relayed to me.

After Jaryd was reported missing and SAR started their work, Allyn's twin brother, Arlyn came out from California to support his brother. Their mom and friends also rallied around the family and tried to continue to keep spirits upbeat. At one point the family asked the SAR team and sheriffs if they could go up the trail and view the place where Jaryd vanished? This is a reasonable and normal request. Remember, the singles group was the last people to see Jaryd. Allyn was at his resort when the group took Jaryd to the trail. Arlyn was in California. There was no way that Arlyn or Allyn were suspects and the sheriffs were telling the family there was no evidence that Jaryd had been abducted. When the family asked to go down the trail, there was a curt response, "No." When the family subtly pushed and inquired about the rationale, they were threatened with arrest if they stepped on the trail. Allyn said he and the family never understood the stiff response. I've never heard of a SAR team or sheriffs member making a statement like that.

At another point early in the search Allyn was at the search headquarters near the trailhead and engaged one of the sheriffs officials in a conversation. He was told that his son was in the river. The water was extremely cold and the body wouldn't be found for four years. Where would anyone get the idea that this was a good idea to tell a parent?

Nearly three days into the search, Allyn and Arlyn were on the highway listening to the news when they heard on the radio that Jaryd had approached a pair of fishermen on the river the day he vanished. Jaryd asked the men if there were bears in the area. The fishermen told them that there were not. Jaryd supposedly walked away. Yes, completely irrational of the fishermen to allow a three year old to walk away into the wilderness without adult supervision. But also unbelievable that the Larimer County Sheriff never told Allyn about this development and allowed them to hear it on the radio. Allyn consistently gave the impression that the communication between the family and the sheriff needed improvement. I asked Allyn if Jaryd had ever seen a live bear, he stated that he didn't think so.

During the point that searchers and canines were working the scene, Allyn was at the search headquarters at the trailhead when two SAR workers came in and asked for a bag in a cupboard. One of the canines needed Jaryd's scent to work the area and the bag supposedly had a piece of his clothing. Allyn grabbed the bag and looked inside and saw a pair of his own shorts. He was dumbfounded. He looked at the SAR leader and asked if this was the bag they were using for scent? He was told that it was.

He asked how anyone could misinterpret a man's pair of shorts for something a small three-year old boy would be wearing? The SAR leader got up towards Allyn' and stated: "We can call off the search right now." This statement infuriated Allyn and the heat in the trailer got high.

I have no idea how anyone could believe that Allyn's shorts could be Jaryd's. I think Allyn's response would be the representative from any father that had their son lost in the woods and then finds out the canines never had Jaryd's scent. The response from the SAR leader is troublesome and confusing. First, they want to keep the Atadero's off the trail and threaten them with arrest. It is then determined that SAR officials aren't using a scent piece from Jaryd, then threaten to quit. It's probably good I wasn't in Allyn's position; I may have been less polite. I may have told the SAR leader to describe how his canines are ever going to find my son without the proper scent? If his mind wasn't in the proper frame to lead the search, get off the mountain and I'd find someone who was committed. I do admire Allyn's refrained mindset under the conditions.

It was about this time that Allyn was having a discussion with SAR and sheriffs about the trail and any opportunity an abductor would have about escaping the valley without being noticed. He was told by officials that there was only one way in and one way out of the river valley and that was via the Big South Trailhead, days later, Allyn determined that this was entirely untrue. There are several ways to exit the valley other then via the trailhead. Again, either the official was incompetent or lying.

Jaryd disappeared in a National Forest, which is under the supervision and law enforcement control of the federal government. The Atadero family had made inquiries to get the assistance of the FBI. They were told that there was no evidence of a crime and the FBI would not get involved. That is a very, very troubling response. I have written about dozens of cases which are very similar to Jaryd's disappearance where the FBI doesn't get directly involved, but they do have an agent or two who stays at the SAR center and monitors the case. Why they distinctly refused to get involved is baffling and not consistent with past practices.

Four long years dragged on until hikers were 500+ feet above the Big South Trail, over two miles from the trailhead when they found scattered clothing. Larimer County Sheriff was notified and deputies went to the scene and found remains that were consistent with Jaryd. Allyn was called and this time they escorted him down the trail to the point just below the remains. Allyn said that it was a very, very steep and rocky incline where two SAR workers helped him up the mountain. Allyn stated he was taken to an area where they showed him the area where his sweatpants were found, but the clothing was already removed from the mountain. He was taken to another location where Jaryd's shoes were found. Allyn made it a point to say that it didn't appear to him that the shoes had been through the elements for four winters. The shoes were clean and the colors were vibrant. Searchers also found the sweater Jaryd was wearing that had some unusual hairs around the neckline. Crime scene technicians found the top of his skull and one tooth in the general area. No other bones were found. Needless to say Allyn was devastated. He told me that he remembers sitting on the bluff looking out at the river thinking that it was a beautiful spot. He said that as he was sitting there, the sheriff's radio blurted out that they had found another item. Allyn thought to himself: "Jaryd, you waited for dad to arrive to make yourself known."

Days after finding Jaryd's remains, the sheriff had a press conference. They had the clothing and shoes up on display boards covered with plastic. Allyn noticed that someone had (pulled the pants to display them right-side out), straightened out one of the legs to the sweatpants and asked the sheriff why they did that. The sheriff asked him what he meant. Allyn told them that when they were found, they were inside out. The sheriff asked him how he knew that. Allyn stated that he was at the scene. The sheriff claimed ignorance to the pant issue and left the displays as they were. Let me state right here, finding a young boys pants turned inside out on the side of a mountain is highly unusual. The sheriff had to have known this, thus straightening them out. One of Jaryd's teeth was located sitting on top of a bed of needles in plain view, a very, very unusual sight. After four winters, you'd expect the tooth to be under the needles and buried by debris.

At the press conference, the sheriff stated he wasn't positive what happened to Jaryd. He thought it was possible that a mountain lion killed him, but there wasn't significant evidence to support that.

The sheriff sent the tooth and the top of the cranium to the Colorado Bureau of Investigation for DNA analysis. They also sent all of the clothing to the bureau to locate blood. They didn't find any blood on any of the clothing. The CBI stated that the cranium had degraded DNA, causing the 85% return, but a DNA expert from Ohio told Allyn at a later date that the tooth was contaminated with more than one person's DNA. Personally, I have no idea what they mean. All DNA experts know that you cleanse the item prior to testing to eliminate any contamination. The sheriff also sent the hair they collected off Jaryd's collar to the lab. They told Allyn that the hairs were non-human and not Mountain lion and not to worry about it. They never gave Allyn the hair report and never told him what the hairs belonged to. Think this through clearly. You are the investigator and you are attempting to understand what killed a small boy. Wouldn't you want to know what those hairs belonged to? Hair and fiber experts know what every animal hair looks like. They have a guide to every hair in the wilderness and it's their job to match them. Why wasn't this completed? Why wasn't Allyn given a copy of the hair report? He was given the DNA report and every other imaginable report, but that one. He still doesn't have it.

Jaryd's personal items that were not found were the lower jaw, teeth, his T-shirt and underwear.

When Allyn and I met, he brought Jaryd's shoes, sweater and pants. The shoes still look pristine. During our conversation, Allyn told me that there were several things about the crime scene that didn't make any sense. Jaryd never tied his shoes. He always left them untied. If something dragged him 500+ feet up a rocky, steep incline, his shoes would be banging or dragging on the ground and would undoubtedly fall off, yet they were found near the clothes. When I examined the shoes, there were no scuff marks or significant scratches near the toes or the back of the shoes, which I believe there would've been if he had been dragged up the mountain. The other point Allyn brought up, the shoes still looked new and the colors were still loud and vibrant, even after being out in four winters. There was no mold inside the shoes or evidence that there had been significant snow and water on them.

Allyn was given all of Jaryd's property, bones, skull, tooth, clothing and shoes. Mr. Atadero is a smart and committed dad. Allyn contacted a group of mountain lion experts, explained the evidence that had been recovered and asked their opinion on what happened to his son. The consensus opinion was that a mountain lion had not killed Jaryd. This was based on a lack of serious damage to the sweater near the stomach and neck. The totality of the circumstances made the experts believe that something else happened.

Near the end of our meeting, Allyn reaffirmed his beliefs that it appeared as though Jaryd's remains were placed there for people to find. Readers, does this sound familiar? The number of times I've written that SAR can't find the missing, yet months/years later, the remains are found in an area that had been searched numerous times.

Many of the facts in this case are reminiscent of others I have documented.

- Jaryd is found uphill from where he disappeared.
- Canines can't find a scent and cadaver dogs can't find the body.
- There is an aircraft crash in conjunction with the search.
- Jaryd was far in front of a group he was hiking with.
- Jaryd is in a cluster of missing from the vicinity Rocky Mountain National park.

Allyn's findings confirm the belief by CanAm investigators that something very unusual happened to Jaryd, that as of today, cannot be explained.

Allyn and I have agreed to meet in the near future and further discuss missing children. My prayers are with he and his family.

—David Paulides

....

The following episode started on September 23, 2014.

Just like any other day, I left work at three thirty and drove home. My family and I had just sat down to eat dinner when the phone rang. I looked at the caller ID, but I didn't recognize the number or name. I get a lot of strange calls, and for the most part, I just let the phone ring because some calls are not that important. I don't know why, but this one was different, and I decided to answer it.

I slowly got up and made my way to the phone. "Hello."

A deep voice on the other end said, "Hi, can I speak to Allyn Atadero?"

"This is Allyn."

"Are you the father of Jaryd Atadero?"

My heart began to pound. "Yes, Jaryd is my son!"

"My name is John Cameron, and I'm a retired cold case investigator out of Great Falls, Montana. I was contacted by a lady from Littleton, Colorado, about your son. She read my book and thought Jaryd could be a victim of a serial killer I wrote about named Edward Edwards."

I thought, *What are you talking about, and why are you calling me?*

My wife, Debbie, could tell something was wrong, and she shrieked, "Who is it…what's wrong?"

I looked at her, and she could tell I was upset. I put my hand over the receiver and said, "This guy says he used to be a cold case detective, and he wants to look into Jaryd's case."

I didn't know what to think. My body started shaking , and I could feel the tears welling from my eyes. I quickly walked into my office and grabbed a pen and paper to take notes. As he talked, he told me this Edwards guy would target Christians and their children. He'd been killing for over sixty years, and he believed Edwards murdered Jaryd.

I couldn't breathe, but I listened to John's allegations concerning the serial killer. He asked me to go to his website, www.coldcasecameron.com, and read about his book and look at the picture of the person he was talking about.

I had a person in mind and thought, *What if it's him? God, please don't let this be true.*

I told John, "If you're right, I'm leaving tonight, and I'm killing him myself!"

John replied, "I'd help you, but Edwards died in prison back in 2011."

I hung up the phone and walked back into the living room where Debbie was patiently waiting. I told her about my conversation and she tried her best to calm me down, but how could she stop my mind from creating chaotic thoughts?

We sat down together and pulled up the website John had asked me to visit. I read many disheartening things about a man who was dedicated to evil and how he tried to destroy everything good that he touched. I tried to digest the information that was presented, but I couldn't imagine how he could have had anything to do with Jaryd's disappearance.

I tried to return John's call that night, but he didn't answer. I got in touch with him the next day, and he apologized because he missed my call. He told me he was totally engrossed in Jaryd's story, and he didn't want anything to bother him and interfere with his investigation. I could tell he was totally convinced this Edwards freak had something to do with my son's plight.

I received the following e-mail from John on September 25, 2014:

> Allyn; Here is a review of just a few of the things pointing to Edwards. There will be many more as I keep reviewing your son's case. Thanks for talking and listening. The skepticism I have been confronted with is par for the course. This investigation has been going on for 4 years now, and since the release of my book, many more murders have been revealed. He killed 500 between 1946 and 1996 and I have only unraveled 130. He was free 13 more years to kill and did. The press and police have ignored this because that is who Edwards targeted his entire life. The results are, ED made them look like fools. That is what the Zodiac killer bragged about in his letters to the "Editors" in the 60's, 70's, 80's, 90's, 2000's. ED just never got caught but had put it all out in publications to be figured out if someone challenged him. We did that in 2010-14. He was never investigated by the FBI because once he got identified in 2010, they realized he had been a paid informant for them since 1951. I am willing to come to Colorado and talk to you and your family.
>
> Respectfully,
> John A Cameron

John and I exchanged books in order to understand each other's stories. John's book was very intriguing, and it truly conveyed and supported his ideas concerning the life of Edward Edwards and his killing ways.

I wasn't convinced, and I was having a hard time buying into John's theory, but there were a lot of similarities, and I understood where he was coming from. I was impressed with his book, and it proved he was an incredible cold case investigator, one with a lot of talent. I believed in him, and I knew he had the ability to uncover truths the average person would overlook. I knew, if there was something to be found, he would find it!

When John received my book, he read it in less than two days and e-mailed me several thoughts concerning Jaryd's case.

John and I have communicated several times concerning his beliefs, but it will take more evidence to convince me Jaryd was taken by a serial killer with a thirst to kill. This all makes for a great story, but I need some proof this happened.

I'm somewhat cynical because I've read stories about Bigfoot, aliens, serial killers, mountain lions, and someone committing a crime of opportunity. Let's not forget about the theory that included me, Jaryd's father, as a person of interest for the disappearance of my very own son.

I know there is more to Jaryd's story, but how long will it take for the truth to surface and manifest itself? One thing for sure, the more eyes on his case, the more likely the truth will be found.

Final Thoughts Concerning the Mountain Lion Theory

Most of my thoughts are never-ending questions or questions that can only be answered with more questions. Was Jaryd taken by a mountain lion that possessed the ability to remove pants and consume its prey without leaving a trace of blood? Yes, that is a question that leads to many other questions.

I don't know the answer, but I've had many experts provide logical opinions and views concerning the mountain theory.

I talked to a mountain lion expert, and he told me they wouldn't classify my son as a mountain lion attack. He said, "I've never seen or heard about a lion pulling the pants off of someone and leaving them inside out."

Jaryd's pants were found inside out. He also said a lion would open the thoracic and abdominal cavity in order to consume the heart and liver. Jaryd's jacket was completely intact.

Again, was it a mountain lion? Jaryd's clothing was tested, and there was no trace of blood or mountain lion hair. This theory is believed by some, but are they truly looking at the situation and evaluating the evidence? I'm not sure, but I believe the lack of evidence speaks for itself.

Jaryd hated wearing shoes, and the day he went missing was no different. He refused to tie his shoes, and he left with the shoestrings dangling to the side. If he would have casually kicked with his foot, his shoe would have come off and flown through the air. What does all of this mean? I doubt Jaryd was dragged 500 feet up a steep mountain, without losing his shoes.

Several seasoned cold case homicide investigators and forensic examiners viewed the photo of the skull and found the striation very unusual. They had never observed fine scratches like that in any skull. It was their opinion that a very sharp object made the marks. They do not know of any animal that has made similar scratches on other skulls in the past. I was told, "*Nobody* had ever seen anything like it, *ever.*"

Another law enforcement expert, who knows everything about Jaryd's case, believes something highly unusual happened.

Will the opinions and theories subside as time passes? I would think so, but they keep rolling in as if they are waves pounding on a beach. For instance, I received the following e-mail from a reliable source on January 3, 2015:

> I can only tell you what I was told. That just because you don't see the Feds that does not mean they are not crawling all over this. On the contrary, nobody wants this, not in this country, not in Russia, not in any country. Remember how long it took them to catch the Unabomber? Its not over Allyn...

Atadero Search and Recovery Report

On March 14, 2015, I received the official report that was written by a necro search team and issued on July 3, 2003. The word "Necro" literally means death, dead tissue, corpse or a dead body or person.

This was the first time I had seen the report because I didn't know it existed nor was it ever offered to me. I got my hands on the report because Josallyn tried, for months, to get the pictures that were taken at the time Jaryd's clothing was found. She finally spoke to a nice lieutenant from the sheriff's department and she had the information within a week. The report was included with the CD containing the pictures of Jaryd's case.

I was sitting at my kitchen table when I first read the report. The room was quiet, but the silence was broken when I yelled, "What, are you serious? I can't believe what I'm reading!"

I thought the report contradicted itself and it contained strange information concerning the behavior of mountain lions.

I was extremely frustrated when I read, "The failure to locate any other remains leaves several questions open, most notably the location of the primary scavenging and decomposition site. Locality 1 seems the best candidate given the presence of the clothing. However, the reported absence of any stains that might have come from either blood or decomposition fluids indicates that they were removed from, or by, the victim prior to the time that any significant bleeding or decomposition took place. Consequently, the clothing cannot be unequivocally assumed to mark the spot of the primary scavenging or decomposition of the remains. "

I had a hard time digesting the part that says, "However, the reported absence of any stains that might have come from either blood or decomposition fluids indicates that they were removed from, or by, the victim prior to the time that any significant bleeding or decomposition took place."

I thought, *that's it, the reason they didn't find any blood, body tissue, DNA or mountain lion hairs was because he either removed his clothing or something else had removed them.*

That didn't make a lot of sense. If Jaryd removed his clothing before he was attacked, then he had to hike to the point where his clothing was found, and that was an impossible task. When I took that hike, it was arduous, time consuming and I had two members of the search and rescue team at my side. This was done because they thought the mountain was too treacherous for me to accomplish on my own.

I continued reading, "Further, no evidence was recovered that would provide grounds for rejecting the view that predation by a large carnivore, possibly a mountain lion is the most plausible explanation of the death of the individual whose remains were recovered in the search reported here. If the remains are demonstrated to be those of Jaryd Atadero, it seems that he was taken by a large carvivore, most likely a mountain lion, in his last foray away from the group with which he was hiking. The activities of other hikers on the trial and the searching subsequent to the discovery of Jaryd's disappearance would have encouraged the animal to move away from the kill site, which must have been fairly close to the Big South trial, to a more secure location."

Again, I was confused because either Jaryd or something removed his clothing before any signs of blood could be left on his clothing. The statement above says the kill site must have been fairly close to the Big South Trail and Jaryd's body was moved to a more secure location. He was moved because there were too many hikers and searchers on the trail.

If this were the case, then Jaryd didn't remove his clothing because they would have been found fairly close to the Big South Trail. His clothing would be in a different location than the cranium . If a mountain lion killed Jaryd close to the trail and carried him to the location where his clothing was found, then there was ample time for blood to have dripped or flowed onto his clothing. It would have taken some time for a mountain lion to carry Jaryd up the side of the mountain.

I know, as a matter of fact, the claws and teeth would have created wounds that produced blood. If the mountain lion removed Jaryd's clothes, it killed him first, took him up the mountain, and then performed this miraculous event.

The report stated the removal of clothing is consistent with mountain lion treatment of prey following a kill. It goes on to state the lack of extensive staining of the clothing indicates that it was removed from the body before any significant damage was done to any tissues or any significant decomposition took place.

If the person responsible for the report really believes Jaryd's clothing could have been removed, then why does the report say the Division of Wildlife experts indicated that it is possible that the missing shirt might have been consumed along with the with the victim's body? If this is correct, the mountain lion removed some of the clothing and consumed the other. That sounds like a confused cat to me!

The best part of the report was the last paragraph, which I've listed below:

In summary, there is no point in the limited body of evidence available that points to any interpretation other than that Jaryd Atadero was the victim of a large carnivore which took advantage of the child's behavior during the hike on the Big South Trail. The primary weakness of this conclusion is the lack of physical evidence. It is primarily based on circumstantial or indirect information. It must be understood that the reconstruction is essentially hypothetical and any new evidence will lead to at least to its extensive revision, if not its outright rejection.

I sat back and tried to comprehend the information I read in the report. The more I thought about it, the less sense it made. Jaryd could not have removed his clothing and been attacked by the Big South Trail. If so, his clothing would have been found near the trail and not up the mountain side. Which was it?

I was extremely frustrated and I set out on a quest to find the truth. I searched the internet and contacted as many mountain lion experts as possible.

I've listed the responses below:

First, as a father of 3, I offer my deepest empathy for your loss. You are suffering every parent's worst nightmare.

I find it most unlikely that a mountain lion could turn pants completely inside out. I won't say "impossible" but I would say "99% unlikely." Inside out with no trace of blood would be about as close to impossible as I can imagine.

—Steve

March 14, 2015

Hi Allyn,

These are the only clues provided to me:
no mountain lion hairs on his clothing
no trace of blood
pants turned completely inside-out
absence of any stains that might have come from either blood or decomposition fluids

Based on these clues, I do not believe that a mountain lion killed and ate your son.

A forensic specialist might be able to advise whether all traces of blood or decomposition could have disappeared in 4 years, but it strikes me as unlikely. I would expect a mountain lion to tear clothing in the process of removing it. I do not believe that a mountain lion could turn pants inside out. It also seems most unlikely that a mountain lion would eat the sweatshirt but remove the other clothes.

I am sorry for your loss.

—Steve

March 16, 2015

Dear Mr. Atadero—I'm sorry to hear about the loss of your son. However, based on the information you provided it doesn't sound like he was a victim of a mountain lion attack. First, when mountain lions attack they usually ambush their prey, jumping on its back and biting the neck. A sign of such an attack would have been quite apparent on the clothing that was found. Second, mountain lions do not "skin" their prey (or shed their clothing.) A shirt would have been torn and bloodied in the area of the chest cavity if a lion was involved.

I hope this information helps you in your search.

—Tim Dunbar
Executive Director
Mountain Lion Foundation

March 25, 2015

Hi Mr. Atadero—Sorry about the delay in getting back to you—I've been out of the office for the past few days. I and my biologist looked at the photos and could discover no signs of a mountain lion attack. At the very least I would have expected to see evidence of blood on the back and shoulders of the jacket.

As I indicated in my previous email I am sorry for your loss, but do not believe that the evidence points to an animal attack.

Tim Dunbar
Executive Director
Mountain Lion Foundation

March 18, 2015

Dear Mr. Atadero,

First of all, on behalf of all of us at the Cougar Network, please accept our deepest sympathies regarding the loss of your son. We are so incredibly sorry to hear of your loss and of course will help however we can in your time of grieving.

Based on the information you provided, it doesn't sound to me like a mountain lion killed your son. However, please keep in mind I am not a forensic scientist and I have only your brief description to go by. But given the circumstances, the fact that his clothes were found (and not ripped to shreds), and that his body was never recovered sounds like something else may have happened. Have you spoken with cougar biologists in Colorado? They most certainly could answer your questions, as they would have local knowledge of the cougar population there, and their behaviors.

In the interest of your sensitivities, I will spare you the details of a cougar kill (usually deer). However, if you would like me to describe a typical kill for comparison (or even provide pictures so you can see what I'm talking about), please let me know.

I hope that this has been helpful for you and please let me know if there is anything further with which I can assist you.

Michelle LaRue, PhD
Executive Director
Cougar Network

March 23, 2015

Hi Allyn,

The strangest thing in my mind, sadly, is the lack of blood on the clothes. I am guessing you and others have raised that question as well? I would think there would be blood present if a mountain lion took your son.

I can't say what clothes being left in the wilderness for 4 years should look like, but I would think they should be a lot more beat up than that, and have DNA evidence of a cougar somewhere.

Again, I'm so very sorry for your loss and I wish I could do more to help you.

Best,
Michelle
Executive Director
Cougar Network

March 17, 2015

Allyn,

First of all, I am very sorry to hear about your son Jaryd. Please know I am praying for you for a peace and answers to your whole ordeal. And please, feel free to ask me anything if it helps. Thank you for taking the time to write me and share your story. Very humbling...

Let me start off by saying I am in no way an expert in forensics, nor any of the sort. I do know a little about mountain lions as you can tell by my own personal attack story at: www.lionkingministries.com.

Only by the Grace of God was I able to get away and down that mountain that day. I know this without question as the peace I felt when I saw the face of Jesus during my screams and run down the mountain.

Per your ordeal, one question I would have is no blood on anything. It would be incredibly rare that the mountain lion wouldn't puncture something on your son's body. Thus, giving way to some sort of blood drip. I know my shirt, shoes, socks, shorts, and hiking pack all had blood as well as the path itself. In fact, the searched path (3 flattened locations under different trees deeper in the mountains) by hounds found small blood spots. Of course I was about 135 lbs at the time and fought back as hard as I could.

Have investigators done any blood samples on the clothing? Or even hair samples? Your story reminds me a little of: http://articles.latimes.com/1997/jul/19/news/mn-14282. Now is it possible that your son's fear overwhelmed him and he passed out. Thus, no fight and the animal was able to easily remove the clothing? Possibly. Having no blood would be my big question. Hopefully, they were able to test the clothing even four years later.

Hopefully, the weather did not destroy any evidence. Not sure if any of this helps at all? I can only pray someday you find peace with all this. I know your son is walking hand in hand with Jesus now and that, my friend, is the most peaceful, most loving place any of us can be.

Praying for you...God Bless Allyn.

—Andy Peterson

Was it a mountain lion, a strange creature, or a deranged person that took Jaryd's young life? I have my opinion, and I'm sure after reading this story, you have your own.

Writings and Frustrations

I have a deep love for my son, and I wanted him to know that he was always on my mind, and there was nothing I wouldn't do for him. The first thing I was told when Jaryd vanished was he's okay, but he couldn't be found. After looking for Jaryd that afternoon, I went back to the resort and emotionally fell apart. I thought about all the things that had transpired and sat down and wrote the following:

> He's Okay
> We Just Can't Find Him
>
> It was a Saturday morning
> when you said good-bye.
> You had a smile on your face
> and a twinkle in your eye.
> Later on that day
> when my friends came home,
> You weren't with them,
> they left you up there alone.
> I drove up the mountain,
> I ran up the trail.
> I called out your name,
> hoping I wouldn't fail.

Jaryd, my son,
I love you so much,
I want to hold you in my arms,
I want to feel your touch.
You may be lost
and we might be miles apart,
But as long as I live
You will always be in my heart.
I love you, son!
Daddy

I was getting a lot of phone calls about Jaryd, and each one of them conjured up several different thoughts.

I remember one person telling me Jaryd was okay because there were eight angels watching over him. She said she had a dream and was given this information. I asked her, "Why are there so many angels watching over my son?"

She said, "One was there to protect him, one was feeding him, another was keeping him warm, and one was keeping the wild animals away from him." She continued, "The others were there to keep him happy."

The thought of eight angels watching over my son brought tears to my eyes, and it inspired me to write the following poem:

They Tell Me

They tell me eight angels
are watching over you.
They tell me you are a miracle
waiting to happen.
They tell me you have brought our country
down to their knees.
They tell me your smile has brought
tears to many people's eyes.
They tell me you're a
very good-looking little boy.
They tell me you
are a blessing.

Jaryd,
There's nothing they can tell me
I don't already know.

The more I thought about Jaryd, the more I wanted to write. I was trying to figure out what he was going through, and I was hoping he was happy.

I imagined my son talking to another son who was missing at one time, and that was Jesus. I tried to imagine what it would have been like when Jesus first met Jaryd. You have to understand, I didn't know if my son was dead or alive.

The thought of the two coming face-to-face inspired my next writing:

What Did Jesus Say?

Hi, Jaryd,
I want you to meet my father.
He's been watching over you
And he thinks you're a very special kid.
Do you remember all the times you fell?
He's the one who picked you up.
Do you remember all the times you cried?
He's the one who dried the tears for you.
Do you remember when you were lost in the woods?
He's the one who sent the angels to you.
I know your dad misses you,
But he knows we have you
And he understands he'll see you again someday.
Don't worry about your dad,
We've sent the Holy Spirit to comfort him.

Every time I read "What Did Jesus Say?" it brings tears to my eyes. Dead or alive, I know God is with my son.

I spent the first few days at home, thinking and crying about Jaryd. I wrote every chance I got because he was my inspiration, and I wanted to express every feeling he ever gave to me. I desperately wanted to hold my son, so I wrote this poem to him:

Jaryd

What I would give
to have you sitting on my lap and holding my hand?
What I would do to
see your smiling face and hear your wonderful voice?
If I could only bring you back,
we could play catch and you could jump on my back.
If I could have one more day
I would look into your big, brown eyes and cry with you.
I would do anything
to see you and your sister laughing and playing together again.
If I could see you,
I'd let you suck your thumb.
If you come home,
I'll let you jump on the bed and write on the walls.
I told you,
If you ever died,
I'd die with you.
I have!

One day while I was thinking of my son, my heart screamed with pain. I thought I was at the end of my rope, and I didn't want to deal with the thought of living the rest of my life without ever seeing Jaryd again. If I didn't have a beautiful daughter and if I didn't believe in the truth about God, I would have looked for a different way to escape my pain.

My mind was drowning in a pool of reality that can only be described as hideous. I went over to my computer and wrote Jaryd a letter, hoping he would get the chance to read it. The following is the letter I wrote to my son:

11/19/1999

Jaryd,

I remember the smile on your face when I gave you permission to go on the hike with Janet. Jaryd, the tears I've shed and the pain I've had to endure are more than anyone can imagine. Jaryd, if you're dead, I want to be with you. I want to hold your hand and tell you I'm sorry! I want to look into your eyes and be your daddy again. Jaryd, you don't understand; every day without you is a day not worth living. I love your sister, but my life was meant for both of you. There are a lot of people left here on earth that can take care of your sister. I want to be with you. I want to hold you and never let you go.

I was looking forward to seeing you play your first football, baseball, and basketball games. I was looking forward to your first day of school and meeting your first girlfriend. I always told your sister you would be the person that would take care of her when Daddy is gone. Son, I'm so sorry. I never wanted to let you down. I was the one who cherished your life, yet I left you to somebody who didn't understand. I never would have let you go, I never would have lost you. Forgive me for not being there with you right now.

I remember your beautiful smile and your thumb in your mouth. You were such a happy little boy, and you brought me so much happiness. I'm sorry, but I have such a hard time looking at your picture because it rips my heart apart. Jaryd, it's so hard to see with so many tears in my eyes.

Where are you? Please don't tell me you've taken the step to the other side. I miss you so much, and all I want to do is hold you. You don't realize you've taken my will to live and made my life meaningless. Every day is so empty without you. The thought of you spending even one night alone in the mountains was more than any father should go through. Jaryd, please don't tell me you're dead. Please don't tell me a wild animal attacked you and destroyed our future.

I miss you so much!

I love you with all my heart,
Daddy

I've written several poems and letters to my son. If he died, I think about all the ways he could have perished, but if he's alive, I try to imagine all the possibilities that could have taken place.

I talk to my son every day, and I tell him I love him. Jaryd has taught me there is no greater love than the love a parent has for their child, and he has also taught me there is no greater pain than the pain one gets with the loss of a child. The following poem is my most recent thoughts concerning Jaryd:

Truth

My eyes can't remember the last time they were dry,
but my memories of you are very clear.
My heart thinks it was made to be broken,
but you are the one who holds it together.
My mind can no longer tell the difference between a
dream and reality.
I'd rather dream about you than face my reality.
My hands long to touch what is not there,
but somehow they hold you close to my heart.
My ears listen for a sound they can no longer hear.
Who said 'Silence is golden?'
If I only had one wish to make,
I'd trade the rest of my life to spend another minute with you.
I love you, Jaryd,
Daddy

One day, I was sitting with Josallyn, and we were talking about her little brother and what it was like living without him. She told me she wanted to write a poem, so we sat down together to write the following:

I Remember

I remember the first day
When I said your name
And I remember the first time
We played our favorite game

I remember everything about you
In every little way
And I'd give anything to see you
Just for one more day
Jaryd, my little brother
What a beautiful name
Without my little brother
My life isn't the same

....

Jaryd,

I know I'll see you again someday, and when I do, I hope
you're not upset with me. I miss you...thank you for being
my son.

I love you,
Daddy!

....

I look forward to the day I get to heaven, and I get to look
into Jaryd's eyes. Will I ask him what happened? No, it won't
matter then!

> The LORD is my shepherd, I shall not be in want. He
> makes me lie down in green pastures, he leads me beside
> quiet waters, he restores my soul. He guides me in paths
> of righteousness for his name's sake. Even though I walk
> through the valley of the shadow of death, I will fear no
> evil, for you are with me; your rod and your staff, they
> comfort me. You prepare a table before me in the presence
> of my enemies. You anoint my head with oil; my cup
> overflows. Surely goodness and love will follow me all the
> days of my life, and I will dwell in the house of the LORD
> forever. (Psalm 23, NIV)

Afterword: Jaryd's Legacy and Congressman Tancredo

Foresight is a gift I've never had. When Jaryd vanished, I was concerned with the very moment at hand, and I never gave the future any undeserved attention. On the other hand, I never realized the impact my son would have on so many people.

The Tuesday after my son had vanished, Brenda, Candice, and I were at the resort, leaning against the counter in the store, talking about trail safety. As I listened to their conversation, I tried to deal with my pain as it continued to eat away at my broken heart. I slowly came to the realization that I might not see my son again, and the thought was terrifying. We questioned the things we could have done to prevent this tragic incident from happening. Candice said, "If Jaryd only had a whistle, he could have been blowing it, and we probably would have found him." In my heart of hearts, I knew she was right. I went along with the conversation as other thoughts swam through my mind. I thought, *A whistle is a great idea, but responsible adults would have brought my son back to me.*

We were talking about whistles when Candice and Brenda came up with the idea to start some type of memorial for Jaryd.

They wanted to order thousands of whistles with Jaryd's name on them, and they wanted to pass out the whistles to young children. As we continued to talk, we decided the whistles should be packaged with a list containing several trail safety tips. It was a great idea but one too late to help my very own son.

As our conversation continued, the word *memorial* was eating me up inside. I was having a hard time dealing with the word because I always associated it with the death of a person. There was no proof my son was dead, and until there was, I would never mourn my son as dead. I voiced my frustration to my friends, and they totally agreed. After talking for several more minutes, we came up with the Jaryd Atadero Legacy.

I wasn't sure why we were having that conversation that night, but it was as if we were acting as though my son would never be seen again. I remember how the thought of my son being lost forever kept trying to climb to the forefront of my mind, but even to this day, my heart refuses to surrender to the idea.

Later that night, we shared our idea with Susan. Susan was excited because she had the funds to implement such a project through the County's Victims Response Team. Susan had never met my son, but there was something inside her that wanted to keep my son's legacy alive forever. I could tell she was feeling the pain I was going through, and I know she did not want to see another parent go through this same ordeal.

About four months after Jaryd's disappearance, the sheriff's department and search and rescue team implemented the Jaryd Atadero Whistle Project. Susan, along with the sheriff's department and the search and rescue team, traveled to several elementary schools in the area and shared the story of Jaryd with the students. They talked about trail safety and how important it is if one becomes lost. At the end of the presentation, each student was presented with a whistle that had Jaryd's name on it.

Susan wanted to visit Stony Creek, my daughter's school, in Littleton, Colorado, to present the whistle project to the younger students. All of Josallyn's classmates knew about Jaryd's disappearance, but I think they truly thought Josallyn's brother would be found.

When Susan arrived at Josallyn's school, she asked me to speak to the kids and be part of her presentation. The thought of speaking made me nauseated because the pain I was experiencing that day was making me feel like I was back on the trail looking for my son again. I told her I would try but not to count on it.

Susan brought Josallyn to the front of the gym and introduced her as her very own special friend. Susan shared pictures of Jaryd as she retold his story. I could tell Josallyn was having the same problems I was having, because I could see her eyes tearing up, and I knew her thoughts were focused on special moments she had shared with her brother.

I had a hard time holding myself together when Susan turned and looked at me. Her eyes seemed to be asking me if I was okay, and I knew she was hoping I would have the strength to share a few words with the young children in the gymnasium. I was terrified at the thought of breaking down and crying in front of all of my daughter's friends, but I convinced myself to walk up to the front of the room to share my feelings about the tragedy that happened to my son. It was as if Jaryd was there whispering into my ear, saying, *Daddy, look at all of these beautiful children. Please help them understand what we're going through because something like this has ruined several families' lives, especially ours.*

As I stood there, I looked at the children and envied their parents. I was thinking how lucky these kids were not to be lost and how lucky their parents were because they still had their children in their lives. When I began talking, I faced a tremendous battle because I could feel my emotions trying to force me to succumb to the very pain from which I was running. Being a teacher, talking in front of a group was second nature, but this was different. The thoughts were there, but the words were holding onto my tongue the same way I would have been holding onto Jaryd's hand the day he vanished. I had a very hard time talking, and when I was done, I walked outside and broke down and cried like a baby. I talked to myself and said my son's name over and over. It was tough, but I knew I needed to purge the pain from my system because I wanted to see the rest of the presentation. It took about five minutes before I felt strong enough to go back into the gym.

I was back in the gym for a short moment when a couple of men walked into the side door. I made eye contact with the second man as he approached me with his arms outstretched, looking for a friendly hug. I opened my arms because this was a man who was becoming a true friend and a person I'd give anything in the world for my son to meet. It was Congressman Tom Tancredo. As we met, we gave each other a friendly yet genuine hug. The congressman was there to talk about trail safety, and he wanted to read a bill he was getting ready to introduce in Congress.

Congressman Tancredo talked to the students, and at the end of his speech, he read the bill to the quiet and somber crowd. The bill was asking Congress to change the name of the trial my son was lost on from the Big South Trail to the Jaryd Atadero Legacy Trail. As the congressman read the bill, I had my eyes closed, hoping to hide the tears that were fighting to escape. It was a sad moment, yet the congressman said something that brought a smile to my face. He told the kids, "I want you to enjoy the Colorado Mountains, and I want you to return home safely with your families. I never want to try to change another trail name because one of you becomes lost. This is something we don't want to do." He was right. Nothing can bring back the happiness and joy my son gave to me. My life was a living hell, and the congressman was helping my family and me remind everyone who visits the Colorado wilderness to keep a constant eye on his or her children. He didn't want to see another family experience the daily horror I have to endure for the rest of my life.

When the presentation was over, the congressman invited Josallyn and me to visit him at his office later that afternoon. The visit was enjoyable because my daughter and I had the chance to present the congressman with a couple of Jaryd's whistles. We also had the opportunity to take pictures with the congressman, and when we left, I was overwhelmed with Congressman Tancredo and his staff's compassion and willingness to help my family.

House Resolution 3817

It was March 2, 2000, and I was at school working and doing anything I could to get through another day when my cell phone rang. I was acting like Pavlov's dog, because each time my phone rang, I hoped it was someone with news about my son. I answered my phone, and the voice on the other end was very upbeat and familiar.

He said, "Hi, Mr. Atadero. It's Matt Knoedler from Congressman Tancredo's office, and I've got some great news. My boss introduced Jaryd's bill into Congress yesterday."

I didn't know what to say because I was both overwhelmed and excited. Matt and I continued our conversation for a couple of minutes, and he informed me that Jaryd's bill was House Resolution 3817 (H.R. 3817), and he gave me the Web address that displayed the actual bill as it was introduced.

I hung up the phone, walked over to the corner of the gym, and sat down and cried. I hadn't seen my son in five months, yet somehow in a strange sort of way, my son was continuing to make me a proud father.

I walked around for the rest of the day with tears in my eyes, and I told everyone about the bill Congressman Tancredo had introduced. My friends at Deer Creek Middle School shared in my bittersweet happiness.

As the day slowly passed, I couldn't wait to pick up Josallyn from school because I knew she would be excited about her brother. I waited until we got home before I said anything, and when I did, we hugged each other and shared tears of both joy and sadness. We sat there for about ten minutes, held hands, and wished our little man were home.

Later, I found my son's bill online. I stared at it for several seconds and couldn't believe what I was reading. I cried as I slowly read the following:

> To redesignate the Big South Trail in the Comanche Peak Wilderness Area of Roosevelt National Forest in Colorado as the `Jaryd Atadero Legacy Trail'. (Introduced in the House)
>
> HR 3817 IH
>
> 106th CONGRESS
>
> 2d Session
>
> H. R. 3817
>
> To redesignate the Big South Trail in the Comanche Peak Wilderness Area of Roosevelt National Forest in Colorado as the `Jaryd Atadero Legacy Trail'.
>
> IN THE HOUSE OF REPRESENTATIVES
>
> March 1, 2000
>
> Mr. TANCREDO introduced the following bill; which was referred to the Committee on Resources
>
> A BILL
>
> To redesignate the Big South Trail in the Comanche Peak Wilderness Area of Roosevelt National Forest in Colorado as the `Jaryd Atadero Legacy Trail'.

SECTION 1. FINDING.

Congress finds that Jaryd Atadero, a 3-year old boy from Littleton, Colorado, was last seen the morning of October 2, 1999, 1 1/2 miles from the trailhead of the Big South Trail in the Comanche Peak Wilderness Area of Roosevelt National Forest.

SEC. 2. REDESIGNATION.

The Big South Trail in the Comanche Peak Wilderness Area of Roosevelt National Forest located in Colorado shall be known and designated as the `Jaryd Atadero Legacy Trail'.

SEC. 3. REFERENCES.

Any reference in a law, map, regulation, document, paper, or other record of the United States to the trail referred to in section 2 shall be deemed to be a reference to the `Jaryd Atadero Legacy Trail'.

SEC. 4. SIGN.

The Secretary of Agriculture shall post a sign at the trailhead of the trail referred to in section 2 that includes a copy of this Act and a picture of Jaryd Atadero.

I think I read the bill about ten times before it actually sank in. I was excited, and I e-mailed the web page to my family and friends. It was strange, but I've never met the people who were putting their time and effort into trying to change the name of the trail where my son was lost; but for some reason, it was as if I had known these special people most of my life.

I looked at the web page that tracked each House bill that was introduced and noticed something frustrating. Most bills took about a year to a year and a half before they were given to the president to be signed into law. I tried to digest the legislative process, and then I prepared myself for a long and drawn-out procedure. I understood anything could happen, including the fact there was a chance the bill wouldn't pass.

It was strange, but I was facing a dilemma that cut like a knife. If my son was dead, I wanted a quiet place to visit. Every parent who loses a child cherishes the spot where their child is laid to rest. It becomes a refuge that allows one to continue the parent-child bond, and it allows a grieving parent to somehow express their long-lasting love. I am not sure if Jaryd is dead or alive, but I yearned for a spot we could call ours; and at the same time, we could bring attention to trail safety and remind other families about the potential dangers faced in the Colorado Wilderness. I know it's not much, but I've been back to the rock several times where Jaryd was last seen, and I've had the opportunity to sit and talk to my son. If he's there, I know he hears me.

It was April 28, 2000, when I talked with Matt Knoedler, from Congressman Tancredo's office, concerning the next phase of Jaryd's bill. He told me the subcommittee would be holding a hearing regarding Jaryd's bill on May 3, 2000, and we would have a better idea about the support we had with the passage of H.R. 3817.

....

May 3, 2000

I woke up and feverishly got ready for school knowing this was the big day. I was edgy, and I looked at my watch every five minutes, hoping that somehow time would understand my frustration and cooperate with me. But I was wrong. Each second seemed like a minute, and every hour was longer than a day. I did have one thing going for me though, Washington, DC, was two hours ahead of us, and I knew I would have some news by 10:00 a.m. Colorado time.

Initially, the National Forest Service did not want to support the bill the way it had been written. They made several recommendations that were agreed to. The following is a copy of the testimony of Jim Furnish, the deputy chief for the National Forest System USDA Forest Service.

H.R. 3817, a bill "To Redesignate the Big South Trail in the Comanche Peak Wilderness Area of Roosevelt National Forest in Colorado as the 'Jaryd Atadero Legacy Trail'," seeks to recognize the tragedy that occurred on October 2, 1999, when Jaryd Atadero, a three year old boy disappeared on this trail.

While we do not support the addition of permanent memorials and the changing of culturally significant place names, we also recognize the terrible loss suffered by the family and those who knew and loved Jaryd. We believe that some form of recognition that also helps to prevent future tragedies is a better way to recognize Jaryd's loss. The Administration would support the enactment of this bill if it was revised to eliminate the requirements to redesignate the name of the trail and to make the corresponding changes to all references to the trail. We propose revising the bill to read as follows:

(a) "The Secretary of Agriculture shall recognize the loss of Jaryd Atadero and the need for increased awareness of child safety in outdoor recreation settings by posting an interpretive sign at the Big South Trail trailhead that (1) describes considerations for safe outdoor recreation with children; and 2) refers to the tragic loss of Jaryd Atadero to underscore the need for such safety considerations; and includes a copy of this Act and an image of Jaryd Atadero.

(b) The sign shall be placed at the trailhead for a period of not less than one year from the date of enactment of this bill.

It was May 8 when Matt Knoedler called me and gave me an update on the new information concerning H.R. 3817. Matt, with a very comforting and reassuring voice, said, "Mr.

Atadero, I have some great news. My boss (Congressman Tancredo) has been talking to all of the congressional representatives from Colorado, and they have all agreed to cosponsor Jaryd's bill."

Matt reassured me everything was going to be great, and he wanted me to keep the faith. I knew he was right, but my body was reeling from the pain the past six months had inflicted upon it.

When I checked Jaryd's bill on May 16, I was overwhelmed when I noticed the names that were under the heading,

COSPONSORS:
Rep Degette, Diana–5/15/2000Rep Hefley, Joel–5/15/2000
Rep McInnis, Scott–5/15/2000Rep Schaffer, Bob–5/15/2000
Rep Udall, Mark–5/15/2000 Rep Duncan Hunter

United States Senate

While Jaryd's bill was in the House of Representatives, Congressman Tancredo and his staff kept me abreast of all the activities surrounding H.R. 3817. I know the bill had already cleared one major hurdle, but there were still two key obstacles in the way before we could actually sit and have our final celebration.

The second hurdle was extremely frustrating because it was hard getting any information from the Senate. I know Jaryd's bill was being considered, but we had to wait and hear everything secondhand after it occurred. The Senate didn't have a Matt Knoedler I could call, so I was forced to get most of my information from the www.thomas.loc.gov website. The website indicated the Senate received Jaryd's bill on July 25, 2000, and it was read twice and referred to the Committee on Energy and Natural Resources.

Sunday, October 1, came upon us quicker than I wanted. I woke up that morning and tried to remember everything that had happened the year before, because it was the last day that I spent with my son. I knew it was going to be a long day because Chris Schauble and I had agreed to meet up at the trailhead of the Big South Trail later that afternoon. We had planned on hiking up to the area where Jaryd was last seen, hoping to get answers to the questions that had eluded us for what turned out to be the longest year of my life.

Monday, October 2, was the year anniversary of Jaryd's disappearance; and as I said before, I spent the morning at the Services of Hope and Healing. It was a rough day, and I'm not sure how I lived through it.

Tuesday, October 3, rolled around, and I was back at school looking at the Internet, hoping to find something from the Senate that would make me smile. The past five days had taken an emotional toll on me, and I was desperately looking for a reason to make my life worth living.

Both October 5 and 6 started off like the past few days, but for some reason, the morning of the sixth was a little different. I started the week by going up the trail to visit and communicate with Jaryd. I sat on the rock where he was last seen, and I told him how much his sister and I missed having him in our daily lives. As I talked with my son that day, my tears flowed from my face, and I watched them drop into the river below to become part of the surroundings that held the answers to my undying questions. I'm sure Jaryd caught every tear I shed, and he knew I was having a bad week. I know it's weird, but I believe Jaryd didn't want the week to end without his daddy hearing some positive news.

I woke up and got ready for work, hoping and praying to hear some news from the Senate. When I arrived at school Friday morning, I taught my first two classes then went into my office at around nine fifty. I took my time logging onto the Internet because I didn't believe there would be any new information. I brought up the page that had the summary for H.R. 3817, and I scrolled down to the bottom where the updated information was posted. I was both disappointed and excited at what I saw on the screen:

10/5/2000
Senate Committee on Energy and Natural Resources discharged by unanimous consent.
10/5/2000
Passed Senate without amendment by Unanimous Consent.
10/5/2000
Cleared for White House.
10/6/2000
Message on Senate action sent to the House.

As I gathered my information, I discovered the Senate had passed H.R. 3817 late on the evening of the fifth of October 2000. I was very excited, but I couldn't understand why someone from Congressman Tancredo's office hadn't called to inform me about the good news.

I decided to give Matt a call to inform him I was aware of the actions that had transpired the evening before. I dialed the phone, and the voice on the other end politely said, "Congressman Tancredo's office, can I help you?"

I anxiously replied, "Yes, can I please speak with Matt Knoedler?"

"May I ask whose calling?"

"Yes, this is Allyn Atadero."

"Hi, Mr. Atadero. Let me get him for you."

Matt was always professional and extremely polite, and he treated me like we had been friends for many years; but in reality, I had never met the man.

Matt got on the phone and said, "Hi, Mr. Atadero. How are you?"

I answered, "Just fine, Matt. I was calling about Jaryd's bill."

Matt was quiet for a few seconds, then he said, "I'm sorry, but we haven't heard anything yet."

That explained everything. The reason they hadn't called me was because they didn't know yet.

I laughed. "Jaryd's bill passed the Senate last night."

"No way! Where did you hear that?"

"I saw it on the Internet about five minutes ago."

Matt didn't believe me because he answered, "I've got to see this for myself. Just a minute. I've got to pull up the web page."

Matt was gone for about forty-five seconds, surfing the Web, looking to confirm the information I had just given him. I didn't have to be sitting next to him to know he had found the web page because I could hear him screaming and yelling in the background, acting like an excited child in a toy store.

Matt got back onto the phone, saying, "I can't believe it! I need to go tell the congressman."

About fifteen seconds later, Congressman Tancredo got on the phone to congratulate me; but in my mind, he was the one who deserved the accolades. As Matt, Congressman Tancredo, and I laughed and shared in each other's excitement, the congressman made the statement of the day. "It took someone from Colorado to call and inform us about what is going on here in Washington, DC." Again, we all laughed then said our good-byes.

The following press release was issued by Congressman Tancredo's office on October 6, 2000:

October 6, 2000

Tancredo Elated as Bill Dedicating Trail to Jaryd Atadero Passes Congress

"Jaryd's memory will forever be preserved and will help educate all of us on the dangers that can accompany recreating in Colorado's forests."

WASHINGTON, DC—U.S. Representative Tom Tancredo (R-CO) spoke to Allyn Atadero today, father of Jaryd Atadero, to celebrate Congress' passage of H.R.

3817, which would dedicate the Big South Trail in the Comanche Peak Wilderness area of Roosevelt National Forest to Jaryd Atadero, a three year-old from Littleton who tragically vanished last year.

"Jaryd's memory will forever be preserved and will help educate all of us on the dangers that can accompany recreating in Colorado's forests," Tancredo said. "Safety must be the number one priority."

H.R. 3817 directs the Secretary of Agriculture to post a sign at the Big South Trail trailhead that describes "safe recreation" outdoors with children, refers to both the tragic loss of Jaryd Atadero and the dedication by Congress of this trail. The bill also requires posting a copy of the bill at the trailhead.

The bill passed the House on July 25th by a voice vote, and the Senate passed the bill unanimously. It now awaits signature into law by the President.

"Working with Allyn Atadero to make this bill a reality was an immensely pleasurable experience, and I want to thank him for the strength he has shown throughout the past year," Tancredo said.

H.R. 3817 Is Presented to President Clinton

Jaryd's bill cleared both the House and Senate, but it needed to be signed by the president to become a public law. I wasn't sure how long it took for the president to look at a bill after it was sent to the White House, so once again, I headed to the Internet to research other bills that became public laws. Through my research, I discovered the president signed most bills into law less than a week after they were presented to him. President Clinton was traveling a lot at the time, so I assumed it would be at least a month.

As I continued my daily ritual of looking up H.R. 3817, I learned the bill had been presented to the president on October 12, 2000. I was excited, and I knew if my research was correct, the bill would be signed into law a week later. I decided to stay off the Internet for the next week because I didn't want to continue torturing myself with the lack of new information.

I went to work on Tuesday, October 24, 2000, without checking the status of Jaryd's bill. At 10:00 a.m., I went to my office and turned my computer on to check my e-mail. I casually responded to a couple of my friends then decided to check on the status of H.R. 3817 before logging off. I wasn't expecting much, but I needed to satisfy my curiosity and quench my desire to see something that wasn't there.

I waited as the web page slowly loaded into my browser, and then I scanned down to the bottom of the page where the new information was posted. My heart pounded and my eyes filled with tears as I saw what Jaryd and I had been waiting for. President Clinton had signed H.R. 3817 into law on October 19, 2000, and it was now Public Law 106-324.

I couldn't believe it. Jaryd's bill had passed, yet I didn't really have any desire to celebrate. I got up out of my chair and walked out of my office. I went through the locker room and into the farthest corner of the gym and sat down and cried for about ten minutes. I would have sat there and cried all day if it wasn't for Jaryd telling me it was okay to be happy. Happiness brought on guilt because I didn't believe I had the right to be happy anymore.

Congressman Tancredo Presents My Family with a Copy of Public Law 106-324

Wednesday, January 17, 2000, Congressman Tancredo presented a framed copy of Public Law 106-324 to Josallyn and me. I was honored because I had proof that Jaryd's legacy would live forever. The congressman and his staff helped me get through the hardest year of my life. I will always be grateful to them.

On October 6, 2001, two years after my son had vanished, Congressman Tancredo, along with my family and friends, visited the Big South Trail and dedicated it to Jaryd's memory. The design of the kiosk was beautiful, and the signs that were displayed brought smiles to those who were in attendance. I was very proud at that moment, but deep down, I still had an unyielding desire to hold my son.

Recreational Safety Awareness Week

After the disappearance of Jaryd, my family and I made efforts to create a license for human trackers in the state of Colorado. I was frustrated because of the politics involved with Jaryd's search, and I thought a state license would help in situations where a missing person was involved. For instance, a tracker with a state license could show up at a search sight and present his license. The search coordinator could assign the tracker to a group of searchers, and the tracker would follow all the rules put into place at each individual search.

How could something like this hurt? If the search is coming up empty, then why would one not take advantage of a person who is properly trained? I thought it made a lot of sense, and the more eyes searching, the greater the chance of success.

In 2008, State Representative Gagliardi and my family pushed for this legislation so Colorado would have a premier system in place for finding missing children and adults. We wanted to take a great design and make it better.

Our bill, to license trackers, was shot down, and those who were against it claimed the first taste of victory. To me, it was only strike one, but I wasn't out, and it was early in the game.

To my amazement, Representative Sara Gagliardi wasn't finished either. She fought hard for what we all believed was the right thing to do, and she continued working with the governor. In 2008, Governor Ritter proclaimed the second week in September as Recreational Safety Awareness Week in honor of Jaryd and the great search and rescue teams here in Colorado. Governor Hickenlooper continues this yearly tradition.

I received the following letter from Governor Ritter:

August 20, 2008

Greetings:

On behalf of the people of Colorado, I would like to express my thanks for your dedicated efforts to promote "Recreational Safety Awareness Week."

Your remarkable commitment to bring awareness to recreational safety will help the thousands of people who come to enjoy the natural beauty of Colorado. This proclamation, inspired by your son, Jaryd Atadero, will serve as solemn reminder of the dangers we face when enjoying the great outdoors. Educating adventurers in the wilderness on basic safety precautions is of paramount importance, and I greatly respect the time and effort you have put into making our state a safer place to live and visit.

Thank you again for reminding us how important safety is. You have my warmest wishes now and for the years to come.

Sincerely,
Bill Ritter, Jr.
Governor

Colorado State Representative Sara Gagliardi became a close friend and our family hero. Recreational Safety Awareness Week is the result of Representative Gagliardi's hard work and dedication.

Comparing Two Different Maps

Map One

The above map was drawn by Seaux on Thursday, October 7, 1999. He numbered the camps sites backward, counting down from four to one. The dot is where Seaux thought Jaryd was located. Remember, the sheriff refused to respond to our request to search this area.

The map below is an actual topographical map of the area where Jaryd's clothes were found. Seaux was guessing on his map, but his guess was right on the spot.

Map Two

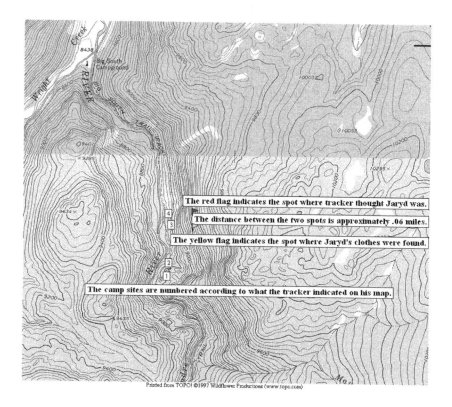

The red flag indicates the spot where tracker thought Jaryd was.

The distance between the two spots is approximately .06 miles.

The yellow flag indicates the spot where Jaryd's clothes were found.

The camp sites are numbered according to what the tracker indicated on his map.

Printed from TOPO! ©1997 Wildflower Productions (www.topo.com)

The following is part of an e-mail I received from Seaux:

> I must admit I took the search for your son very personal because I was looking for Jaryd on my son's 3rd birthday. The tracks told the story and I think he was gone the first night. My goal at that point was to provide evidence and give closure to such a tragic incident. What I got in return from the SAR coordinator and the Sheriff's department

was ridicule and disbelief. When Tom, a different tracker, came in I tried to return to the scene to have him prove to me his theory of the boy being across the river! As you remember, several controversial figures showed up to give their opinions because of the amount of media coverage. I am sorry your loss became such a promotional cat fight. I went back to the mountain the next summer and spent a couple days all alone looking and tracking in hopes of finding something. All the trails were there even after a year but I just ran out of steam. I re-enlisted in the Army and was stationed in Kentucky in 2000.

Since then the war has kept me very busy. I tried several times to introduce tracking as a means to find the elusive enemy but every general seems to insist on expensive electronics instead of the old method of following evidence. I returned back to Colorado the summer of 2005 to the Special Forces group there and was happy to learn that because of your son's incident, a group of trained and experienced trackers has been formed called Rocky Mountain Trackers Association. This small group is an amazing little gang of people who dedicate their time and resources training the right way, and they are volunteers who are called out to searches and they find people alive or provide the end statement needed for resolution. I was lucky to be the primary tracker for the search of a young autistic boy named Evan Thompson last Memorial Day. The search was successful, and I told the boy's uncle about Jaryd and how I had been waiting to heal my own emotional wounds for a long, long time.

Contacting Allyn Atadero

Thank you for reading Jaryd's story. If you or your book club is interested in discussing Jaryd's story any further, or if you have any questions or comments, I invite you to contact me at allynatadero@yahoo.com.

Thanks again,
Allyn Atadero
www.atadero.com

The following websites are associated with David Paulides:

- http://www.canammissing.com/jaryd-atadero.html
- https://www.youtube.com/watch?v=5QjBFM56EC8
- The following websites are associated with John Cameron:
- http://coldcasecameron.com/killers-timeline/2000-2011/
- http://coldcasecameron.com/

Some of the names have been changed in this book to protect the privacy of those involved.

Allyn and Arlyn Atadero face the media
during the final press conference.

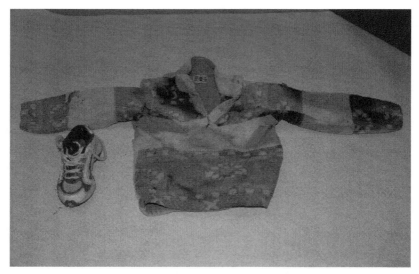

Jaryd's jacket and shoe

June 24, 2000
The Arapahoe Rescue Patrol joins the Atadero Family to
search for clues to what may have happened to Jaryd

The Atadero Family meets with Governor Ritter

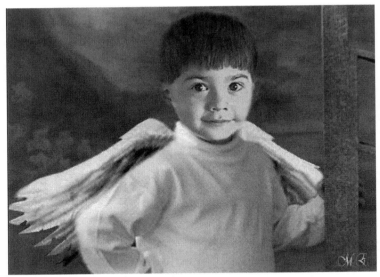

Missing angel rendering of Jaryd Atadero created by artist Marty Edwards (Shylee) who posts her artwork of missing children on the Internet.

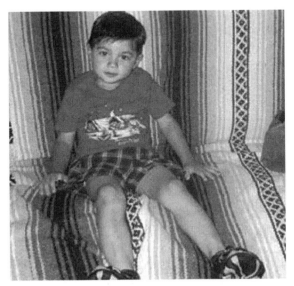

Photo of Jaryd Atadero circulated with the media.

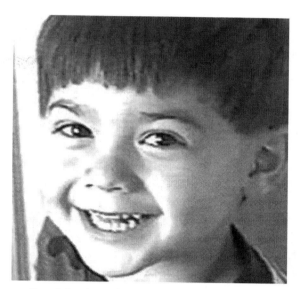

Jaryd Atadero always had a smile every day!

Jaryd's shoe as found by hikers.

Jaryd's pants laying inside out next to a log.

Allyn Atadero climbs the mountain to the area
where Jaryd's clothing was found.

Jaryd's pants as found by hikers. Rodents and birds in the area reportedly used fibers from the clothing as material for nesting.

Robyn Atadero, Aunt of missing three-year-old Jaryd Atadero, is consoled by a member of the victim response team after officials had informed family members that searchers had found Jaryd's footprints.

National and local media gathered at the trailhead of the Big South Trail

Atadero family meets with Colorado State Representative, Sara
Gagliardi, at a news conference outside the State Capitol in Denver.

Reprented with permission of Evergreen Newspapers

The tooth that was found on the mountain three years and eight months after Jaryd vanished.

The top of the cranium that was found along with the tooth.

Congressman Tancredo talking to Allyn Atadero during
the dedication of the trail to Jaryd's memory.